4-10-01

First published 1999 by Cornell University Press

Printed in the United States of America

Library of Congress Cataloging-in-Publication Data
Adams, Marilyn McCord.
Horrendous evils and the goodness of God / by Marilyn McCord Adams.
p. cm.
Includes bibliographical references and index.
ISBN 0-8014-3611-7 (alk. paper)
1. Good and evil. 2. Theodicy. I. Title.
BJ1401.A435 1999
231'.8—dc21
98–31382

Cornell University Press strives to use environmentally responsible suppliers and materials to the fullest extent possible in the publishing of its books. Such materials include vegetable-based, low-VOC inks and acid-free papers that are recycled, totally chlorine-free, or partly composed of nonwood fibers. Books that bear the logo of the FSC (Forest Stewardship Council) use paper taken from forests that have been inspected and certified as meeting the highest standards for environmental and social responsibility. For further information, visit our website at www.cornellpress.cornell.edu.

Cloth printing   10 9 8 7 6 5 4 3 2 1

FSC FSC Trademark © 1996 Forest Stewardship Council A.C.
SW-COC-098

For Nelson

Contents

Acknowledgments

During the eighties, I began to unfold some of the core ideas of this book in a series of overlapping articles, written for different occasions and a variety of audiences. Although in the book most of these thoughts have undergone significant development, transformation, and recontextualization among new materials, readers of the following articles will recognize familiar themes:

"Redemptive Suffering: A Christian Solution to the Problem of Evil," in Rationality, Religious Belief, and Moral Commitment, ed. Robert Audi and William Wainwright (Ithaca, N.Y.: Cornell University Press, 1986), 248–67.

"Duns Scotus on the Goodness of God," *Faith and Philosophy* 4 (1987): 486–505.

"Problems of Evil: More Advice to Christian Philosophers," *Faith and Philosophy* 5 (1988): 121–43, by permission.

"Separation and Reversal in Luke-Acts," *Philosophy and the Christian Faith*, ed. Thomas Morris (Notre Dame, Ind.: Notre Dame University Press, 1988), 92–117.

"Theodicy without Blame," *Philosophical Topics* 16 (1988): 215–45, by permission.

"Horrendous Evils and the Goodness of God," *Proceedings of the Aristotelian Society*, supp. vol. 63 (1989): 299–310, by courtesy of the Editor of the Aristotelian Society: © 1989. Reprinted in *The Problem of Evil*, ed. Marilyn McCord Adams and Robert Merrihew Adams (New York: Oxford University Press, 1990), 209–21.

"Sin as Uncleanness," *Philosophical Perspectives*, vol. 5, Philosophy of Religion, ed. James E. Tomberlin (1991): 1–27, by permission of Ridgeview Publishing Company.

"Julian of Norwich on the Tender Loving Care of Mother Jesus," in *Our Knowledge of God*, ed. K. J. Clark (Dordrecht: Kluwer Academic Publishers, 1992), 203–19, with kind permission from Kluwer Academic Publishers.

"Symbolic Value and the Problem of Evil: Honor and Shame," in *Interpretation in Religion*, ed. Shlomo Biderman and Ben-Ami Scharfstein (Leiden: E. J. Brill, 1992), 259–82; by permission of E. J. Bill Publishing Company.

"Aesthetic Goodness as a Solution to the Problem of Evil," in *God, Truth, and Reality: Essays in Honor of John Hick*, ed. Arvind Sharma (London: Macmillan; New York: St. Martin's Press, 1993), 46–61, by permission.

"God and Evil: Polarities of a Problem," *Philosophical Studies* 69 (1993): 39–58.

"The Problem of Hell: A Problem of Evil for Christians," in *Reasoned Faith*, ed. Eleonore Stump (Ithaca, N.Y.: Cornell University Press, 1993), 301–27. Used by permission of the publisher, Cornell University Press. Copyright © 1993 Cornell University.

"Evil and the God Who Does Nothing in Particular," in *Religion and Morality*, ed. D. Z. Phillips (London: Macmillan; New York: St. Martin's Press, 1996), 107–31; Comments and Responses, Voice F, 310–21, esp. 310–16, by permission.

"Chalcedonian Christology: A Christian Solution to the Problem of Evil," in *Philosophy and Theological Discourse*, ed. Stephen T. Davis (Hampshire and London: Macmillan; New York: St. Martin's Press, 1997), 173–98, by permission.

Work on this book, which has stretched over two sabbatical periods, has been supported by grants from the American Council of Learned Societies and the University of California President's Humanities Fellowship, by a Guggenheim fellowship, and by Yale University. I offer thanks to all of these agencies. I am also grateful to UCLA and to Yale University for the opportunity to teach a range of courses relevant to my topic and interact with many stimulating students, some of whom have now moved on to distinguished careers of their own. I mention especially Derk Pereboom, Holly Thomas, Keith DeRose, William Fitzpatrick, Houston Smit, Brian Lee, and Andrew Chignell, whose challenges have shaped my thoughts at particular points, as have those of colleagues Robert Merrihew Adams, Rogers Albritton, Nicholas Wolterstorff, and Serene Jones. During my seminary days, James Loder furnished crash courses in the conceptuality of developmental psychology. Later, the experiences of many members of the Los Angeles area congregations I served—most notably, Trinity Hollywood, St. Augustine's Santa Monica, and St. Mary's Palms—became the litmus test for my reflections on God and evil, while many and deep conversations with A. Orley Swartzentruber and Jon Hart Olson crystallized key questions and connections.

Thanks of another kind go to Nelson Pike. When, as an undergraduate in 1963, I read his now celebrated article "Hume on Evil," I recommended it to all and sundry as the solution! This led to my enrolling in a summer reading course on the problem of evil when he visited the University of Illinois and subsequently to my going to Cornell in 1964 to study philosophy of religion with him. Besides his devotion to analytical clarity and precision, and his persistent instinct to profit from the history of philosophy and theology, Nelson evidenced a remarkable capacity to focus on and help the student develop *her* own ideas. To whatever extent I have also been shaped by other influences and commitments, his training has formed not only my approach to the problem of evil, but also the way I teach and do philosophy generally. That is why I dedicate this book to him.

M. M. A.

Horrendous Evils
and the
Goodness of God

Introduction

Evil as topic and symbol is fascinating, alluring. It sucks into itself everything that is "out of bounds," not only forbidden but unthinkable, "beyond
the pale." Undefined, it is chaotic, energetic, disruptive, full of possibility.
Unquarantined, evil is pervasive, insideous, infiltrating nook and cranny and
winding itself around roots and arteries until it is impossible to separate out
from the good. By contrast, good may seem boring, banal, superficial. Even
writing or reading about evil affords opportunity to taste that delicious
dread of picking and tasting fruits primordially disallowed.

Evil as concrete fact of human life is no less gripping but understandably
loses much of its charm. It takes hard work to make planet Earth a hospitable place. Life's necessities seem to be in short supply. Food, water,
shelter, and clothing are difficult to secure. Relative to the hazards we en-
counter, our psycho-physical capacities are quite limited and easily damaged. At the biological level, we are vulnerable to predators, disease, and
death. Coping with nature, eeking out survival, requires human collaboration, which brings its own problems. For we human beings do terrible
things to one another, sometimes deliberately but also unintentionally, un-
deniably as individuals but certainly collectively, occasionally with carefully
calibrated precision but often with unforeseen consequences that mush-
room out of control.

In our struggle to survive and flourish, "knowledge is power." Intelligence gives us an advantage relative to other animals. We can try to understand the world around us, to form theories about the place of humans in

the universe. We can study ourselves, try to discover what patterns of character and forms of social organization frustrate human life and what make it flourish. Religion and science respond to this need to get our bearings, albeit in different ways. Both draw pictures of the cosmos, offer estimates of human being and its prospects. Both are fruitful with corollary recommendations as to better and worse ways to negotiate life.

Nevertheless, in relation to what it would be helpful to know, human cognitive powers are limited. Whether individually or collectively, we are inveterate oversimplifiers, marginalizing some data in order to come up with tractable systematizations, over time striving for more complexity without sacrificing too much simplicity, only eventually to face such massive misfits as to have to begin again. Idealized scientific method takes this successive approximations approach for granted; its program of testing hypotheses even goes looking for falsifying evidence. Religions are more conservative; as complex social institutions and practices, they have their own patterns of adjustment and evolution. But they too face crises, especially when their accounts are inadequate to handle the very features of life for which they are most needed.

Evil belongs to the syllabus of religion, which is expected to say something about its nature, source, and consequences: how and to what extent it takes root in human beings, whether and how it can be eradicated, how in the midst of it we should conduct ourselves through life. Where biblical religions are concerned, with their strong doctrine of an omniscient, omnipotent, and perfectly good God Who created everything other than Godself, evil has always been a challenge. The Bible's authors themselves struggle with it in an impressive variety of ways (contrast Job with Ecclesiastes with the Servant Songs of Isaiah with the synoptic Gospels). Typically, Jewish and Christian writers from the first four centuries up through the Middle Ages sought the origin of evil in the material composition of the world or in the free choice of personal creatures and explained Divine permission of evils in terms of God's overall creative projects and commitment to maintaining optimal cosmic order. If ancient and medieval attention was trained on sin and disordered human agency, on the metaphysical fact of death, and on material resistance to order, writers from Hume onwards have shifted the spotlight back onto personal pain and suffering, to its apparent arbitrariness, to the frequency of its occurrence, often—whether through wars or natural disasters—on a grand scale. In contemporary philosophical debates, 'evil' functions as an umbrella term that covers both foci, indeed all the minuses of life.

Although I discuss many traditional ideas in this book, my approach here is not by way of historical review but by way of analysis of the structure of some problems that evils cause for biblical religions generally and for Christianity in particular, as well as through examination of how varied conceptual resources constrict or expand the prospects for a solution to these problems. My point of departure reflects my own history with philosophical discussions of these problems. In 1955, J. L. Mackie published his now classic article "Evil and Omnipotence," arguing that theism is *positively* irrational because the existence of evil is *logically* incompatible with that of an omnipotent, omniscient, and perfectly good God. Its sharp analytical focus readily attracted attention and in fact centered roughly thirty years of debate among analytic philosophers of religion. Much important work was produced within this framework, including fresh formulations, in-depth reflections, and probing critiques of the best-of-all-possible-worlds and free will approaches to the problem of evil. For me as for many who grew up in philosophy during those years, these rich articles were our starting point for reflecting on the problem of evil.

After many years of teaching through the syllabus of these materials, I began to feel the discussion had bogged down, somehow stymied. Cost-benefit analyses of major responses to Mackie had been laid on the table. None seemed to satisfy all the way down. Despite supplementary and partial suggestions, no comprehensive way forward appeared on the horizons. I began to look for a diagnosis of what was going wrong.

My own nutshell answer is that the debate was carried on at too high a level of abstraction. By agreeing to a focus on what William Rowe came to label "restricted standard theism," both sides avoided responsibility to a particular tradition; neither took care—whether in arguments for the incompossibility of God and evils, or in their rebuttals—to construe the value-premises and attribute-analyses as that tradition does; neither felt any pressure to explore its distinctive resources or to admit its peculiar liabilities.[1] In fact, Christian theism embraces a richer store of valuables than secular value-theories recognize, while some versions of Christianity countenance worse evils as well. Further, our philosophical propensity for generic solutions—our search for a single explanation that would cover all evils at once—has permitted us to ignore the worst evils in particular (what I shall call horrendous evils) and so to avoid confronting the problems they pose.

In this book, I develop these reflections and their consequences in some detail. I begin, in Part 1, by deconstructing Mackie's problem. I argue that his elegant formulation is based on (often implicit) methodological as-

---

1. William L. Rowe, "Evil and the Theistic Hypothesis: A Response to Wykstra," *International Journal for Philosophy of Religion* 16 (1984): 95–100.

sumptions which were usually (if sometimes tacitly) accepted by parties to the dispute. I maintain that by operating within these parameters, our discussion has not only passed over the worst evils, but also mistaken the proportions between Divine and human agency and overestimated the relevance of *moral* goodness to the issues at stake. In Part 2, I first call attention to alternative metaphysical models for understanding Divine agency in relation to creatures. Then I further challenge the value-theory imperialism of morals by reintroducing a range of neglected values. Appealing to social anthropology, I show how the calculus of purity and defilement, on the one hand, and the honor code, on the other, each remodel Divine-human relations. I also put an end to the eclipse of aesthetic goodness in analytic philosophical discussions of the problem of evil. In Part 3, I draw these materials together to show how the wider resources of Christian theology can be deployed to formulate a family of solutions to the so-called logical problem of evil. I close with a brief consideration of the relation of philosophical reflection to praxis.

This book is addressed to a broad readership that includes both analytic philosophers of religion and Christian philosophers. I live in both worlds. Thus, the issues raised ought to be read by analytic philosophers of religion as a reflection on our recent "family history." Standing within that circle, I warn Mackie's heirs against "short way" inconsistency proofs that fail to pay detailed attention to subtlety and nuance in the belief system under attack. At the same time, standing within the circle of Christian philosophers, I challenge us to show the courage of our convictions by drawing on the wider resources of our religion to explain how an omnipotent, omniscient, and perfectly good God could both permit and defeat even horrendous evils. Insofar as I "practice what I preach," this is also an essay in philosophical theology. One subtheme of this book is that these disciplines are not so distinct as is commonly thought.

Worries about evils and the problems they cause, resist confinement, however. They not only spill across academic boundaries, but well up in the hearts of most every human being. The basic intuitions that first motivate my critique and then inspire my constructive position are not technical in nature. Not only are they highly accessible, these same intuitions are often voiced by those who suffer, by their intimates who keep watch, and by those who agonize over the ruinous harms they have caused. I hope this book may also be of use to this wider audience, insofar as it offers a fuller articulation of what I have learned from these many voices.

Part One

DECONSTRUCTING
A PROBLEM

[1]

Problems of Evil

If God exists, how can evils be explained? For an omnipotent being
would have the power to prevent any and all evils if it wanted to;
an omniscient being would know all about them; and a perfectly
good being would want to prevent/eliminate all the evils it could.
Thus, it seems, if God existed, and were omnipotent, omniscient,
and perfectly good, there would be no evils.

NELSON PIKE, Good and Evil

When, in philosophy, a number of prima facie plausible premisses seem
to generate a problematic conclusion, the resultant argument can be said to
formulate a problem, and that problem can be dealt with in various ways.
One can simply accept the argument as sound and its surprising conclusion
as true. Alternatively, one may remain confident that the conclusion is false
but see the argument as creating a difficulty for anyone who rejects it: that
of explaining how the prima facie plausible premisses are not all so acceptable, the inferences not so evident, as they seem. To respond the latter way
is to take the argument aporetically, as generating a puzzle. What is important to note is that the same argument can be taken in both directions.
Sometimes consensus gathers around one reading—as when most philosophers took Zeno's paradoxes and Parmenides' arguments against the possibility of change as aporetic. In other cases, both usages persist, but one pre-
dominates—as in the case of skeptical arguments about the existence of
other minds and/or a physical world, about the possibility of knowledge,
and so forth.

The traditional problem of evil stated above participates in this ambiguity. In this chapter, I show how the different ways of taking it generate con-

trasting methodologies and chart how preoccupation with one of them has limited progress towards a solution to the deepest of religious problems.

1. The Aporetic Version

Understood aporetically, the traditional problem of evil gives crisp focus to a difficulty in understanding the relationship between God and evil. In particular, there is a prima facie obstacle to consistently maintaining both

> (1) God exists and is omnipotent, omniscient, and perfectly good,

and

> (2) Evil exists,

not because there is an explicit logical contradiction between them,[1] but because our pre-analytic understandings of 'omnipotent' and 'perfectly good' construe the maximizations straightforwardly, in such a way as to render

> (P1) A perfectly good being would always eliminate evil so far as it could, and

> (P2) There are *no limits* to what an omnipotent being can do,

plausibly true. (1), (2), (P1), and (P2) seem to constitute an inconsistent quartet, so that there is a valid inference from the conjunction of the last three to the denial of the first. When taken aporetically, the challenge of this argument is constructive: it is an invitation to probe more deeply into the logical relations among these propositions, to offer more rigorous and subtle analyses of the divine perfections. (P1) and (P2) are not held to have anything more than prima facie plausibility in their favor. And the aporetic argument serves a positive function of structuring the discussion and enabling one to pinpoint and contrast various resolutions in a precise way.

Notice, even those who (like many of the great medieval philosophers) accepted (2) as empirically obvious and held (1) as demonstrable a priori or as a nonnegotiable item of faith could recognize a problem in understanding how (1) and (2) are compossible—of articulating (1), (2), and one's un-

---

1. Cf. Alvin Plantinga, "Self-Profile," in *Alvin Plantinga*, ed. James E. Tomberlin and Peter Van Inwagen (Dordrecht: D. Reidel Publishing Company, 1985), 38.

derstanding of the divine attributes fully enough to explain why they have seemed compossible.

2. The Atheistic Argument from Evil

In the modern period, David Hume started a trend of using such an argument from evil to give a positive disproof of divine existence.[2] In "Evil and Omnipotence," that neo-Humean J. L. Mackie sets out to establish "not that religious beliefs lack rational support, but that they are *positively irrational*" by showing that "the several parts of the *essential* theological doctrine"—namely, (1) and (2)—"are inconsistent with each other."[3] Once again, Mackie recognizes that (1) and (2) are not explicitly contradictory; one needs "some additional premises, or perhaps some quasi-logical rules connecting the terms 'good', 'evil', and 'omnipotent'." But, to his mind, these are readily supplied by (P1) and (P2) above. To be sure, Mackie admits, a theologian might try to rebut his atheistic argument from evil by making "a minor modification of one or more of the constituent propositions [namely, (1), (2), (P1), and/or (P2)], which would, however, still satisfy all the essential requirements of ordinary theism."[4] But on Mackie's deployment of the argument, (P1) and (P2) are now advanced, not as preanalytic guesses as to what is meant by 'omnipotence' and 'perfect goodness', but as principles having presumption in their favor. Mackie now talks as if the burden of proof is on the theologian to show that some revision of (P1) and/or (P2) is still both reasonable and true to ordinary religious belief.[5]

3. Pike's Clarification

In his model article, "Hume on Evil," Nelson Pike discovers that the Humean atheistic argument from evil requires reformulation, for, (P1) does not accurately reflect *our ordinary moral intuitions,* according to which we do not always blame a person for permitting (not preventing) evil that was within his/her power to prevent: "As a general statement, a being who per-

2. Nelson Pike, "Introduction," *God and Evil* (Englewood Cliffs, N.J.: Prentice-Hall, 1964), 4.

3. J. L. Mackie, "Evil and Omnipotence," in *The Problem of Evil*, ed. Marilyn McCord Adams and Robert Merrihew Adams (Oxford: Oxford University Press, 1990), 25–37, esp. 25–26. (Italics mine.)

4. Ibid., 25, quote on 28.

5. Thus, Mackie notes, as if it were a disadvantage, that the metaphysical contention 'Good cannot exist without evil' resolves the contradiction between (1) and (2) "only by qualifying some of the propositions that constitute the problem" (ibid., 28).

mits (or brings about) an instance of suffering might be perfectly good pro-
viding only that there is a morally sufficient reason for his action"[6] If God
had *a morally sufficient reason* for permitting (bringing about) instances of
suffering, then His nonprevention of such evils would not count against His
perfect goodness. To generate a logical contradiction from (1) and (2), one
would have to maintain

> (P3) It is logically impossible for an omniscient, omnipotent being to
>   have a morally sufficient reason for permitting (bringing about)

evils, a premiss which derives some plausibility from the fact that, ordinar-
ily, morally sufficient reasons for permitting (bringing about) evils arise
from some ignorance or weakness in the agent thus excused. Conversely,
those who wish to rebut Mackie's atheological challenge will have to undermine (P3), either by furnishing a logically possible, morally sufficient
reason for permitting (bringing about evils) that even an omnipotent and
omniscient being could hold, or by giving some other reason to think
that—for all we know—there is such a reason.

Pike's reformulation brings to the surface two assumptions implicit in the
Humean atheistic argument from evil: (i) that 'goodness' is to be understood
in terms, not of metaphysical or natural goodness, but rather of *moral* goodness; and (ii) that God is understood to be a moral agent whose creative activities are governed by moral obligations.[7] Accordingly, (iii) to say that God
is *perfectly* good is to imply that God fully lives up to those obligations in
creation. That is why, assuming (P1), the existence of evil seems to count
against it.

Moreover, following J. S. Mill, Pike understands 'moral goodness' here in
the *ordinary* sense. Expanding on (i), Mill does not deny that there is such a
thing as metaphysical or natural goodness, which might be possessed in infinite degree by "the Absolute," or God, and be a property that pertains to
God as He is in Himself. However that may be, Mill insists that to count as
worthy of worship, a being must be perfectly good in the ordinary sense of
that term, a sense which is "relational" in that it implies that its possessor
would deal with the world and treat created persons in certain ways and not

---

6. Nelson Pike, "Hume on Evil," *Philosophical Review* 72 (1963): 180–97, quote on p.
188.

7. Although Plantinga is far from explicit about this in his published writings, in a letter to me on January 23, 1987, he suggests that he agrees with this account of God as subject
of moral obligations regarding the conduct of creation: he complains that Scotus's principle
"that God has no obligations to creatures to will one thing rather than another" "isn't at all
obviously true" but rather "seems *to me* questionable at best" (my emphasis).

others. Mill chides those who move to cut off such implications by equiv-
ocating on 'perfect goodness' as being almost so misleading as to lie.[8]

Finally, in the article "Hume on Evil," Pike assumes the perfections—
omniscience, omnipotence, and perfect [moral] goodness in the ordinary
sense—to be *essential* to God, at least in the sense that the statement 'for all
x, if x is God, then x is omniscient, omnipotent, and perfectly good' is true
by definition, or analytic. That is how the conjunction of (2) with (P1) and
(P2) or with (P3) is supposed to imply that God does not exist, rather than
that God exists but lacks one or more of these perfections.

4. The Myth of Shared Values

Pike seems perfectly at ease with the notion of a religion-neutral value
theory that is common to atheologian and believer. In his anthology, he
consistently draws on "ordinary" moral intuitions and seconds Mill's insistence that unless God is perfectly good in the ordinary sense of moral
goodness applied to human beings, He is not worthy of worship.

No doubt, Pike is influenced here by the fairly wide-ranging agreement
(even within our pluralistic society) about the sorts of acts that are morally
wrong and/or praiseworthy, the character traits that count as virtuous or vicious, and the individuals who are saints and heroes. Such extensional
agreement underlies the government of pluralistic society by common laws,
its entertainment by common literature and dramatic fare, and other shared
aspects of culture.

Moreover, Pike wrote "Hume on Evil" at Cornell in the early 1960s,
when the Philosophy Department there was still in the grip of ordinary
language philosophy. Recall that according to this methodology, philosophers who want to find out truths about mind and body, morals, and so on,
should not go about inventing philosophical theories, but should set out to
analyze the concepts of mind, body, moral goodness, and so on, implicit in
our ordinary use of language. Insofar as meaning is a matter of social con-
vention, the philosopher proceeds to examine linguistic usage with a view
to making those conventions explicit.

Many, perhaps most, analytic philosophers have abandoned the ideals of
ordinary language philosophy (and rightly so, in my judgment) and re-
sumed the traditional activity of theory construction. Once theorizing begins, however, the hope of universal agreement in value theory is shattered,

---

8. Pike, "Introduction," 3. Cf. J. S. Mill, "Mr. Mansel on the Limits of Religious
Thought," in Pike, *God and Evil*, 37–45.

the wide-ranging extensional overlaps notwithstanding. Witness, for example, the divide in secular ethics between "consequentialists" who assert that lying can sometimes be justified if it optimizes the consequences, and "deontologists," who contend that lying is always wrong, no matter what!

If such disagreements in moral theory arise among philosophers who share a common understanding of what there is, how much more should theories diverge where ontological commitments are significantly different. An ontology that holds roughly that "what you see is what you get" may recognize such valuables as sensory pleasures (the beauty of nature and cultural artifacts, the joy of creativity, and loving personal intimacy), but it will be less rich than ontologies which posit a transcendent good (such as the form of the Good in Platonism, or God, the infinite being and supremely valuable object, in Christianity). Insofar as the highest human happiness is usually conceived of as involving some relation to the best good(s), and moral precepts direct humans to their individual and collective ends, different ontologies will produce different accounts of the human good and varying moral precepts.

Moreover, we should expect moral theories to differ with respect to the origin and structure of personal obligations, depending upon whether or not all the persons recognized by the ontology share a common ontological status—in particular, whether all the persons are human or, instead, whether there are suprahuman persons. Whereas nontheistic value theories assign all persons a common ontological status as humans and find it natural to see all persons as woven into a common web of rights and mutual obligations, many Christian thinkers regard God as of the wrong ontological category for such entanglements (see Chapter 4). Of crucial importance for the present discussion is the fact that different ontological commitments with their different stores of valuables widen or narrow the range of options for defeating evils with goods. Secular value theories can offer only packages of immanent goods; some religious theories posit an infinite transcendent goodness and invite relationship to it; while mainstream Christianity believes the infinite good to be personal and locates the happiness of finite persons in loving personal intimacy with the divine persons.

5. The Snares of Equivocation

Given such value-theory pluralism, disagreements between Christians and atheologians about whether and what sorts of goods could balance off or defeat evils are bound to emerge. But these differences will yield varying, nonequivalent notions of 'perfect goodness' and contrasting evaluations of evils and, so, lead to *equivocal* interpretations of our original propositions (1) and (2). Indeed, insofar as these perfections are analytically predicated of 'God', such variations in the notion of 'perfect goodness' beget different concepts of God; insofar as they are regarded as nonessential predications of relative goodness, these differences yield widely divergent ascriptions of character. The upshot is that the structure of any fair-minded debate about the problem of evil will be much more complicated than the literature in analytic philosophy of religion over the last thirty years has made it to seem.

Suppose we take the atheologian like Mackie at his word, that the problem he has in mind in alleging the inconsistency of (1) and (2) is "a logical problem, the problem of clarifying and reconciling a number of beliefs."[9] We must ask, "Whose beliefs?" and "According to whose interpretations?" Mackie has deployed the problem of evil as a disproof for the existence of God in the hope of showing the religious beliefs of others contradictory and irrational. If he simply construes (1) and (2) and the range of possible morally sufficient reasons from the presumptive standpoint of his own value theory, it would be a brilliant defensive maneuver for the believer to show how the compossibility of (1) and (2) follows even within the atheologian's point of view. But this would be a mere preliminary to making explicit their disagreements in value theory and the way they yield two different problems of evil: the question of whether (1) and (2) are compossible on the atheologian's reading, and that of whether they can stand together on the believer's rendering. Insofar as Mackie wished to show the believer's view contradictory and irrational, he must take an interest in whether (1) and (2) can be understood as compossible on the believer's construal of those claims. Likewise, it would be a hollow victory for the believer to stop with showing that the God that Mackie doesn't believe in (essentially omniscient, omnipotent, and perfectly good in Mackie's senses) could coexist with evils, if that God is not the one the believer confesses.

6. Further Distinctions, More Problems

6.1. Abstract versus Concrete Formulations.

If value-theory pluralism renders (2) systematically ambiguous, possibilities for equivocation remain even when the framework is held fixed. For, as Michael Tooley points out, 'evil' can be understood "abstractly" to refer to some evil or other, or "concretely" to refer to evils in the amounts and of the

9. J. L. Mackie, "Evil and Omnipotence," 25.

kinds and with distributions of the sort found in the actual world.[10] Most would agree, however, that it is quite a different thing to argue that Divine permission of some evil or other (such as five minutes of wincing from a torn hang nail) is compossible with omniscience, omnipotence, and perfect goodness, than to argue that Divine noninterference with the horrors of Auschwitz is. Yet failure to distinguish sharply between abstract and concrete formulations invites defenders to focus on the former in producing rebuttals of (P3), while sliding forward to the latter when claiming victory (see Chapter 3).

I agree with Tooley that the abstract problem of evil—while not uncontroversial—is of marginal theoretical interest. It is the *concrete* version that captures our attention because of the depth of its correlative existential and pragmatic implications. Some philosophers concede abstract compossibility but argue that God's existence is incompatible with some quantity of evil, while others focus, not on quantity but on *certain types* of evil. Dostoyevsky's Ivan Karamazov instances the unjust tormented suffering of children, while liberation theologians target massive communal suffering in circumstances of war and political oppression.[11] In the next chapter, I shall try to capture these especially offensive types of suffering under the umbrella of horrendous evils.

6.2. Logical versus Evidential Problems

Mackie is eager to distinguish his approach from other attempts that argue merely that concrete evils are good evidence against the truth of theism, insofar as they render the existence of an omnipotent, omniscient, and perfectly good God unlikely. They are content to contend that if (2) is true, then (1) is probably false. Mackie reaches for the stronger conclusion that theism is "positively irrational" because inconsistent with obvious facts. For much of the last forty years, this logical problem of evil has held center stage. Yet, already in his 1974 book, *The Nature of Necessity,* Plantinga—confident that he has dispatched the logical problem—returns to the evidential problem of evil, arguing that objections from the quantity of evil had no purchase. Five years later, in a series of articles, Rowe revived the argument that certain types of evils are manifestly pointless and so constitute good evidence for the nonexistence of God.[12] Rowe's papers have in turn

10. Michael Tooley, "The Argument from Evil," *Philosophical Perspectives* 5, Philosophy of Religion (1991): 89–134, esp. 91–93.

11. See, e.g., Rebecca S. Chopp, *The Praxis of Suffering: An Interpretation of Liberation and Political Theologies* (Maryknoll, N.Y.: Orbis Books, 1986), esp. 1–2.

12. William L. Rowe, "The Problem of Evil and Some Varieties of Atheism," *American Philosophical Quarterly* 16 (1979): 335–41; Rowe, "Evil and the Theistic Hypothesis: A Response to Wykstra," *International Journal for Philosophy of Religion* 16 (1984): 95–100; "The Em-

prompted the full range of responses. *Total refutations* boldly deny that evils are even prima facie evidence against God's existence because God's ways are so much higher than ours that we would not expect to be aware of Divine reasons for their permission if there were any.[13] *Defenses* trot out armies of possible reasons why God might permit such evils, contending that even if we don't know the actual reasons, the greater the number of apparently available reasons, the less obviously pointless are the evils in question.[14] *Theodicies* suggest actual reasons, whether on grounds of revelation or of common sense.[15]

Participants in this recent debate have shown considerable ingenuity and insight. Moreover, Rowe's discussion has the merit of burning off the fog of abstraction and riveting attention on particularly troublesome evils. And I agree with Rowe's claim against the total refuters, that certain sorts of evils do (or would, should they occur) create a strong presumption against the existence of an omnipotent, omniscient, and perfectly good God. Nevertheless, in this book, I restrict my attention to discussions of the "logical" problem for twin reasons. First, my strategy for solving the special problem posed by horrendous evils is simpler within the framework of the logical problem of the consistency of (1) and (2). Once again, in my view, Mackie and his fellow atheologians found theism an easy target precisely because they were unacquainted with the details and subtleties of more particular traditions. My approach repairs this ignorance by bringing wider theological resources back into play. Naturally, atheologians would not concede the probability, much less the truth, of these further tenets. But where the logical problem is concerned, this does not matter. It is enough if they are plausibly self-consistent and logically compatible with the other belief items at stake. Second, and in any event, debate about whether certain sorts of evil are plainly pointless quickly re-

---

pirical Argument from Evil," in *Rationality, Religious Belief, and Moral Commitment,* ed. Robert Audi and William Wainwright (Ithaca, N.Y.: Cornell University Press, 1986), 227–47; Rowe, "Ruminations about Evil," *Philosophical Perspectives* 5, Philosophy of Religion (1991): 69–88.

13. Notably, Stephen J. Wykstra, "The Humean Obstacle to Evidential Arguments from Suffering: On Avoiding the Evils of 'Appearance'," *International Journal for Philosophy of Religion* 16 (1984): 73–93. Cf. Peter Van Inwagen, "The Problems of Evil, Air, and Silence," *Philosophical Perspectives* 5, Philosophy of Religion (1991): 135–65.

14. E.g., William P. Alston, "The Inductive Argument from Evil and the Human Cognitive Condition," *Philosophical Perspectives* 5, Philosophy of Religion (1991): 26–67.

15. For an interesting anthology of articles on the evidential problem of evil, see Daniel Howard-Snyder, ed., *The Evidential Argument from Evil* (Bloomington: Indiana University Press, 1996).

turns to territory shared with the logical problem: namely, whether there are any (many) reasons compossible with omnipotent, omniscient, perfect goodness for permitting (producing) evils of that kind. Consequently, my focus on the logical problem created by horrendous evils will cover some of the same ground.

[2]

Global Goodness and
Its Limitations

1. Pike's Best-of-All-Possible-Worlds Defense

Having reformulated the atheological argument from evil in terms of the contention that the statements

(1) God exists and is omnipotent, omniscient, and perfectly good,

(2) Evil exists,

and

(P3) It is logically impossible for an omniscient, omnipotent being to have a morally sufficient reason for permitting (bringing about) evils,

constitute an inconsistent triad, Pike offers the believer what I shall call an epistemic defense against it. Assuming that (2) refers not merely to some evil or other but to evils in the amounts and of the kinds and with the distributions found in the actual world, Pike rules out as unpromising the piecework approach of arguing that one sort of evil could be logically connected with one sort of good (say, injury with forgiveness) and some other sort of evil with some other sort of good (perhaps, danger with courage). Just as the atheologian cannot prove (P3) by enumerating putative excuses for permitting (bringing about) evils and rejecting them one by one, be-

cause he "could never claim to have examined all the possibilities";[1] so also
it is hopeless to catalog the evils and display logically necessary connections
with great enough particular goods. We may fare better, however, if we look
for a single good that could at once provide a general morally sufficient reason for the permission of all the evils.[2] Pike turns for materials to the best-
of-all-possible-worlds theodicy, which asserts

> (P4) God, being a perfectly good, omniscient, and omnipotent being,
>   would create the best of all possible worlds,

and

> (P5) The best of all possible worlds contains instances of suffering as
>   logically indispensable components.

Pike reasons that if (P4) and (P5) were true, they would state a morally sufficient reason—namely, the aim of creating the best of all possible
worlds—that even an omniscient and omnipotent being could have for
permitting (bringing about) evils. Thus, the conjunction of (P4) and (P5)
entails the falsity of (P3); just as the conjunction of (1) with (P4) and (P5)
entails (2).[3]

If we could know (P4) and (P5) to be true, or even possible, we would
thus be able not only to defeat the above atheistic argument from evil—by
showing (P3) to be false—but also to demonstrate the compossibility of (1)
and (2) (let us call this a demonstrative defense). Unfortunately, Pike reckons
(P5) to be a proposition which is possible if and only if necessary. And he
admits that he sees no way to establish (P5) apart from (P4)—in particular
apart from an a priori proof for the existence of God (such as Leibniz
thought he had). Consequently, Pike does not think his borrowings from the
best-of-all-possible-worlds theodicy put us in a position to make the positive assertion that (1) and (2) are compossible. But since the atheist is in no
better position to show (P5) false than the theist is to prove it true, Pike concludes that the atheist is not entitled to his claim of inconsistency either.
Since, for all he or the theist knows, (P5) is true; for all he or the theist
knows, (P3) is false; and a Scottish verdict of "not proven" must be rendered.[4]

---

1. Nelson Pike, "Hume on Evil," in *The Problem of Evil*, ed. Marilyn McCord Adams and
Robert Merrihew Adams (Oxford: Oxford University Press, 1990), 41.
2. Pike made these points in undergraduate lectures on the philosophy of religion given
at Cornell University in the falls of 1964 and 1965.
3. Pike, "Hume on Evil," 42–45.
4. Ibid., 47–48.

2. Plantinga's Defensive Apologetics

In his formally elegant and widely influential writings on the problem of evil, Alvin Plantinga has concentrated on formulating a demonstrative defense against atheological arguments such as we have been discussing.[5] Reviewing the logical structure of a defense, Plantinga writes, "One way to show that P and Q are consistent is to find some other proposition R such that P and R are consistent, and such that P and R together entail Q."[6] In the special case of the atheistic argument from evil, what is wanted is some proposition R which (i) is itself logically possible, (ii) is logically consistent with (1), and (iii) either alone or together with (1) entails (2). Plantinga emphasizes that it is not necessary in addition that R be (iv) true, (v) probable, (vi) plausible, or (vii) believed by either the atheist or the theist.[7] On the other hand, conditions (i) to (iii) would be trivially satisfied by some R for any pair of propositions that is logically consistent. Since Plantinga aims to convince the atheologian of the consistency of (1) and (2) by locating an appropriate R, he elsewhere indicates that R must satisfy the following additional conditions: both (viii) its logical possibility and (ix) its compossibility with (1) must be fairly clear.[8] Similarly, if "the R you propose has to fit the audience you mean to address," it would be too polemical to present an R that the defender himself does not regard as meeting conditions (i) and (ii).[9]

Assuming, once again, that (2) asserts not merely the existence of some evil or other, but evils in the amounts and of the kinds found in the actual world, one might try to construct R piecemeal, as the conjunction of logically possible morally sufficient reasons for evils of each type found here in the world as we find it. Like Pike, Plantinga thinks it would be a mistake to try to "get specific" about morally sufficient reasons this way and prefers to proceed "on a quite general level."[10]

Focusing on the other principal response to the problem of evil, the free will defense, Plantinga constructs his actual candidate for R with an eye on Mackie's main objection to it—namely, that if God existed and were going

---

5. This is his own self-description in "Self-Profile," in *Alvin Plantinga*, ed. James E. Tomberlin and Peter Van Inwagen (Dordrecht: D. Reidel, 1985), 37; see also Plantinga, *God and Other Minds* (Ithaca, N.Y.: Cornell University Press, 1967), 115–54; Plantinga, *The Nature of Necessity* (Oxford: Clarendon Press, 1974), 164–95.

6. Plantinga, "Self-Profile," 42–43.

7. Plantinga, "Self-Profile," 43–44; see also Plantinga, *The Nature of Necessity*, 165.

8. This comes out in his correspondence with me, his letter of January 23, 1987.

9. Plantinga to Norman Kretzmann and Eleonore Stump, February 23, 1987, and Plantinga to the author, February 27, 1987.

10. Plantinga, "Self-Profile," 34–35.

to create free creatures, He could have and therefore should have created only sinless ones. Thus, Plantinga proposes

> R*:   God has actualized a possible world A containing significantly free creatures (angels, human beings, other kinds, what have you) with respect to whose actions there is a balance of good over evil (so that A is on balance a very good world); some of these creatures are responsible for moral and natural evil; and it was not within God's power to create significantly free creatures with respect to whose actions there would be a better balance of good over evil than that displayed in A.

Both the possibility of $R*$ and its compossibility with (1) rest on highly subtle understandings of divine goodness and power—alternative to (P1) and (P2). Thus, in *The Nature of Necessity*, Plantinga argues at length that there are some possible worlds that not even an omnipotent God can create, contrary to (P2).[11] And he assumes, contrary to (P1), that a perfectly good God might well accept evils (in the amounts and of the kinds found in the actual world) as the price of goods related to free creatures. $R*$'s entailment of (2) is obvious.

3. Defeat versus Balancing off

We have already noted how Pike works within the parameters of common-ground, "ordinary" moral intuitions and seeks to provide (what for all we know may be) a morally sufficient reason for Divine permission of evils in terms of a generic and global good—the best of all possible worlds. In effect, his candidate for R would be

> R**:   God created the best of all possible worlds, and the best of all possible worlds contains evils as logically indispensable constituents.

If the second conjunct could be known to be possible, Pike thinks $R**$ would be the basis for a demonstrative defense. Failing that, since $R**$ cannot be known to be impossible, it provides an epistemic defense.

Not only do best-of-all-possible-worlds defenders draw on the consequentialist assumption

> (P6) an agent is always morally permitted to bring about the morally best state of affairs he can,

11. Plantinga, *The Nature of Necessity*, 164–93.

they also presuppose a distinction, spotlighted by G. E. Moore and further explored by Roderick Chisholm, between two ways value-parts may be related to one another and to value-wholes.[12] The balancing-off relation is arithmetical and additive: value-parts are balanced off within a larger whole if other parts of opposite value equal or outweigh them. Alternatively, value-parts may be integrated into a whole to which they bear (in Moore's words) "no regular proportion" via relations of "organic unity." In these latter cases, not only may the whole have a different value from the part, but also

> (P7) a significantly smaller, negatively (or positively) valued part can contribute to a greater overall positive (or negative) value in the whole;

in which case (to borrow Chisholm's label) the negative (or positive) value of the part may be said to be "defeated" within the whole. Aesthetic examples illustrate this principle—for example, in Monet's study of Rouen cathedral in early morning, the ugliness of the bilious green color patches is defeated by their integration into the vast beauty of the artistic design. Obviously, if the value-parts were networked to the whole possible world only by additive relations, it would be impossible that the best of all possible worlds should contain evils. Thus, best-of-all-possible-worlds approaches must take possible worlds to be like impressionist paintings in this respect, so that (P7) applies.[13]

---

12. G. E. Moore, *Principia Ethica* (Cambridge: Cambridge University Press, 1960), 27–36. See also Roderick Chisholm, "The Defeat of Good and Evil," in Adams and Adams, *The Problem of Evil*, 53–68; for Chisholm's alternative analysis in an earlier version of the paper, see "The Defeat of Good and Evil," *Proceedings of the American Philosophical Association* 42 (1968–69): 21–38.

13. In "The Defeat of Good and Evil," Chisholm's own ingenious attempts to give the contrast between balancing off and defeat technical precision seize on the idea that balancing off occurs when a whole includes mutually distinct parts of comparable but opposing values, while defeat is never merely a function of the opposing values of mutually exclusive parts. Chisholm's definitions make the two relations exclusive, however, by stipulating that the value of a part *p* is defeated within the whole *w* only if any of *w*'s parts whose values are opposed to *p*'s are themselves parts of *p*. This strikes me as wrongheaded and unnecessary. What is crucial is not whether the whole has mutually exclusive parts of opposing value, but rather what the relations are that the values of the parts bear to one another. In the case of Monet's painting, the aesthetic values of the color patches that constitute the painting would seem to be related both by addition and by organic unity—in which case the ugliness of the bilious green patches might not be balanced off if there were fewer pretty color patches than ugly ones, while being nevertheless defeated via organic integration into the artist's design.

4. Vagueness in Pike's Epistemic Defense

Pike's account justifies God's choice in terms of a global good, because being best possible is a feature of the world as a whole; it is generic, because it is at once justification of each and every one of the evils that the world in question contains. The further point I wish to make is that this putative morally justifying reason is thereby vague, twice over: First, as acknowledged by Pike, it eschews any attempt to say *how* any given piece or specific type of evil might fit in or contribute to making a given possible world the best. Second, by the same token, Pike does not tell us which sorts of goods contribute to that result. Insofar as Pike has followed the atheologian in focusing on a moral evaluation of God's productive activity, he would seem to suggest that Divine permission of evils could be excusable if such evils were suitably ordered into a package of merely immanent (created) goods of the sort recognized by the religion-neutral value theory. On this reading, Pike would be appealing to the epistemic possibility that evils (in the amounts and of the kinds found in this world) be defeated by some appropriate combination of created goods. On the other hand, Pike never denies that God, the being a greater than which cannot be conceived, is a valuable the proper ordering to which is necessary for the defeat of evils. Pike's epistemic defense based on $R^{\star\star}$ is thus vague as to whether the permission of evils is to be exonerated in relation to the immanent goods of secular value theory or as to whether appeal must be made to the transcendent good.

5. Defensive Distortions

Unlike Pike, Plantinga is explicit that a full-blown Christian value theory will diverge considerably from a merely secular one with regard to the range of valuables it includes. In a moving passage, he draws on the Heidelberg catechism to suggest how God, the supreme good, relates Himself to the evil of created suffering:

> As the Christian sees things, God does not stand idly by, cooly observing the suffering of his creatures. He enters into and shares our suffering. He endures the anguish of seeing his son, the second person of the Trinity, consigned to the bitterly cruel and shameful death of the cross. Some theologians claim that God cannot suffer. I believe they are wrong. God's capacity for suffering, I believe, is proportional to his greatness; it exceeds our capacity for suffering in the same measure as his capacity for knowledge exceeds ours. Christ was prepared to endure the agonies of hell itself; and

God, the Lord of the universe, was prepared to endure the suffering conse-quent upon his son's humiliation and death. He was prepared to accept this suffering in order to overcome sin, and death, and the evils that afflict our world, and to confer on us a life more glorious than we can imagine.[14]

But so far as the project of demonstrative defense is concerned, Plantinga wishes to find an R that both he and the atheist can agree on as logically pos-sible, compatible with (1), and—whether alone or together with (1)—entail-ing (2). And so Plantinga's $R^\star$, like Pike's $R^{\star\star}$, is generic and explicitly ap-peals only to global goods—the existence of significantly free creatures, whose actions collectively yield a favorable balance of moral good over moral evil—which could be recognized within an atheologian's value theory.

Since Plantinga aims at persuasion, one might expect that those explicitly mentioned good-making features are supposed to suffice, by themselves, to convince the atheologian that God could be morally in the clear in choosing a possible world containing evils (in the amounts and of the kinds found in the actual world). In correspondence, however, Plantinga makes clear that he does not intend that these features by themselves would constitute a morally sufficient reason for divine permission of evils. On the contrary, he writes,

> What would be the morally sufficient reason for allowing the devils to per-petrate moral evil is the good of the entire possible world God could thus actualize, a good as great or greater than any he could achieve if he didn't permit the devils to carry on their evil ways. But of course the good in question would not be the mere exercise of free will on the part of the fallen angels; that would be a minuscule part of it. The good in question would consist instead in such things as freely done good actions on the parts of angels, human beings, and no doubt personal creatures of other kinds, of the natural good of the whole world, and of the unthinkably great good of the incarnation and the redemption.[15]

This thought was prefigured in his 1979 paper "The Probabilistic Argument from Evil" where he writes that the views of the theist and atheist

> may differ, for example, with respect to the proportions of good and evil in the universe at large; the Christian theist will no doubt concur with St. Paul: "For I reckon that the sufferings we now endure bear no comparison with the splendor, as yet unrevealed, which is in store for us." (Romans 8:18) They

14. Plantinga, "Self-Profile," 36. The hypothesis of Divine suffering will be discussed fur-ther in Chapters 4 and 8.
15. Plantinga to Kretzmann and Stump, February 23, 1987.

may also disagree as to the *extent* or *amount* of good the universe contains. From a Christian point of view, there is immortality and the expectation of a better world; and, towering above all, the unthinkable splendor of God's gift to mankind in the suffering and death and resurrection of His Son.[16]

Elsewhere, Plantinga suggests that the supernatural good of God's existence might combine with the natural and moral goodness of the world to out-weigh evils (in the amounts and of the kinds and with the distribution found in the actual world), even apart from the Incarnation and Atone-ment.[17] Admittedly, the natural goodness of the world and the supernatural goodness of divine existence and/or the Incarnation and Redemption are *not* explicitly mentioned in Plantinga's $R\star$; but they aren't explicitly ex-cluded either. It is because $R\star$ is compatible with these further goods, that Plantinga recognizes $R\star$ as satisfying conditions (i) to (iii) above.

But then we may ask how $R\star$ is supposed to serve its function? For ei-ther the atheologian will accept the explicit list—the good of created free-dom and the favorable balance of moral good over evil (a more favorable balance than which God could not ensure)—as sufficient to establish $R\star$'s satisfaction of conditions (i) to (iii) above, or he will not. If he does not, it would seem that Plantinga cannot hope to convince without making ex-plicit additions. If the atheologian does, but Plantinga does not, proferring $R\star$ as it stands seems misleading and unacceptably polemical (by Plantinga's own lights).

Plantinga, in correspondence, explains that $R\star$ is not designed "to exhibit the main types of goods that outweigh the evils those worlds contain; rather, I refer to the goods connected with free creatures because these are the goods such that possibly God may have to put up with evil in order to actualize them."[18] Insofar as the atheologian has conceded (for his own reasons) that a world would be good enough for God to make except for feature F (in Mackie's example, the sins of free persons other than God), $R\star$ need only mention a condition acceptable to the atheologian that exhibits the compos-sibility of F with (1); it would not be necessary for $R\star$ to list all the other good-making features of such worlds. $R\star$ thereby wins neutral ground: the atheologian will accept $R\star$ for his reasons (supplementing the explicit list of goods one way), while Plantinga underwrites it for other reasons (filling out the list in a Christian way). Put otherwise, $R\star$ is an abstract general proposi-

16. Alvin Plantinga, "The Probabilistic Argument from Evil," *Philosophical Studies* 35 (1979): 46–47.
17. Plantinga to author, June 12, 1987.
18. Ibid.

tion picking out an infinite family of possible worlds. The atheologian looks at one branch, finds God and evil there, and concedes the compossibility of (1) and (2). Plantinga explores a different branch, finds God and evil there, and feels satisfied about the compossibility of (1) and (2). So far as the aims of the free will defense are concerned, Plantinga will be thus satisfied.

By thus masking differences about the store of goods, Plantinga's proce-dure already fosters equivocation (see Chapter 1, section 5). But there is a companion peculiarity where evils are concerned. With startling candor, Plantinga actually commends his generic and global approach on the ground that it enables us to avoid specific consideration of evils, so appalling and so horrifying that we not only do not know why God permits them, we can-not even conceive of any plausible candidate reasons.[19] (consider, for exam-ple, the lingering death by leukemia or cancer of young children or their mothers, the ironic evil of a father's accidentally running over his beloved child, and the demonic evils of the death camps in which a mother is forced to choose which of her children will live.) At the same time, Plantinga seems to want to respond to the concrete and not merely the abstract problem of evil. Yet, his chosen $R\star$ (as detailed in section 2 of this chapter) does not en-tail the existence of such horrifying evils, but only that some significantly free creatures cause some or other moral and natural evils, and so does not entail (2) concretely construed. Neither does the conjunction of (1) with his

(3) Every essence suffers from transworld depravity,[20]

and

(4) God actualizes a world containing moral good.

19. Plantinga, "Self-Profile," 34–35.

20. Plantinga defines transworld depravity for persons as follows: "A person *P suffers from transworld depravity* if and only if for every world W such that P is significantly free in W and P does only what is right in W, there is a state of affairs T and an action A such that (1) God strongly actualizes T in W and W includes every state of affairs God strongly actualizes in W, (2) A is morally significant for P in W, and (3) if God had strongly actualized T, P would have gone wrong with respect to A." Thus if a person suffers from transworld depravity, "it was not within God's power to actualize any world in which that person is significantly free but does no wrong—that is, a world in which he produces moral good but no moral evil" (*The Na-ture of Necessity*, 186). Similarly, given his metaphysics in which individuals are the instantia-tions of essences, he defines the transworld depravity of an essence as follows: "An essence E *suffers from transworld depravity* if and only if for every world W such that E entails the prop-erties *is significantly free in W* and *always does what is right in W*, there is a state of affairs T and an action A such that (1) T is the largest state of affairs God strongly actualizes in W, (2) A is morally significant for E's instantiation in W, and (3) if God had strongly actualized T, E's instantiation would have gone wrong with respect to A" (*The Nature of Necessity*, 188).

Thus, in boasting the triumph of his free will defense, he equivocates between concrete and abstract construals of (2).[21] To satisfy the requirements
of his own strategy, Plantinga will have to formulate another candidate
R★★★ that includes the condition that patterns of participation in such horrifying evils by significantly free creatures are no better transworldly than
they are in the actual world. Nothing is free in philosophy! I turn now to
examine this marginalized category of evils more closely to show how it
comes back to haunt him.

6. Horrendous Evils—Defining the Category

Among the evils that infect this world, some are worse than others. I
want to try to capture the most pernicious of them within the category of
horrendous evils,[22] which I define (for present purposes) as 'evils the participation in which (that is, the doing or suffering of which) constitutes prima
facie reason to doubt whether the participant's life could (given their inclusion in it) be a great good to him/her on the whole'. The class of paradigm horrors includes both individual and massive collective suffering, and
it encompasses the appalling evils mentioned by Plantinga. Further examples include the rape of a woman and axing off of her arms, psycho-physical torture whose ultimate goal is the disintegration of personality, betrayal
of one's deepest loyalties, child abuse of the sort described by Ivan Karamazov, child pornography, parental incest, slow death by starvation, the ex-
plosion of nuclear bombs over populated areas.

6.1. Reason to Doubt

I believe most people would agree that such evils as listed above constitute reason to doubt whether the participants' life can be worth living,
because it is so difficult humanly to conceive how such evils could be
overcome. In terms of Chisholm's contrast between balancing off and defeat,[23] horrendous evils seem prima facie, not only to balance off but to
engulf any positive value in the participant's life with which they are not
organically connected. In most (if not all cases) their destructive power
reaches beyond their concrete disvalue (such as the pain and material deprivation they involve), into the deep structure of the person's frameworks

21. See Plantinga, *The Nature of Necessity*, 189–90.
22. I defined this category first in my paper "Theodicy without Blame," *Philosophical Topics* 16 (1988): 215–45, and discussed it further in "Horrendous Evils and the Goodness of God,"
reprinted in Adams and Adams, *The Problem of Evil*, 209–21.
23. Chisholm, "The Defeat of Good and Evil," 53–68.

of meaning-making, seemingly to defeat the individual's value as a person, to degrade him/her to subhuman status. The Nazi death camps aimed, not merely to kill, but to dehumanize their victims, treating them worse than cattle to break down their personalities and reduce their social instincts to raw animal aggression and self-preservation. Organizing and running such institutions also degraded the Nazis, who caricatured human nature by using their finest powers the more imaginatively to transgress the bounds of human decency. Similarly, inasmuch as taboos constitute hedges erected to maintain minimum standards necessary for human community, taboo violations degrade their perpetrators, by exhibiting their unfitness for human society; they appear subjectively to degrade by socially disorienting their victims, exploding role expectations at the most fundamental of levels.

I intend this criterion for horrendous evils to be objective, but relative to individuals. The example of habitual complainers, who know how to make the worst of a good situation, shows individuals not to be incorrigible experts on what ills would defeat the positive value of their lives. Nor, as evidenced by the curmudgeon, is a person's explicit testimony an unfailingly reliable guide. Nevertheless, nature and experience endow people with different strengths; one bears easily what crushes another. And the individual's own estimate is a major piece of evidence as to whether his/her life has been a great good for him/her on the whole.

6.2. Finding the Right Rubric

I define the category horrendous evils as I do because I wish to focus on precisely those evils, Divine permission of which clearly calls into question Divine goodness towards the individuals who participate in them. I do not define them as outrageous injustices (the classification that Ivan Karamazov prefers), although some horrendous evils do involve injustice to their victims. One reason is that not all horrors involve injustice (for example, the father's nonnegligent accidental running over of his beloved infant son, or a person's slow, degrading death by cancer). Conversely, where injustice is involved, the concept of injustice rarely plumbs the depths of what is so bad about it (for example, a mother's eating the corpse of her already dead son). For the same reasons, neither do I define 'horrendous evil' in terms of cold-bloodedness (a feature Tolstoy used to express his moral revulsion at technically ingenious state executions) because it fails to be comprehensive and fails to get to the bottom of what is so bad about the evils in question. Rather, what makes horrendous evils so pernicious is their life-ruining potential, their power prima facie to degrade the individual by devouring the possibility of positive personal meaning in one swift gulp.[24] Moreover, I do not equate horrors with massive collective suffering[25] because I want to focus on what such evils do to the individual persons involved and because individuals may participate in horrors even when others are faring well (consider, for example, the Bible's Job, the father who nonnegligently runs over his beloved child, and those who suffer from schizophrenia or deep clinical depression).

On my conception, horrors afflict persons insofar as they are actual or potential meaning-makers. With this focus, I leave to one side the question of whether God is *good to* individual inanimate objects or plants. Likewise, my analysis of both problem and solutions will pertain to animals only to the extent that their cognitive and affective capacities constitute something like meaning-making powers. Folk psycho-biology would place worms and clams well below horrors' reach but might equivocate about chimpanzees or dolphins, perhaps even dogs or cats. If all mammals and perhaps most kinds of birds, reptiles, and fish suffer pain, many naturally lack self-consciousness and the sort of transtemporal psychic unity required to participate in horrors. By contrast, human children of all ages—except for the severely brain deficient—are nonetheless potential meaning-makers. I count them among participants in horrors because childhood traumas significantly damage the individual's powers to make positive sense of his/her existence later on.

6.3. Defeating What?

Confronting the problem of horrendous evils requires consideration of whether anything could balance off, much less defeat them. It is worth pausing here to forestall terminological confusion. In stating my definition, I mention prima facie reasons; I talk about the defeat of good and evil; and we also speak of judgments and reasons as defeasible. My notion is that reason to doubt can be outweighed, if the evil *e* can be defeated. The evil *e* can be defeated if it can be included in some good-enough whole to which it bears a relation of organic (rather than merely additive) unity; *e* is defeated within the context of the individual's life if the individual's life is a good whole to which *e* bears the relevant organic unity. If the evil *e* is defeated within the context of an individual *x*'s life, the judgment 'the life of *x* can-

---

24. Stewart Sutherland's comments on my article "Horrendous Evils and the Goodness of God" at the 1989 Joint Session of the Mind Association and the Aristotelian Society showed me the need for these clarifications.

25. This is what Rebecca Chopp does in her book *The Praxis of Suffering: An Interpretation of Liberation and Political Theologies* (Maryknoll, N.Y.: Orbis Books, 1986), esp. 1–2.

not be worthwhile given that it includes *e*' would be defeated, but the judgment '*e* is horrendous' would stand; this is because *e*'s inclusion in a good-enough whole (even where the whole is *x*'s complete life span) to which it is related by organic unity does not prevent it by itself from counting as a prima facie reason for doubting the positive value of *x*'s life. Similarly, '*e* is defeated within the context of *x*'s life' does not entail '*e* was not so bad after all' because '*e* is defeated' is compossible with 'the inclusion of *e* in *x*'s life is a prima facie reason to doubt whether *x*'s life can be worth living'. That *e* constitutes even a prima facie reason for thinking *x*'s life is thereby ruined, is enough to make *e* daunting. Again, '*e* is defeated within the context of *x*'s life' does not entail 'the judgment that *e* is unjust, is defeated' or '*e* was not unjust after all'. Rather, my definition holds open the possibility that genuinely unjust horrors might be defeated, not by being turned into justice after all, but by being relevantly integrated into *x*'s relation to a great enough good.

Here I mimic the way most participants in the present discussion have spoken. Most begin with a confidence that certain types of phenomena are evil, a confidence that exceeds their commitment to any general ethical theory. Even where they recognize the possibility of overbalance or defeat, they do not suppose that such overcomings mean the phenomena were not really evil but only prima facie evil or that the phenomena's negative value has been taken away. As both Pike and Chisholm point out, our epistemic access to defeaters—especially to global and generic defeaters—is poor. If defeated evils were just apparently and not really evil, we could not be sure whether anything was evil or not. We pay tribute to the seriousness of evils by respecting our own epistemic confidence that their negative value is evident.[26]

7. The Impotence of Global and Generic Approaches

This definition of the category of horrendous evils spawns a pair of distinctions (i) between two dimensions of Divine goodness in relation to creation—namely, "producer of global goods" and "goodness to or love of individual created persons"—and (ii) between the overbalance/defeat of evil

26. See Chisholm, "The Defeat of Good and Evil," 66–68. Naturally, I do not mean to claim that alternative theories could find no way to accommodate such intuitions. Those who reject the notion of intrinsic value (apparently including Rowan Williams, "Reply: Redeeming Sorrows," in *Religion and Morality*, ed. D. Z. Phillips [New York: St. Martin's Press, 1996], 132–48, esp. 135–36), which I join Pike and Chisholm in accepting for the sake of argument, could say that the evaluation of evil-in-the-narrow-context stands even when the verdict good-in-the-wider-context has been rendered. Likewise, even what is not really evil would remain prima facie evil.

by good on the global scale, and the overbalance/defeat of evil by good within the context of an individual person's life.[27] Correspondingly, we may separate two problems of evil parallel to the two sorts of goodness mentioned in (i).

By trying to cover all evils at once and fixing on global and generic features of worlds taken as wholes, both Pike and Plantinga have in effect restricted their attention to defending Divine goodness qua producer of global goods in the face of many and great evils. Thus, Pike mounts an epistemic defense, urging that, for all we know, evils such as we observe are logically indispensable constituents of the best of all possible worlds. Plantinga's claim of a demonstrative defense depends on his contention that $R^\star$ is evidently compatible with (1). Yet, if he has mustered considerable (if controversial) argumentation to persuade us that $R^\star$ is compatible with Divine knowledge and power, compossibility with perfect goodness gets short shrift. Once again, where the abstract logical problem is concerned, this last presumption would likely be granted by most (but not all) atheologians, including Mackie. Where entrenched horrors are figured into the bargain, however, it is far from obvious that a perfectly good God would accept them as the price of a very good world with as favorable a balance of moral good over moral evil as God could weakly actualize. Certainly, it is epistemically possible that entrenched horrors are constituent ingredients of a world exhibiting Leibnizian maximum variety with maximum unity. Perhaps if we bracket worries about the conceptual coherence of middle knowledge and counterfactuals of freedom[28]—that is, about whether it makes sense to say that God knows what merely possible free creatures would do if they existed in this or that circumstance—we might also find it epistemically possible that entrenched horrors infect worlds with the most favorable balance of moral good over moral evil that God can weakly actualize—in which case Plantinga could retreat to Pike's "for all we know" position. If it is claimed that it is logically possible that such considerations constitute the whole reason why God permits entrenched horrors, this might constitute an epistemic defense of Divine goodness along the dimension 'producer of global goods'.

A cosmic creator and/or governor who operated with such reasons alone would not thereby be one who placed a high value on human personhood

27. I owe the second of these distinctions to a remark by Keith DeRose in our fall 1987 seminar on the problem of evil at UCLA.

28. Robert Merrihew Adams challenges the coherence of these notions in his article "Middle Knowledge and the Problem of Evil," reprinted in Adams and Adams, *The Problem of Evil*, 110–25.

in general or individual human persons in particular. On the contrary, such government would thereby show itself to be at best indifferent, at worst cruel. Rather, I contend that God could be said to value human person-hood in general, and to love individual human persons in particular, only if God were *good to* each and every human person God created. And Divine *goodness* to created persons involves the distribution of harms and benefits, not merely globally, but also within the context of the individual person's life. At a minimum, God's *goodness* to human individuals would require that God guarantee each a life that was a great good to him/her on the whole by balancing off serious evils. To value the individual qua person, God would have to go further to defeat any horrendous evil in which s/he par-ticipated by giving it positive meaning through organic unity with a great enough good *within the context of his/her life*. By skirting the special prob-lems horrendous evils pose for Divine goodness to individual created per-sons, global and generic approaches win no ingenious strategic victory. They simply fail to solve them.

The Dignity Of Human Nature?

The Stature of Self-Determination

We have just seen how Plantinga's influential free will defense promotes Divine goodness at world-producing to the neglect of God's *goodness to* created persons. Plantinga avowedly appeals to created freedom because of its connection with global and generic goods that—under conditions of transworld depravity—God couldn't get without evils. To be sure, the notion that freedom is *good for* created persons might be one of the covert considerations motivating his own and/or Mackie's judgments about which possible worlds are very good. But this factor—like the problem that horrendous evils pose for God's *goodness to* created participants—never comes explicitly into play.

By contrast, classical free will approaches hope to integrate Divine global goodness with Divine *goodness to* created persons by arguing that free will is a very great benefit, while evil is tolerated as a possible or actual accompaniment of this gift. They begin with the observation that persons—humans and angels—crown creation because they alone have the dignity of being "made in God's image." God endows us with free will, makes us thereby imitate Divine aseity, in order that through its right exercise we might become still more Godlike—namely, in being self-determining with respect to uprightness. Unfettered exercise of freedom is necessary to achieve this purpose however, and this opens the correlative possibility that personal creatures might sin instead. Contemporary versions stress how

God lends great significance to created freedom by allowing personal creatures, not only freedom to choose, but also to live out the consequences of
their own and others' actions—to do so, not only in this antemortem
world, but also in a postmortem life to come. Moreover, recent authors insist that such Divine policies express God's respect for created personal
agency. Thus, Richard Swinburne insists not only that God accords each
human being the dignity of freely determining its own destiny, but also that
God has no more right than society to stand in anyone's way to prevent
them from destroying their own souls.[1] Jerry L. Walls agrees that created
persons have a right to the unencumbered exercise of their libertarian freedom, a right to persist even if they do themselves irreparable harm, a right,
that God respects by not acting unilaterally to change morally significant
preference structures.[2] Shifting imagery, Eleonore Stump holds that God
would not violate created free wills by stepping in uninvited miraculously
to obstruct sinful choices or alter their orientations. Nor will God change
our natures or annihilate us, but rather He allows us to choose our way into
characters and values and to eternally experience the natural and intrinsic
consequences of being who we have become.[3] These writers are convinced
that the gift of free will makes personal agency *sacrosanct*, holy ground on
which not even God may tread uninvited without violation.[4] Divine aid
may be offered, but everyone ought to respect created autonomy, its twin
rights—to accept and flourish or to refuse and lose.

Broadly speaking, classical free will approaches branch into two varieties:
"free fall" theories according to which created free agency begins in excellent condition in highly advantageous if not utopian circumstances and then
"falls" into our present condition through misuse of free choice; and "soul-
making" approaches according to which human beings are created immature in an environment conducive to self-determined development towards
maturity. Because both types are offered as explanatory theodicies, their
focus is on God's actual reasons for permitting evils such as the actual world
contains and, so, on the concrete rather than merely the abstract problem of
evil. My contention will be that free fall approaches founder while soul-
making theodicies at least teeter on the rock of horrendous evils.

1. Richard Swinburne, "A Theodicy of Heaven and Hell," in *The Existence and Nature of
God*, ed. Alfred Freddoso (Notre Dame, Ind.: University of Notre Dame Press, 1983), 37–54,
esp. 49.

2. Jerry L. Walls, *Hell: The Logic of Damnation* (Notre Dame, Ind.: University of Notre
Dame Press, 1992), esp. 134–37.

3. Eleonore Stump, "The Problem of Evil," with comment by Michael Smith and reply
by Stump, *Faith and Philosophy* 2 (1985): 392–435.

4. See Chapter 5.

2. "Free Fall" as the Origin of Evil

Classical free fall theodicies begin with the intuition that Divine opposition to evil is less equivocal than best-of-all-possible-worlds approaches require. In particular, free fall theories are convinced that Divine Goodness would never directly or deliberately introduce evil into the world. Thus, Augustine declares that neither sin nor its natural and punitive consequences are necessary to the perfection of the universe.[5] On the other hand, free creatures *are* a great good, central to Divine aims, even necessary for cosmic excellence.[6] By creating instead of omitting them, God introduces the *possibility* of evil into the universe, which free creatures in fact actualize. Nevertheless, responsibility for the origin of evil falls on the shoulders of created free agents who sin, because evil is not something God intends (as end or chosen means) but rather a known side effect: not something God *does* but something God *allows* other intervening agents to do.[7] Augustine, pace Plantinga, insists that free creatures do not jeopardize God's project of creating a maximally perfect universe because God can maintain maximal cosmic perfection simply by imposing a retributive order on their choices.[8] Moreover, this guarantees that the evils that happen to them have meaning for the persons who suffer them because they will be reckoned into the category of *just deserts for sin.*

3. Double Effect, Doing/Allowing, New Intervening Agent

Act-utilitarianism evaluates acts and, derivatively, agents in terms of the total consequences of the acts. Other approaches to ethical theory partition an act's consequences in such a way as to hold the agent responsible for some acts rather (more or less) than others. Famous among the operative principles are the following:

Double Effect. An agent is responsible for the end and chosen means thereto in a way that s/he is not responsible for the known but unintended side effects of the action.

---

5. *Augustine, De libero arbitrio: Libri Tres,* ed. William M. Green, vol. 74, *Corpus scriptorum ecclesiasticorum latinorum* (Vienna: Hoelder-Pichler-Tempsky, 1956), 3.93 [bk. 3, sec. 93].

6. Augustine, *De libero arbitrio* 3.113–16.

7. Augustine, *De libero arbitrio* 2.201–4; see also 2.7, 2.179, 2.188, 2.191.

8. Augustine, *De libero arbitrio* 3.66, 3.93–102, 3.113–24.

Doing/Allowing. An agent is responsible for his/her actions in a way s/he is not responsible for those s/he merely permits or allows or does not prevent when s/he could.

New Intervening Agent. An agent bears diminished or no responsibility for those consequences of his/her action that are produced by a new intervening agent.

Medical ethics is a mine field of alleged double effects. For example, suppose the only way to save a pregnant woman's life involves a hysterectomy to remove a cancerous uterus. Hysterectomy will result in the death of the fetus, although killing the fetus is not a means to the end. Alternatively, suppose in a difficult delivery the only way to save the child's life involves making incisions that will result in the death of the mother, although it is not the mother's death but the incisions that are a means to saving the baby's life. Philippa Foot's rescue scenario illustrates the intuition behind the doing/allowing distinction: in a forced choice situation, I can either perform an action that will result in the rescue of one person, or another action that will result in the rescue of five people; if I rescue the five and let the one die, I am not so responsible for the resultant death as I would be if I shot the one with a pistol. For an example of *novus agens interveniens*, consider the highway commissioner who builds splendid new roads which are much safer to travel on than the old roads between point A and point B. S/he is said not to be responsible for the increase in the number of traffic deaths that occurs because more people decide to travel between point A and point B on the new road. Similarly, if a blackmailer threatens to kill my sister unless I burn incense to the genius of the emperor, *novus agens interveniens* says I am not responsible for my sister's death should I refuse.

Obviously, such principles and examples are highly controversial within ethical theory. Even their advocates recognize restrictions. Doing/allowing and *novus agens interveniens* apply only where the other new agents who are "allowed" to "do their thing" have a certain *independence* relative to the agent from whose shoulders responsibility is to be shifted; *novus agens interveniens* requires proportionate competence as well. Likewise, double effect excuses only where the negative side effects are inevitable or avoidable only at unacceptable cost and only where the total package—means, end, and side effects—is a great enough good. In their normal application, all of these principles require good enough reasons; none licenses the gratuitous allowance of evils.

4. The Horror of Humankind

Classical free fall approaches make human agency so robust as to stand between God and evil; the dignity of human nature and its self-determining action are taken to be so great as to outweigh or defeat any evil side effects or means. In my judgment, these estimates should not survive sober consideration of human entrenchment in horrors.

4.1. Radical Vulnerability, Entrenched Propensity

I begin with some straight forward observations of fact. First, human history is riddled with horrendous evil. Second, it is comparatively easy for human beings to cause horrendous evils (or at least be salient members of causal chains leading to them). Consider, for example, the father who nonnegligently runs over his beloved infant son. Third, an individual human being's capacity to produce suffering—horrendous and otherwise—(or be a salient member in a causal chain leading to it) exceeds his/her ability to experience it. This is evident, so far as quantity is concerned: Hitler engineered a holocaust of millions; it required relatively small groups of government leaders, scientists, and military personnel to produce the atomic explosions over Hiroshima and Nagasaki. It is trivially true as to quality, because each person's suffering is unique. More significantly, can childless male soldiers experience suffering anything like that of a mother whose child is murdered before her eyes? Fourth, since where suffering is concerned, capacity to conceive follows capacity to experience, in such a way that we cannot adequately conceive what we cannot adequately experience, it follows that our ability to cause horrors exceeds our powers of conception. Just as the blind person's color concepts are deficient because lack of acquaintance deprives him/her of the capacity for imaginative representation of colors, despite lots of abstract descriptive knowledge about them; so lack of experience deprives an agent of the capacity empathetically to enter into what it would be like to suffer this or that harm, despite more or less detailed abstract descriptive knowledge of such suffering. Such empathetic capacity is especially important for assessing just what is so bad about that suffering and hence for appreciating how bad it would be to produce it.

Nor is this human capacity to participate in individual and collective horrors superficial. On the contrary, it seems deeply rooted in our nature as personal animals. We not only use bodies as instruments as a pilot does the ship, but our psyche also reflects our biology, at both conscious and unconscious levels, in some ways scientists now predict and in other ways that go unnoticed even by them. Of course, this fact can be interpreted metaphys-ically in many ways. But it led prominent medieval philosophers—Thomas Aquinas, Duns Scotus, William Ockham and others—to reject dualism, and to say instead that our soul is the form of an organic body.[9] In this world, we humans trace an animal life cycle: birth, growth, maturity, decline, death. Pscyho-spiritually as well as biologically, we are developmental creatures: We human beings start life ignorant, weak, and helpless, psychologically so lacking in a self-concept as to be incapable of choice. We learn to 'construct' a picture of the world, ourselves, and other people only with difficulty over a long period of time and under the extensive influence of other nonideal choosers. Human development is the interactive product of human nature and its environment, and from early on we humans are confronted with problems that we cannot adequately grasp or cope with and in response to which we mount (without fully conscious calculation) inefficient adapta-tional strategies. Yet, the human psyche is habit forming in such a way that these reactive patterns, based as they are on a child's inaccurate view of the world and its strategic options, become entrenched in the individual's per-sonality. Typically, they are unconsciously acted out for years, causing much suffering to self and others before (if ever) they are recognized and undone through a difficult and painful process of therapy and/or spiritual forma-tion. Having thus begun immature, we arrive at adulthood in a state of *im-paired freedom*, as our childhood adaptational strategies continue to distort our perceptions and behavior.

Our animal life cycle combines with our instinct towards self-preser-vation to produce an underlying anxiety about death, based on our "knowl-edge" that we contain the seeds of our own demise. These psycho-biological factors make resources seem scarcer than they are. Nevertheless, there is the additional fact that we live in a physical environment that is prima facie inhospitable to human life. Nature is more powerful than we and hostile to our survival; collectively, human survival has been won through wit and technology. Nevertheless, the understanding of nature is sufficiently beyond us that we cannot anticipate the consequences of mea-sures taken for present survival; and past apparent advances have had envi-ronmental consequences that threaten future disaster. Moreover, we are placed in an environment of scarcity, with apparently not enough to go around for everyone to live comfortably. No wonder there is a Hobbesian

---

9. Cf. Marilyn McCord Adams, "The Resurrection of the Body according to Three Me-dieval Aristotelians: Thomas Aquinas, John Duns Scotus, William Ockham," *Philosophical Top-ics* 20 (1993): 1–33.

war for the survival of the fittest, resulting in the stronger exploiting the weaker.

Free fall theodicies, so far from denying human vulnerability to horrors, make it an aspect of the primordial human condition. For they stipulate that God created and so arranged the universe that should rational creatures remain sinless, evil would never enter the world; but were they to sin, evils would ensue, in the amounts and of the kinds and with the distributions known to us. On the merely human scene, Adam's fall set off the causal and/ or punitive chain producing humanly insurmountable psycho-spiritual disorder (in Augustine's language, *ignorance* of what is right and *difficulty* in making and following through on right choices for the right motives) in all his offspring. Thus, even in Eden Adam and Eve are credited with an agency easily able to trigger horrendous evils of cosmic proportions!

4.2. Atlas Crushed!

My further contention is that free fall attempts to shift responsibility for horrors from God to humans fail, for at least two reasons. First, the *necessary* disproportion between human agency and horrendous evils makes it impossible for humans to bear full responsibility for their occurrence. For we cannot bear full responsibility for something to the extent that—through no fault of our own—"we know not what we do." But (as noted above) where horrendous suffering is concerned, our ability to produce it radically and inevitably exceeds our ability to experience and thus adequately to conceive how really bad it is. It follows that we cannot be fully responsible for those dimensions of horrendous evil that are inevitably inadequately conceivable by us. Insofar as culpability is directly proportional to responsibility, we cannot be fully to blame either. (To deflect charges of hypocrisy, let me readily concede that a parallel argument bars the way to our taking full credit for inevitably inadequately inconceivable goods!) Note, my argument does not deny even great moral responsibility or culpability for deeds thus inadequately conceived of by their agents. Hitler's generic grasp of genocide and his means thereto would be more than sufficient to rank him among history's worst sinners. But even where abstract descriptions expose the evils as horrors, there will be immense dimensions to that horror which only the experienced could adequately conceive of and for which the unavoidably inexperienced would not be fully responsible or culpable. This would be true in spades for Adam and Eve who—prior to the fall— would have no experience at all of evil or suffering.

These considerations are reinforced by the further observation that—according to free fall theories themselves—the great chain of horrors does not depend on created free choice alone, but on the environment into which it is inserted. Yet most causally salient features of human nature and the environment lie outside the creature's control and are produced by God instead. Consider the following two analogies. *The Stove Analogy*: Suppose a parent introduces a three-year-old into a room which contains gas that is not harmful to breathe but will explode if ignited and also contains a stove with brightly colored nobs which if turned will light the burners and ignite the gas. Suppose further that the parent warns the child not to turn the nobs and then leaves the room. If the child turns the nobs and ignites the gas, blowing up the room, surely the child is at most marginally to blame, even though it knew enough to obey the parent, while the parent is both primarily responsible and highly culpable. *The Terrorist Analogy*: Suppose a terrorist announces his intention to kill one hundred citizens if anyone in a certain village wears a red shirt on Tuesday. The village takes the threat seriously, and everyone is well informed. If some adult citizen slips up and wears his favorite red shirt on Tuesday, he will be responsible and culpable, indeed seriously so. But the terrorist, who set up the situation, will be far more responsible and culpable.

Free will defenders who posit fully competent, well-disposed and adequately informed creatures, in an environment which will produce further evils if and only if they sin, seem to liken free creatures to the red-shirted citizen in the Terrorist Analogy. Those that start with immature choosers make them analogous to the three-year-old in the Stove Analogy. Neither model allows the created choosers to bear the full or even the primary moral responsibility or culpability for the evils consequent upon their choices. Turning the appeal to *novus agens interveniens* on its head, there is another, fully competent and independent agent whose actions in setting up the world "intervene" between created free choices and their horrendous consequences. And this agent is none other than God!

5. Augustinian Integration—Horrendous Balance as Just Deserts?

At best, the principle of double effect excuses an agent from the foreseen but unintended harms of his/her actions only if the over all package (means, side effects, and end) is a great enough good. Augustine thinks this condition easy to satisfy where Divine government of the world is concerned because he is confident that God can weave any evils that creatures cause into a maximally perfect universe via an order of retributive justice which at the same time attends to the meaning of evils within the context of individual lives.[10] In my judgment, radical human vulnerability to horrors thwarts this strategy.

5.1. Exploded Proportions

Retributive justice contributes to the value of the universe as a whole by awarding individuals and groups the just deserts of their actions. If I drive my car in such a way as to damage yours, other things being equal, it is fitting that I should compensate you for the damage, even pay the government a fine for the trouble I caused. The state of affairs in which I damage your car and pay money to you and the government in consequence is, other things being equal, plausibly morally better than that in which I damage your car but get off scot-free. Yet, as critics of retributivism commonly point out, retribution is a matter of proportion, whereas the notion of proportionate return demanded by the *lex talionis* already breaks down in ordinary cases where numbers are large. For example, suppose I knock one tooth out of the mouth of each of thirty-two people each of whom has a full set of teeth and then the authorities knock out all thirty-two of my teeth by way of punishment. Is my having no teeth not much worse than their each having thirty-one teeth? Or suppose I interrupt television transmission of the superbowl game, thereby causing twenty million fans one hour of fury and frustration each. Surely, my suffering twenty million hours of fury and frustration is much worse.[11] Harms are not atomistic, their cumulative effect not simply additive; and so for large amounts, the notion of proportionate return already loses "precise" definition—all the more so where the enormity arises, not from the amount, but from the *kind*, as is the case for horrendous evils that we cause but unavoidably lack the capacity to experience.

5.2. Horrors, Balanced or Multiplied?

Again, even where possible, retributive balance can fill Augustine's bill only if it is a good thing. Originally, of course, the *lex talionis* was a hostility-limiting principle equivalent to "*no more than* an eye for an eye" and was not even meant to suggest that destroying two eyes was better than taking out one! Ivan Karamazov voices the standard criticism that retributive balance does not serve justice where sufficiently outrageous evils are concerned. Matching the prima facie ruin of the victim's life with the prima facie ruin

10. Augustine, *De libero arbitrio* 3.93–102, 3.113–24.
11. I used these examples in my early paper "Hell and the God of Justice," *Religious Studies* 11 (1974): 433–47.

of the perpetrator's would not make the world a better place, much less defeat the disastrous harm to the victim. "An eye for an eye"—if powerless to restore the original victim's sight—was supposed at least to vindicate his/her honor (see chapter 6 below). Horrendous evil stalemates such vengeance. Horror's power to stain exceeds that of moral guilt—spreads over victim, perpetrator, even unwitting occasion. To return horror for horror does not erase but doubles the individual's participation in horrors—first as victim, then as the one whose injury occasions another's prima facie ruin. What kind of integrity do we have left if attempts to restore our integrity dissolve not only our own, but the integrity of others at the same time?

5.3. Conditional Benevolence?

Seemingly less controversial is the point that such punishment policies would not vindicate Divine *goodness to* perpetrators of horrors in the sense of guaranteeing each perpetrator a life that is a great good to him/her on the whole and a life in which participation in horrors is defeated within the context of the individual's life. If the second horror would not be surd but could be given meaning as punishment for the first, its significance would be overwhelmingly *negative*, multiplying reasons to doubt whether his/her life could have any positive meaning on the whole and in the end.

In fact, Augustine and many Christians make this problem more acute with their additional conviction that any sin against God renders the individual creature immeasurably culpable and, so, deserving of eternal punishment in hell, where hell is a condition that represents, not merely the prima facie ruin, but a decisive defeat of good by evil within the context of the individual sinner's life! (For convenience, I will refer to this conception as the "grim hell.") Moreover, they contend that many, perhaps even the vast majority of created persons, ultimately qualify for this decisively ruinous fate.[12]

As for Divine *goodness to* created persons, some grim hell advocates simply concede that Divine Goodness finds its primary expression in the world as a whole, so that Divine government may sacrifice the well-being of individual created persons as much as that of particular swallows and ants for the benefit of the common good. Closer to the heart of free will approaches

---

12. William Craig, " 'No Other Name': A Middle Knowledge Perspective on the Exclusivity of Salvation through Christ," *Faith and Philosophy* 6 (1989): 172–88. Craig supports this grim estimate by appeal to Matt. 7:13–14.

is the notion that the shape and extent of Divine *goodness to* created persons depends upon their free cooperation: that is, God will guarantee to each that its life is a great good to it on the whole and in the end *except through some commensurate fault of its own*. Boldest by far is Augustine's Christian Platonist appeal to metaphysical goodness: to be, is to be good, because it is either to be God (Who is Goodness Itself) or to be somehow Godlike. He concludes not only that God is *good to* any creature simply by conferring the gift of existence along with other natural endowments, but also that the value of such goods to their created possessor trumps any disvalue constituted by deprivations of its well-being. Thus, even the damned in hell have reason to give thanks and praise to God![13]

Augustine's reach for metaphysical goodness—like the global focus of Pike and Plantinga (see Chapter 2 above)—combines with his desire to blame created persons for the existence of evil, to prevent him from taking seriously the power of horrendous evil to make participants wish (like Judas, according to Matthew 26:24 and Mark 14:21) never to have been born. Augustine's charge of hypocrisy—that people would commit suicide if they didn't secretly regard existence as an overriding good—misses its mark. Even if suicide could end a horrendous career (a thought belied by Augustine's doctrine of hell), it would be powerless to erase the past. Even if we were to grant that existence is a prima facie good because every creature is somehow Godlike, Augustine himself recognizes a hierarchy in Godlikeness, rising from existence to life to understanding. What participants in horrors are suggesting is that horrendous evil so caricatures Godlikeness at the top level as to defeat the positive value of the bottom level, indeed provides weighty reason for them to wish that their lives—prima facie so ruined and/or ruinous to others—had never occurred. Without further argument, Augustine's remarks are too superficial to silence the complaint. (I shall return to the issue of whether existence can be a great good to those whose concrete welfare is a lost cause in Chapters 6 and 8.)

5.4. Utopian Integration?

Augustine and I share confidence in Divine competence and intention to defeat evils thoroughly with good. I desire to flatter Divine resourcefulness by interpreting good (as Augustine does only sometimes) to mean that Divine government can and will accomplish the utopian integration of cosmic excellence with the good of individual persons in such a way as to

---

13. Augustine, *De libero arbitrio* 3.65, 3.70–71.

insure the defeat of evil or, at least evils of horrendous proportions within the context of each individual's life.[14]

Given this premiss, it is easy to see how retributive horrors would defeat God's purposes, for the existence of horrendous evil constitutes prima facie reason to doubt whether the person's life can be a great good to him/her on the whole and, so, reason to doubt whether evils will be defeated within the scope of it. The attempt at retributive balance will only make matters worse, by multiplying reasons to doubt whether evil will be thus defeated. Hitler committed and his victims suffered horrors that called the positive meaning of their lives into question; putting Hitler into a medieval hell of eternal torture would only guarantee the defeat of good by evil in his life. Judas betrayed, Peter denied, the religious leaders of their society arranged the execution of God's Messiah. Taking horrendous vengeance for these crimes would only multiply evils' victories.[15]

6. Living out the "Natural" Consequences?

6.1. Shifting the Model

Augustine operates with a political model, which makes God the supreme governor of the universe and justice the heart of Divine Goodness, and which casts rational creatures as the premier subjects whose insubordination threatens chaos, whose retributive punishment restores harmony in the cosmic realm. The connection between human sin and grim hell is not represented so much as natural, but as juridical and legal, what a just judge would do by way of rendering to sinners what they deserve. By contrast, other free will approaches (including those recently sponsored by Richard Swinburne, Jerry L. Walls, and Eleonore Stump) defend a mild hell as one of the ways God pays respect to created free agency.[16] On their view an omni-

14. I assume that small- or medium-scale evils—such as a childhood case of measles or not getting into the best graduate school—might simply be overbalanced in a good life. Unless horrendous evils, which call into question whether one's life can be worth living, are defeated, however, evil's victories will be too large.

15. For Judas's betrayal, see Matt. 26:14–16, 20–25, 42–48; Mark 14:53–65; Luke 22:3–6, 22, 47–48; for Peter's denial, see Matt. 26:33–35, 69–75; Mark 14:29–31, 66–72; Luke 22:31–34, 60–62; for the religious leaders' role, see Matt. 26:57–68; Mark 14:10–11, 17–21; Luke 22:54–59, 63–71.

16. Richard Swinburne, "A Theodicy of Heaven and Hell," in *The Existence and Nature of God*, ed. Alfred Freddoso (Notre Dame, Ind.: University of Notre Dame Press, 1983), 37–54; and "Knowledge from Experience and the Problem of Evil," in *The Rationality of Religious Belief: Essays in Honour of Basil Mitchell*, ed. William J. Abraham and Steven W. Holtzer (Oxford:

scient, omnipotent, and perfectly good God might preserve human beings in postmortem existence the better to live out the *natural* consequences of their choices, eternally to *be* the persons they have chosen to become.[17] Because heavenly bliss depends in part on the beatified creatures' wanting (willing, choosing) what they get and/or what God wants, human beings can "cut themselves out" of such bliss by becoming persons who have no taste for what heaven offers[18] and/or what God enjoins.[19] Nevertheless, God could house them in other environments where, despite physical suffering and mental anguish, they are still able to take some satisfactions—whether in stimulating intellectual discussions about foreknowledge and free will, or in trivial earthly pursuits such as gin rummy or darts.[20] Such "living" hell(s) would be *mild* because allegedly preferable to nonexistence and hence apparently compatible with positive meaning in the individual's life.[21]

6.2. "Natural" Self-Development

By definition, *natural consequences* are a function of the nature itself. Mild hell advocates share distinctive assumptions about the nature of human agency. (1) They agree that there is a fact about human nature that "fully" "deep" human happiness centers on God[22]—variously characterized as union with God,[23] intimate and harmonious fellowship with God and others,[24] the chance to worship God and be recognized for successfully performing Divinely appointed tasks.[25]

(2) They espouse a developmental view of human nature, according to which human beings are born uncoordinated and need to acquire habits—

Clarendon Press, 1987), 141–67; Jerry L. Walls, *Hell and the Logic of Damnation*; Eleonore Stump, "The Problem of Evil," 392–423.

17. Swinburne, "A Theodicy of Heaven and Hell," 51–52; Swinburne, "Knowledge from Experience and the Problem of Evil," 143, 163; Stump, "The Problem of Evil," 401; Walls, *Hell and the Logic of Damnation*, 143, 150, 153–54.

18. Swinburne, "A Theodicy of Heaven and Hell," 43–46.

19. Stump says that union with God involves freely willing only what is in accordance with God's will ("The Problem of Evil," 400, 402).

20. Swinburne, "A Theodicy of Heaven and Hell," 52; Stump, "The Problem of Evil," 400–401; Walls, *Hell and the Logic of Damnation*, 127–29, 137.

21. Swinburne, "A Theodicy of Heaven and Hell," 52; Stump, "The Problem of Evil," 401–2, 411; Walls, *Hell and the Logic of Damnation*, 137.

22. Swinburne adopts a want-satisfaction account of happiness which he overlays with distinctions between true versus false and shallow versus deep happiness, depending upon whether the perception that wants are satisfied is true and whether the objects at which the wants aim are relatively worthy ("Theodicy of Heaven and Hell," 40, 43).

23. Stump, "The Problem of Evil," 400.

24. Walls, *Hell and the Logic of Damnation*, 150.

25. Swinburne, "A Theodicy of Heaven and Hell," 41.

of thinking, wanting, valuing, and doing—if they are to pursue happiness in an effective way. Thus, Swinburne stresses, God endows humans with free will, so that we might determine our own destinies, influence those of others, even share with God in molding the world.[26] Such destiny-determining freedom is given scope not only to choose its way into virtue or vice, but also to shape the knowledge systems of ourselves and others.[27] Swinburne maintains that if humans were motivated by reason alone we would always choose the apparent best. He concludes that the power for opposites required for moral freedom—the ability to choose evil as well as to choose good—comes with God's implanting a certain amount of depravity in our natures in the form of desires to do what we correctly believe to be evil.[28] Humans form themselves by choosing whether or not to control such impulses, whether or not to pursue relevant information, and so forth. Similarly, Walls sees antemortem humans as embarked on a process of moral development, whose successful course would involve freely adopting second-order desires for the good and subordinating first-order desires to them, and whose happy issue would be a character oriented fully Godward.[29]

(3) Swinburne and Walls agree that the ability to grasp evaluative truths is a function of moral development. Walls accentuates the positive: our capacity for recognizing goods is a function of our readiness to love them; only when moral development is complete is our love of the good so entrenched that Divine Goodness becomes vivid and obvious to us.[30] Swinburne probes the negative: because a thing's goodness furnishes a reason to desire it, we believe in its goodness if and only if we prima facie desire it. Consequently, habitually acting to the contrary undermines the belief, leaving us unable to appreciate the goodness of things we have spurned. In their view, we begin, not with full knowledge, but with abstract dicta and hints that we can choose or refuse to pursue.[31]

(4) They recognize that haphazard choices and behavior can produce a state of habituated disintegration. Swinburne imagines "lost souls" whose persistent refusal to order their desires is an abdication of the throne of agency without possibility of return, an act which transforms these souls

26. Ibid., 51; Swinburne, "Knowledge from Experience and the Problem of Evil," 143–44.
27. Swinburne, "Knowledge from Experience and the Problem of Evil," 151–52, 155–56.
28. Swinburne, "A Theodicy of Heaven and Hell," 47; Swinburne, "Knowledge from Experience and the Problem of Evil," 143–44.
29. Walls, Hell and the Logic of Damnation, 123, 130–31.
30. Ibid., 130–31.
31. Swinburne, "A Theodicy of Heaven and Hell," 46–49; Walls, Hell and the Logic of Damnation, 130–31, 133.

into "mere theaters of conflicting desires," the strongest of which automatically dictates their actions. Similarly, Walls recognizes "weak evil" persons who abort the selves God calls them to be by conforming their second-order desires, to their first-order desires instead of the other way around.[32]

(5) Although many neo-Aristotelians would deny the possibility of more-than-temporary functional centering on anything other than the thing's *telos*, mild hell advocates assume the possibility of stable focus around what is in fact evil. Thus, Walls considers that the damned must have made a "decisive response" to God's offer, which involves a harmony of second-and first-order desires in turning away from God towards what is in fact evil, a response in which the second-order desires perhaps aim towards independence from God or the moral law. Swinburne entertains the possibility that persons whose ante mortem careers revolve around the trivial pursuits of this world might be preserved in an environment where they could pursue them forever. Taking her inspiration from Dante's *Inferno*, Stump sees no reason why persons deprived of union with God might not continue in something like their antemortem states, deprived of union with God but yet experiencing a tolerable mixture of frustration and satisfaction.[33]

(6) While Swinburne is willing to countenance the possibility that God would annihilate persons whose choices make them unfit for heaven, Stump finds existence arguably better than nonexistence even in their case, and Walls insists that it makes our antemortem careers more significant if we have to live with their consequences eternally.[34]

6.3. Consequences: How Natural?

Swinburne, Walls, and Stump/Dante begin by taking human psychology very seriously: the fact that entrenched habits of character, established tastes, and concomitant states of inner conflict are *naturally* consequent upon sinful patterns of choice is supposed to explain the *intrinsic* connection between the sinner's earthly behavior and his/her exclusion from heaven and/or consignment to hell. But their effort to keep the mild hell from collapsing into the grim one depends upon their curiously hybridized portrait of human psychology in which (5) seems misfitted to (1)–(4). With the first

---

32. Swinburne, "A Theodicy of Heaven and Hell," 48; Walls, *Hell and the Logic of Damnation,* 123.

33. Walls, *Hell and the Logic of Damnation,* 123, 129, 138, 143, 150; Swinburne, "A Theodicy of Heaven and Hell," 52; Stump, "The Problem of Evil," 400–402.

34. Swinburne, "A Theodicy of Heaven and Hell," 52; Stump, "The Problem of Evil," 401–2; Walls, *Hell and the Logic of Damnation,* 136.

four assumptions, they seem to take a page from neo-Aristotelian teleological theories such as Aquinas espoused. Nature is like art. Just as running a
machine contrary to its design leads to premature breakdown, so also with
biological organisms. Human metabolism, made to flourish on a diet of dry
food, cannot run on caffeine and chocolate indefinitely. When mild hell
advocates affirm (1) that union/intimacy/fellowship with God is the *only*
thing that will make humans fully flourish, it sounds as if they are identifying such relationship with God as the human end, and so should accept
the consequence that permanent satisfactory focus around something else
is impossible (contrary to (5)). True, assumption (5) draws plausibility from
the empirical fact that vice sometimes organizes a person's character
around evil ends, and trivial pursuits become the center of a person's life
for a medium run of twenty or even the proverbial three score and ten
years. Teleological perspectives count this evidence insufficient because
vice is a psycho-spiritual disorder and forever is a long, long time. My own
view resonates with C. S. Lewis's suggestion, in *The Problem of Pain*, that
vice in the soul preserved beyond death eventually brings about a total dis-
mantling of personality, to the torment of which this worldly schizophrenia and depression (much less Swinburne's lost souls) are but the faintest
approximations.[35]

6.4. Dubious Honor?

Swinburne, Walls, and Stump agree that Divine omnipotence could obstruct such natural consequences, miraculously reach in and reorient our
personalities by transforming our habits, but insist that Divine Goodness
would not do this, because to do so would violate our personhood and/or
transgress our rights. Yet, whether Divine creation and (eternal)noninterfer-
ence with free agency constitute respect for it, depends on its strength and
the perniciousness of its consequences. A parent or teacher can be *good to* a
three-year-old in awarding it the dignity of self-determination with respect
to issues slightly beyond its cognitive and emotional grasp. But benevolent
pedagogy allows this to take place only within a controlled framework in
which neither choice courts disaster. Radical human vulnerability to horrors proves that such conditions do not obtain within our antemortem situation. Swinburne and Walls explicitly comment on how "weak evil" persons and "lost souls" forfeit their agency, dis-integrate before the grave.
Horrors wreck agency another way, by prima facie evacuating life of any
positive meaning. Nor could such presumptive ruin be defeated by God's

35. C. S. Lewis, *The Problem of Pain* (New York: Macmillan, 1979), 124–26.

furnishing the opportunity for us eternally to be the persons we have thus become. Where the antemortem persona is stained by undefeated horror, the hell of its eternal persistence is, by definition, not mild but grim!

Matters are (if possible) worsened by the fact that human agents are often causally salient in raining down horrors not only on themselves, but on others; not only on individuals, but also on collectives of which they are a part. Particularly relevant for mild hell approaches is the way circumstances quite beyond the individual agent's control—for example, physical and sexual abuse in childhood or the traumas of war—pose obstacles out of developmental order, confront agents with problems beyond their capacities to solve. The predictable result is that individuals choose their way into a range of misery-making adaptational strategies which easily become entrenched often beyond the powers of psychotherapy to uproot. Swinburne rushes by such facts with "[it] is good . . . that agents other than God have a share in moulding the world and each other, and the deep responsibility that involves."[36] My countercontention is that God would not thereby *honor* but *violate* our agency by crushing it with responsibility for individual and cosmic ruin. Any god who turns us, perhaps the whole creation, over to the eternal natural consequences of our action, pays us inappropriate respect!

Walls meets his Wesleyan worries, that not everyone has a fair antemortem chance, with the proposal that God will extend the "deadline" for such individuals, to guarantee each the opportunity to make a "settled response" under "the most favorable circumstances."[37] Yet, where created agency is twisted by horrors (as above), this fresh start would require massive miraculous repairs, drastic alterations of a sort Walls otherwise thinks we have a right against God not to produce. A second-round "decisive response" for God might mean the balancing off of antemortem horrors over the total span of the individual's life. But Walls's scenario does not represent a way for God to honor the persons such victims have become, because erasing the slate and repeating the test would not by itself *defeat* the antemortem horrors that so caricatured their lives.

My overall complaint is that mild hell approaches fail to appreciate how horrendous the natural consequences of human antemortem careers can be. They transform the traditionally pedigreed if empirically implausible claim that self-determination is one important way in which we image God into the exaggerated suggestion that it trumps everything else. This tendency

36. Richard Swinburne, "Knowledge from Experience and the Problem of Evil," 141–67, 143.

37. Walls, *Hell: The Logic of Damnation*, 90.

finds its quintessential expression in Swinburne's judgment that God is obliged to leave lost souls as they are because the person they were when they still had agency did not will a pattern of self-control. Underlying this error is the persistent mistake of all free will approaches examined in this chapter so far: namely, that of underestimating the "size gap" between Divine and created personhood. My own suggestion (to be further developed in Chapters 4–6) is that the relation between God and human adults is less inaccurately modeled by that of the mother or nursery school teacher to the infant or small child, than by that of parents to their adolescent or adult children. Within the context of human society, adults and older teenagers may perhaps assert their right that certain self-destructive behaviors (overeating, smoking, private use of alcohol)not be interfered with by others. With infants and small children, the matter is different. The role of the mother or nursery school teacher is not one of controlling but of evoking and enabling the child's agency. In educating the child, they do not seek authorization in the child's original permission or present consent, but look forward to the alleged fact that *the agent that the child will become* would approve. When interactions between the child and its environment go badly so that the child is traumatized and its development impaired, mother and teacher pay their respects to nascent agency by helping the child to recover and move on. Mild hell advocates come close to assuming that God and human adults are moral peers in insisting that we (like adolescent and adult children) have the right to reject God and to erase as completely as possible any trace of family resemblance. My own view is that this is not the right sort of respect for a being like God to pay to creatures like us. Consequently, it is not a medium through which Divine *goodness to* us can be expressed.

7. Horror-Strewn Classroom, Graduation Bliss!

7.1. Irenaean Intimations

When Swinburne and Walls portray antemortem human careers as the scene of character development, the scene of personal formation in which our choices are key, they take their cue from John Hick, whose 1966 publication of *Evil and the God of Love* gave renewed prominence to soul-making approaches to problems of evil.[38] Like many free fall theorists, Hick understands free created response to God to be central to Divine purposes.

38. John Hick, *Evil and the God of Love* (New York: Harper and Row, 1978).

But he thinks the notion of a historical fall runs contrary to the findings of evolutionary biology. Moreover, he argues that a close look at rational agency defeats free fall attempts to shift responsibility for the origin of evil off Divine shoulders and onto ours.[39] Hick reaches for a free will approach that recognizes that God is directly responsible for producing human beings in an environment with actual existing evils and the possibility of many more. Without assuming that God has obligations to creation, Hick claims that God's doing so will be compatible with Divine Love, only if He does it for a good reason. Drawing his inspiration from Irenaeus (as against Augustine), Hick assigns God, not a *retrospective* reason in terms of a past fall from perfection, but a *prospective* or *teleological* explanation in terms of God's developmental goal for created persons. Hick's proposal can be summarized in a series of three claims.

First, God creates humans in two stages. In stage one, God acts alone or through an evolutionary process to produce man as a personal moral being, capable of entering into relationship with God (that is, He produces humans in His "image"). In stage two, God acts in cooperation with the free creature and a stable physical environment in order to mature the individual into one of such a character as will be intimately related to God in the future.

---

39.   Unlike my arguments in section 5 above, Hick's argument takes off from a distinctive theory of human motivation and runs as follows:

(i)   A nondefective, rational, free nature will always choose what it perceives to be in its best interest.

(ii)   A nondefective, rational, free nature enjoying a vision of God would know that continuing in that state was in its best interest.

(iii)   Therefore, a nondefective, rational, free creature enjoying a vision of God would choose to remain in that state. (i, ii)

(iv)   Therefore, if a rational free creature chooses something else in preference to seeing God, it is either because it is defective or lacks the appropriate knowledge. (iii)

(v)   If a rational, free nature is defective or lacks the appropriate knowledge, God is responsible for that, not the creature.

(vi)   Therefore, if a rational, free creature chooses something in reference to seeing God (and thus sins), God is responsible for that, not the creature. (iv,v)

Anselm's action theory contrasts with Hick's regarding (i), maintaining that a nondefective, rational creature *ab initio* would have a power for opposites and so be able to choose justice above its own advantage as well as to choose its own advantage instead of justice. Once the creature has knowledge of God's punishment policies, it is in a position to see that it cannot be ultimately to one's advantage to choose against justice. In fact, it is questionable how consistently Hick endorses (i), since he later claims that spiritual growth is away from egocentrism and towards self-sacrificing Christlikeness, or God-centeredness, or other-centeredness.

Many free fall theorists, including Anselm, accept (iv) and (v), but claim that God has a good reason for not shining through the veil of ignorance with the news that God will punish sin eternally unless satisfaction is made—namely, to set up conditions for self-determined justice. This is strikingly parallel to Hick's own move—that God sets us in this Vale/veil of ignorance so as not to coerce our choices, to allow for free response to God.

Second, God fashions the rest of the world with a view to creating an environment conducive to soul-making. Nonrational creation may have positive value in itself, but the interests of nonrational creation do not take precedence over those of rational free creatures, but the other way around. According to Hick's picture, a world lacking evils in the amounts and of the kinds and with the distributions found in the actual world would not be conducive to soul-making.

Third, stage two of God's creation will be completed in the life to come. Evil will not last forever, and it is morally certain that an infinitely resourceful God will ultimately win the cooperation of *all* rational free creatures. This is because humans have a built-in bias towards God, which maturation will release us to follow. Hick's doctrine of eventual universal salvation sets him at odds with most philosophers and theologians (for example, Augustine, Anselm, Aquinas, Scotus, and Ockham, in the medieval period; Swinburne, Stump, Walls, and Craig, nowadays) who embrace a free will approach.

7.2. Complicating Clarifications

Hick equivocates as to whether or not it is metaphysically impossible for God to "ready-make" mature rational humans, or whether such instant virtue is merely less valuable than that won via a developmental struggle. If the former were true, then not even an omnipotent God could do it. And the immaturity of human cognitive and emotional capacities might themselves be enough to explain our initial cognitive distance from God and our originally self-centered motivational structure. Other times, Hick argues that rational creatures could not refuse an "obvious" God, and therefore can freely respond only if God keeps His cognitive distance, by placing us in a religiously ambiguous environment such as we now experience. This hypothesis of *God's* placing us at a cognitive disadvantage—deliberately setting us back in such a way as to necessitate the (according to Hick) long and painful process of development, extending beyond this world—would be superfluous if it were metaphysically impossible to ready-make mature humans. Either way, sin becomes a virtually inevitable necessary condition of God's getting a free, unmanipulated response of faith, love, and trust.

7.3. A Catalogue of Explanations

Hick's strategy requires him to account for actual evils—evils in the amounts and of the kinds and with the distribution found in the *actual* world—principally in terms of their pedagogical contributions to the soul-making process. Marching in where Pike and Plantinga feared to tread,

Hick adopts a piecemeal approach and marshalls many familiar arguments. Thus, he reasons, if evil choices never had harmful consequences they wouldn't be evil. Again, suffering is the condition of developing many virtues—unselfishness, good faith, courage, commitment, truthfulness. The capacity for love is deepened by trials and so on. Eventually, Hick's cataloguing brings him to "dysteleological" evils—that is, evils that seem neither to serve as punishments nor to further spiritual development. He frankly acknowledges the existence of evils that "can break the victim's spirit," evils that issue in "no gain to the soul, whether of the victim or of others," evils that are "ruthlessly destructive" and "utterly inimical to human values," "affliction" that "instead of ennobling" crushes character and wrests "from it whatever virtues it possessed."[40] Nevertheless, Hick ingeniously subsumes these data under his soul-making hypothesis, with the suggestion that such dysteleological evils lend the universe a quality of mystery that *is* conducive to soul-making. Mystery, he suggests, is wholesome, because we would not sympathize with those who suffered their just deserts or suffered for what was clearly their own good. Likewise, if patterns of reward and punishment were too clear, we would never transcend ourselves to love the good or pursue the right for its own sake.

7.4. Dysteleological Horrors!

Hick assigns meaning to dysteleological evils insofar as they are necessary to an environment generally conducive to soul-making. But horrendous evil is dysteleological for those who participate in it. That God would permit some to participate in horrors in order that others might profit from a better soul-making environment seems a poor defense of Divine *goodness to* the participants. For horrors not only fail to advance the participants' progress, but also prima facie defeat the positive significance of their antemortem careers.

Hick's first response would be to remind us of his universalism, as well as his hypothesis that education continues beyond the grave, perhaps through many lifetimes. Even if antemortem horrors remain undefeated between birth and the grave, each soul will finally be perfected and brought into intimacy with God, a good great enough to balance off—indeed engulf—even horrendous evils. Is this not enough to show that Hick's God is *good to* each and every created person when their whole career (even many lifetimes' worth) is taken into account?

My own answer (predictable from chapter 2 above) is that while even-

40. Hick, *Evil and the God of Love*, 330–31.

tual beatific intimacy with God would ensure that the participant's life was a great good to him/her on the whole, Divine *goodness to* creatures would not only balance off but *defeat* horrendous evil, and defeat it not simply within the context of the world as a whole but within the frame of the individual's own existence.

Stout-hearted Hickians might argue that this condition is likewise met over the long haul of many lifetimes. For participation in horrors that remains undefeated within the individual's antemortem career contributes to the sense of mystery that makes a positive contribution to the soul-making of others. Since one is at least a cause, sometimes even an agent-cause of the willy-nilly sacrifice of one's antemortem good, participation in horrors would constitute some sort of shift from self-centeredness to other-or God-centeredness. Even if this putative positive dimension of participation in horrors is swamped by its negative aspect when considered within the framework of the individual's antemortem career, retrospectively, from the vantage point of the end of the journey, the person one eventually becomes would be glad to have made the sacrifice. Participation in horrors can thus be integrated into that overall development that gives positive meaning to his or her life, and so be defeated within the context of the individual's existence as a whole.

I respect the resourcefulness of this reply and do not find it altogether untenable. Nevertheless, my sense of the depth of horrendous evils drives me to demand more. Would not Divine Love focused on created persons lend positive meaning, not only to the individual's life as a whole, but also to any careers in which he or she participates in horrors? The sacrifice of participation in horrors is pedagogically inept as a first lesson because it can damage the person so much as to make much further antemortem progress from self-centeredness to other-or God-centeredness virtually impossible. This combines with the delay in gratification to another life—or perhaps many other lives—later so as to de-emphasize the importance of this life, leaving the impression that it would have been better skipped by those whose spiritual development was significantly set back through participation in horrors. To give this life, or any career involving participation in horrors, positive significance, some parameter of positive meaning for horrors other than "educational" benefit must be found!

8. A Methodological Moral

Many philosophers of religion insist that the problem of evil can be solved only if we can identify some (logically possible) morally sufficient reason why God would (though omnipotent and omniscient) permit evils. Pressed to meet this demand, many seize on considerations that may plausibly play some role in God's creative choices—for example, the desire to make a world of the highest possible overall excellence, the desire to people it with incompatibilist free creatures and allow them choices of moral and perhaps eternal significance, or the fact that suffering can have pedagogical value and figure in complex goods—and elevate these considerations to the status of "morally sufficient reasons why" or reasons why sufficient by themselves to render the permission of such evils compossible with omnipotent, all wise, goodness.

In my judgment, this has proved a bad idea, first because trying to make these considerations do all the work of explaining why God permits evils in the amounts and of the kinds and with the distributions found in this world, often only adds to the problem of how a being thus motivated could be good in the relevant sense. Such attempts show rather that where horrors are concerned, not only do we not know the *actual* reasons why of Divine permission; we can scarcely think of any candidates for a complete explanation. I do not say that God has no reasons why; on the contrary, God is personal, and so the sort of agent that can act for a reason. Moreover, if good to created persons, we may suppose that, in permitting individuals to experience horrors, God would act for a reason—and not capriciously—in matters so momentous for them. Nor do I want to say that we cannot know or think of any *partial* reasons why God might permit horrendous evil, in the sense of considerations that could have some weight or other in God's creative choices. On the contrary, I assume the desire to have personal creatures who have some free play and the desire to have a very good world on the whole are among God's reasons. And I have already stipulated an unwillingness on God's part to permit any horrors God couldn't defeat within the context of the individual's life. I am about to add a more specific partial reason why in the next section. Nevertheless, I agree with Anselm, that any reasons why that we may discover are only partial, and that for any disclosed to us, there are and always will be deeper ones we cannot fathom. I also concur with Anselm that the mystery of Divine goodness is permanently inexhaustible by us and permanently partially inaccessible by us; exploring it will keep us fascinated for eternity.[41]

41. I was originally tempted to think that explaining how God could defeat horrors within the context of an individual's life and insure to each participant a life that was a great good to him/her on the whole would be enough, apart from any suggestion of partial reasons why, to defend the logical compossibility of the existence of an omniscient, omnipotent, perfectly good God with the existence of evil. Against this, Keith De Rose insisted that the

If our knowledge of reasons why is only partial, how can the problem of evil generally, and of entrenched horrors in particular, be solved? My suggestion is that we can explain the compossibility of God and evil (even the evils of entrenched horrors) if we can offer a (logically possible) scenario in which God is *good to* each created person, by insuring each a life that is a great good to him/her on the whole, and by defeating his/her participation in horrors within the context, not merely of the world as a whole, but of that individual's life.

---

fact that God could defeat horrors was itself a partial reason why (a necessary precondition) of Divine permission of them. His arguments have persuaded me to modify my position.

Part Two

CONCEPTUAL
ENRICHMENTS

Introduction to Part Two

Mackie sets the stage for focus on Divine moral goodness, and Pike follows his lead, reformulating the question raised by evil as whether an omniscient and omnipotent being could have a morally sufficient reason for not preventing or eliminating evil? Terence Penelhum cautions that relevant answers must hold God responsible to the very same moral standards to which believers hold themselves.[1] J. S. Mill warns us not to let Divine metaphysical "class," God's high rank in the society of beings, distract us from what is at stake here: namely, whether evil does not call into question God's perfect goodness in the "ordinary," "relational" sense that implies that its possessor would deal with the world and treat created persons in certain ways and not others?[2]

The ensuing debate puts God on trial. Mackie, and his team of atheologians, make the argument for the prosecution, that God would be "damned if He didn't" prevent or eliminate evils (in the amounts and of the kinds and with the distributions found here). Free will defenders counter that God would be "damned if He did," because—as one moral agent among others—God has an obligation not to interfere with free creatures. Some

---

1. Terence Penelhum, "Divine Goodness and the Problem of Evil," in *The Problem of Evil,* ed. Marilyn McCord Adams and Robert Merrihew Adams (New York: Oxford University Press, 1990), 69–82, esp. 75–76.

2. Nelson Pike, "Introduction," *God and Evil* (Englewood Cliffs, N.J.: Prentice-Hall, 1964), 3; cf. J. S. Mill, "Mr. Mansel on the Limits of Religious Thought," in Pike, *God and Evil,* 37–45.

defense lawyers extend the notion of mandatory Divine respect for created agency to impersonal, material creatures as well. On the one hand, Richard Swinburne and Maurice Wiles maintain, noninterference in nature is part and parcel of respecting created persons, insofar as it preserves the integrity of scientific inquiry and thus makes possible human autonomy in learning to negotiate its environment. Alternatively, how could God be consistent of purpose in making creatures only to obstruct their natural functioning? Perhaps the most extravagant defense is Wiles's argument from fairness, that although omnipotence would be able, God *should* never intervene in creation, not even to prevent horrors. For it would be arbitrary for God to avert some and not others, while systematic interference to prevent them all would constitute a substantial infringement of created autonomy. Therefore, a righteous God would never interfere with natural processes or free agents to prevent evils, even of horrendous proportions! Still other defenders stir the courtroom with political rhetoric: would not God play the despot or the tyrant were He arbitrarily to coerce His subjects to act (or not to act) contrary to their natures or wills?

As arguments bounce back and forth across the court room, many jurors find themselves persuaded that Mackie's god does not exist, not because prosecution arguments are so powerful, but because the whole spectacle leaves them feeling that the god thereby conceived is "too small," merely a giant-sized authority figure, differing only in degree from political monarchs and parents of adolescent children, as fallible as Cleanthes' designer, as subject to moral censure as the Greek pantheon. Surely worthiness of worship demands Deity to be more distinctive, requires relations between Divine and created agency to be otherwise configured!

I have already (in Chapters 1 and 3) tipped the hand of my sympathy with this last demand for theological remodeling. In Chapter 4, I turn my attention to Divine agency and its explanatory functions and examine two families of alternatives to the "leveled" personhood of the god on trial. After estimating what sort of agency it would take to defeat horrors within the context of the individual participant's life, I turn to neglected values. I have already argued (in Chapter 3) that moral categories are inadequate to grasp what is so bad about horrendous evil. On the one hand, horror perpetration is no simple function of moral wrongdoing, both because humans are unavoidably unable to conceive some of the horrors we are able to produce and so cannot be fully responsible for them, and because sometimes we produce them contrary to our fully conscientious efforts and intentions. On the other hand, victims are not only tainted with their ruinous power independently of moral desert; retributive justice is powerless either to compensate them or to make the total state of affairs morally better. Noting that neither the Bible nor the great medieval and reformation theologians assert that God is *morally* good, I take a page from social anthropology which calls attention to the fact that quite different systems of interpersonal evaluation—the categories of purity and defilement, honor and shame, legal right and wrong, moral good and bad—have arisen, evolved, and dominated in turns with changing systems of social organization.[3] So, too, history of religions can be suggestive, hypothesizing primary loci for each system—honor and shame for clan and village, law for expanding, political unit, purity and defilement for cult. Interesting, and already evident in the Bible, is how frameworks once introduced are rarely lost, at most go underground, and in different contexts color the evaluative mix in subtle and bold ways. In Chapters 5 and 6, I examine two such alternative schemes—the purity and defilement calculus and the honor code—both of which loom large in the conceptuality of the Bible and traditional Christian theology. My belief is that each casts distinctive light on Divine-human relations and calls attention to neglected value dimensions that outdo morality both in grasping what is so bad about horrendous evil and in identifying currencies with which God can compensate it.

In Chapter 7, I turn briefly to another neglected value category whose relevance to problems of evil has been widely misunderstood by analytic philosophers of religion. My claim will be that 'horrendous' is itself an aesthetic category and that aesthetic goodness can play a significant role in Divine defeat of evils.

3. Seminal here are Arthur W. H. Adkins's *Merit and Responsibility: A Study in Greek Values* (Chicago: University of Chicago Press, 1960), and the collection *Honour and Shame: The Values of Mediterranean Society,* ed. J. G. Peristiany (London: Weidenfeld and Nicolson, 1965). Such material is being readily absorbed into Biblical studies, as exemplified in the work of Bruce J. Malina (e.g., *The New Testament World: Insights from Cultural Anthropology* [Atlanta: John Knox Press, 1981]). John H. Elliot, "Patronage and Clientism in Early Christian Society," *Forum* 3, no. 4 (1987): 29–48, summarizes and reviews relevant literature on the related topic of patrons and clients.

[4]

Divine Agency, Remodeled

1. Models of Explanation

Philosophical theology commonly identifies God as an ultimate explanatory principle and then unfolds its doctrine of God by assigning Deity the features needed to fill the role(s) in question. Unsurprisingly, portraits vary with the theory of explanation presupposed, according to different views about what needs explanation, how much and of what sort, and about what confers explanatory power. Mackie's critique gets its purchase from the assumption that God is omnipotent in a sense that includes efficient causal power to produce any conceivable effect as well as to obstruct any other agent. If British and *Wienerkreis* empiricism gave a reductive twist to modern classical focus on efficient causality, the alternatives about to be surveyed follow medieval philosophical theology in taking their inspiration from Greek philosophy, which understands the explanatory task in rather different and wider terms.

Recall how in the *Timaeus* Plato attempts a "likely story" regarding things here below. Among the theoretical entities that he posits are the Forms, the true beings that are eternally and immutably as they are, and the receptacle that serves as a mirror in which a moving likeness of eternity (the realm of becoming) is reflected. The Forms function as exemplars, whose contribution consists in their *being* eternally as they *are* in themselves (indeed, their doing *consists in* their being). Similarly, given the eternal Forms, the receptacle is such as to "catch" the (albeit moving) likeness. In the

Timaeus, Plato overlays this account with the myth of the demiurge, who—like the artist—sees the exemplars and tries (with only partial success) to impose their patterns onto the receptacle. Both the Forms and the receptacle are "givens"; it is the order in the moving likeness that is to be explained.

Aristotle illustrates his famous doctrine that there are the four distinct types of causes or explanatory principles by the sculptor making a statue. The *formal* cause is the art or plan in the sculptor's mind; the *material* cause is the clay on which the shape is imposed through the *efficient* causality of the sculptor's skilled motions; the *end* or *final* cause is the bust of Caesar and/or the completion of the shrine in his honor in the market place. At the same time, Aristotle's paradigms of qualitative change suggest an "infection" theory of efficient causality: for example when a heatable is brought close enough to fire, the heatable simply catches heat from the heat in the fire; the latter does not have to *do* anything, or rather its *doing* something reduces to its *being* itself and to a suitable receptacle's coming close enough to catch it. Of course, not just anything is suitable for receiving heat; to be an appropriate receptacle presupposes certain features as opposed to others.

Neoplatonists and some middle-Platonists alter (in part by demythologizing) the *Timaeus* account in a number of ways. Some follow Aristotle's intuition that the top of the ontological hierarchy should be pure thought and so merge the demiurge together with the Forms, making the latter thoughts in the mind of a thinker that is (like Aristotle's unmoved mover) identical with its object when it thinks. Plotinus calls this eternal being "Intelligence" but reserves first place for the One (like Plato's Form of the Good) which is beyond being and thought but the source of both. Moreover, to emphasize that the One is the source not only of perfecting structure but also of the being of *everything* else, Plotinus speaks of lower levels *emanating* from higher ones—the One emanates Intelligence which emanates Soul which emanates the material world—the lower evidently being "metaphysically oozed" into existence by a kind of natural necessity. Yet, the exemplar function is retained insofar as the lower reflects the higher with the result that effects imperfectly resemble their causes. Thus, the lower are also said to *participate* in, to be imperfect because they are more complex likenesses of, the higher from which they derive. Christian Platonist versions soon agreed, God could not be the material cause of creation, much less an inherent form, but rather stands as the exemplar source of all being.

The first family of views I consider locates the uniqueness of Divine agency in Its role in conferring *being;* the second, in Its world-organizing exemplar function as the root of all *goodness.* Unsurprisingly, my own portrait is governed by another rubric. I therefore, select from the reviewed positions a collection of features that promise to make a contribution to *horror-defeating power.*

2. The Source of All Being!

Parties to the debate Mackie spawned seem mostly to agree both that *only* persons are moral agents, and that *any and all* persons—no matter whether human, angelic, or Divine—are moral agents, networked into a system of mutual rights and obligations. One sure way to skirt his logical problem of evil, along with the tangle of "damned if he does, damned if he doesn't" estimates of God's moral obligations, would be to deny that God is personal at all (in the sense of an agency that acts through thought and choice). Certainly, ancient and honorable tradition reaching back through Plotinus to Plato secures metaphysical distinctiveness by placing the source of all being, itself beyond being, so that *a fortiori* it transcends thought and choice. Another way is to deny that persons are necessarily moral agents. Medieval Christian theologians such as Anselm, Aquinas, Scotus, and Ockham, did not begin from below, with human agency, and then conceive of God's agency to be of the same kind, so that Divine and human capacities for thought and choice differ only in degree. Rather they started at the top, assigning to God both the simplicity, immutability, and eternity of Plotinus's One and the paradigmatic thought of Plotinus's Intelligence as well. Medieval philosophical theology undertakes the homework of adjusting these concepts to one another in a consistent and coherent way and thereby understands God to be of the wrong metaphysical category to have obligations to creatures. Both moves are recapitulated in twentieth-century theology. Let us see how the second move—that seeks to resize Deity without sacrificing Divine thought and choice—charts itself off of a version of the first.

2.1. God as Ground of Being

Revising Neoplatonic, Christian Platonist, and post-Kantian idealist views, Paul Tillich counters idolatry by assigning God a unique ontological niche as the Ground of Being, the power of being that overcomes nonbeing. As such, God is not *a* being, one being as distinct from and alongside others, but rather that in which all beings participate, that which overcomes nonbeing in them. Beings are finite; they only *have* their being from another, by participation. Beings both have and lack being, insofar as they are such as to come into being and pass away. The Ground of Being is infinite, eternally conquers the nonbeing which belongs to It. It is a form of being that prevails against nonbeing in ourselves and in our world—being-as-such that precedes any qualifications. Tillich admits that finite persons may *experience* the Ground of Being as personal, insofar as nothing *less than* what is personal could answer to the ultimate concern of finite persons. Nevertheless, the Ground of Being has to be (like Plato's Form of the Good or Plotinus's One) *beyond* personality, beyond the divide between personal and impersonal, because it is the source of both (that in which both participate).[1] "The God who is *a* being is transcended by the God who is Being Itself, the ground and abyss of every being. And the God who is *a* person is transcended by the God who is the Personal Itself, the ground and abyss of every person. . . .[T]his means that being and person are not contradictory concepts. Being includes personal being; it does not deny it. The ground of being is the ground of personal being, not its negation."[2]

Further, insofar as God is not *a* being alongside others, but beyond beings, and the source of all beings, neither is God a cause among others, alongside all others, competing with others for causal influence. Rather Divine causal power operates on a different level, to empower finite causes by virtue of being the power through which they exist.

Corollary to this is that the Ground of Being does not make finite causes produce one effect as opposed to another. It supports them in being, while they do whatever they do. True, different finite creatures participate in the Ground of Being to different degrees. But—just as in old-fashioned Platonism—this is not a function of anything different that the Ground of Being initiates in relation to them, but rather a function of their own natures. Where free beings are concerned, differences arise because of their varying postures towards It and not because God literally has different intentions and purposes for different creatures. For Tillich, God is not *literally* a personal agent.

Another corollary is that God does not interact with finite causes generally, how much less with other persons in particular (the way Buber's *I and Thou* claims). To say that God reacts differently to different human actions would be to make Divine action partly dependent upon 'creatures'. But "how can a being act upon being-itself, how can being-itself be mutually related to any particular being? How can a being influence the ground of being in which and out of which it lives?" For Tillich, to speak

1. Paul Tillich, *Biblical Religion and the Search for Ultimate Reality* (Chicago: University of Chicago Press, 1955), 13, 16, 24–26, 33–34, 59, 74, 82–84.

2. Ibid., 82–83.

of God as personal and interacting with finite persons is symbolic; and we have to understand that God transcends, comprises, and empowers both sides of the reciprocity.[3] God is a source which creatures tap into in different degrees and so vary in their power to symbolize what God is. Consequently, for Tillich, the notion of Divine intervention to obstruct or replace natural causal processes would be as much of a category mistake as would be the notion of the intervention of the Platonic Forms of Being or Justice or Goodness Itself to do so. From a metaphysical point of view, Divine and created agency are mutually noninterchangeable: if no creature could step into God's causal role, equally, neither could God step into theirs.

2.2. Repersonifying Variations

David Burrell wants to profit from Tillich's distinction between the Ground of Being (which is God) and beings that can differ from one another the way contraries under a genus do. He recognizes affinities between Tillich's claims and those of Thomas Aquinas, who identifies God with *ipsum esse,* altogether unlimited, infinity uncompromised by any distinction between the receiver and that into which it is received, the One in Whom created natures participate to receive their finite being. Accordingly, Burrell sets himself against "the endemic tendency of philosophers treating divinity to assign God *a place in the universe,* albeit the largest or the first or the most significant" as well as against their attempts to characterize the relation between God and creatures using "categories tailored to the universe itself." Rather the metaphysical gap between God and creatures is reflected in a semantic gap. Burrell resonates with Wittgensteinian segregation of talk about Divine agency into one language game and created agency into another. Echoing Aquinas, he insists that 'agent' and 'cause' function analogously when applied to God and creatures, and accuses "those who persist in thinking about God as another actor in the world" of envisioning God as a Demiurge instead of a creator. God is the "universal cause," not in the sense of general as opposed to particular, but in that God is the all-pervasive cause-of-being, whose proper effect is the bestowal of existence on things. Burrell denies that the notion that 'creatures exist in a relation of total and immediate dependence upon God' entails that 'God is the total cause of each created event'.[4] After all, Aquinas teaches that "divine provi-

3. Ibid., 30, 81; quote on 31.
4. David Burrell, "Human Freedom in the Context of Creation," in *The God Who Acts: Philosophical and Theological Explorations,* ed. Thomas F. Tracy (University Park, Penn.: Pennsylvania State University Press, 1994), 103–9, esp. 106–7.

dence works through intermediaries [with] God . . . from the abundance of divine goodness imparting to creatures also the dignity of causing."[5] In Burrell's view, "God's bringing about the existence of both cause and effect in a cause-effect relationship means that each is brought to be *as* what it is, so that what exists as cause exercises its activity in such a way as to effect what results in the other."[6] Burrell seems to be saying that—as a matter of metaphysical necessity—it belongs to the created causal power (naturally or freely) to *specify* the act (for example, for fire, to make it an act of heating; for Adam or Eve, to make it an act of obeying or flouting God's command), while it pertains to Divine agency to supply the active created cause with being. Thus, God confers being, not simply on things, but on creatures insofar as they are acting and being acted upon. Thus, God is not like the parent who acted in the past to give his/her adolescent children being and who now competes with them to determine the content of their actions. Rather, God enables created agency by giving being in the present to creatures who are determining their acts in specific ways. For Burrell as for Tillich, Divine and created agencies are mutually noninterchangeable.

Nevertheless, like Aquinas, Burrell believes this vivid appreciation of the vast metaphysical difference between God and creatures can be consistently combined with the conviction that the God of Biblical religion is the free creator of the universe.[7] Although 'intellect' and 'will' would be predicated *analogically* of God and creatures, the semantic gap intended thereby seems to be less than Tillich posits in treating Divine personality as merely symbolic. For while Aquinas consistently denies the possibility of any strict Aristotelian definition of the Divine essence, his later treatments insist against Maimonides that the *res significatae* of perfection terms—such as wisdom or justice—do pertain to God.[8] Moreover, as free, God apparently decides to bestow being on some active and passive things as opposed to others, and thereby establishes "the external and internal context in which we act" to do or suffer one thing rather than another, in such a way that "God's agency envelopes and pervades our own."[9]

5. *Summa Theologica* 1.22.3 (part 1, question 22, article 3).
6. Burrell, "Human Freedom in the Context of Creation," 106.
7. Ibid., 104, 107–9.
8. For the development of Aquinas's views on the semantics of Divine names, see John Wippel, "Quidditative Knowledge of God," in *Metaphysical Themes in Thomas Aquinas* (Washington, D.C.: Catholic University of America Press, 1984), 215–41.
9. Burrell, "Human Freedom in the Context of Creation," 109.

2.3. Tanner's Twists

Inspired equally by Burrell's reading of Aquinas as by the reformed theologian Karl Barth, Katherine Tanner sets out to secure a distinctive locus
for Divine personal agency by deploying the spatial metaphors of distinct
axes, planes, or levels. The horizontal plane is the domain of created causal
activity and interactions. Natural and free causes among creatures are distinguished by their relations to other agents in the horizontal plane. Divine
creative activity occurs along the vertical dimension and consists in "calling
forth" or "suspending" the whole plane of creation. Tanner emphasizes
that—so far as creatures are concerned—the scope of Divine action is *universal*, its manner *direct,* and its efficacy *unobstructable.* Thus, Divine agency
does not vie for causal influence with creatures the way created agents
compete with one another. Nor does God bring about a created state of affairs indirectly by bringing about some other state as a means to the end.
Divine agency is not interventionist: God does not need to enter the horizontal level to get the desired result, because God exercises full control by
direct action to produce creatures acting in a certain way. Following
Aquinas (on some readings), Tanner insists that created freedom is compatible with Divine determinism, since the distinction between natural and
free, free and coerced, is a matter of how created causes relate to one another. Taking a page from Reformed theology, Tanner does not find infal-
lible providential control tyrannical; instead created dependence on God
should inspire humility and gratitude to Divine beneficence that reserves
for us "a piece of the action."[10]

When Tanner turns to confront the problem of evil in the form of
human sin, however, she takes a further step away from Tillich's picture. It
turns out that the "restriction" of Divine agency to action along the vertical axis is not a matter of metaphysical necessity but a function of contingent Divine policy; God *could* intervene, but there would be no point. Likewise, although Tanner tries to avoid the consequence that created sin is an
exception to the universal scope of Divine providence by treating it as a de-
fect that lacks existence rather than a being that would need to be supported by Divine power, she sometimes admits that sin's "occurrence" com-
plicates Divine providence, so that God has to issue a series of conditional
decrees to forward Divine purposes with or without sin. This makes it look
as if God aims at a whole whose parts are after all *constitutive means,* so that

10. Katherine Tanner, "Human Freedom, Human Sin, and God the Creator," in *The God
Who Acts: Philosophical and Theological Explorations,* 111–35, esp. 113–14, 118–20.

God does will some creatures for the sake of others. Alternatively, it makes Divine action interdependent upon because partially reactive to created action, in a way Tillich's Ground of Being could not be. She even admits that God could—if need be—act directly to cause a nonsinful choice instead of letting the defective one occur.[11]

2.4. Resized Divine Agency

All three views try to avoid leveling Divine agency by enforcing a "causal gap"—that is, by identifying distinctive causal roles that only God can fill. Standing closest to the Neoplatonic tradition, Tillich speaks of the relation between God and creatures in terms of the latter's *participating* in the former as their Ground. Insofar as Burrell and Tanner find their inspiration in Aquinas, they are heir to his conflation of participation with efficient causal relations. Like Aquinas, they repersonify from the top, maintaining that a being that acts by thought and choice could be the source of all being and, so, do the causal work that Tillich's Ground of Being is assigned. In particular, *ipsum esse*—Whose *intelligere* and *velle* are identical with Its *esse*—enables created agency, by furnishing being to creatures-in-action.

The rhetoric behind these positions—the desire to preserve the integrity of created agency and so avoid the charge of Divine despotism or tyranny—leads us to expect a God Who can't squeeze into the creature's shoes either. Tillich certainly succeeds in making Divine and created agency mutually noninterchangeable. Although repersonifying Divine agency, Burrell shares this aim, emphasizing how Divine and created agency differ in kind by insisting that neither could occupy the other's causal role. For Burrell, talk of Divine intervention would likewise be ill-formed because predicated on the assumption that Divine agency could stand in competition with creatures' agency. On Tanner's scheme, only God could act along the vertical axis, and Divine determinism in no way compromises the distinction between voluntary and natural agency, between free and coerced actions. Yet, in the end, she allows, God *could* take the creature's place, or at least compete with created agency by obstructing it. It is only as a matter of Divine policy that this does not happen. Both Burrell and Tanner describe a God "too big" to have moral obligations to creatures. Yet, insofar as their God is free, problems of evil rearise— not as questions about whether God fulfills His moral obligations, but about whether Divine policy has chosen to furnish being to a very good

11. Ibid., 120, 134–35.

or optimal world, and whether God has chosen to be *good to* individual created persons.

3. Suffering for the World's Redemption

In his ever less-than-precise but highly suggestive book, *The World's Redemption,* C. E. Rolt joins the protest against any doctrine that Divine omnipotence includes irresistible power to coerce creatures to do/be whatever God wants (including overriding natural laws and the like). Such a view is "immoral, irrational, and anti-Christian" among other things because it pictures God as "a great and mighty despot" and drives us to falsify the size of evils by making excuses for why God does not exercise Divine coercive power to prevent them. As a Christian, Rolt makes it his *theological* axiom that Divine power is most accurately revealed in Jesus Christ whose "spiritual power consists in weakness and spiritual triumph in suffering," in "unselfishness" that "cannot use compulsion or exact obedience and service" but is "humble and lowly". So then God's power is the power of Love which is "weakness" or "the power to suffer pain," so that "God in heaven cannot resist through all eternity, but must be dumb and silent." Rolt's *philosophical* axiom, which dichotomizes matter and spirit, correlating coercive force with matter and weakness or power to suffer with spirit, finds its interpretation in a modified Platonism, which can perhaps be most easily approached by stages.[12]

3.1. God and Evolution

Begin with Plato's picture in the *Timaeus* (leaving the myth of the Demiurge aside). Now alter the picture by letting God Who is Goodness Itself replace the forms and by understanding the receptacle in terms of turn-of-the-century evolutionary theory (34–35, 79–82, 87). Thus, Rolt envisions a primal chaos of stuff that has nevertheless built-in tendencies to act in different ways in different circumstances. At first every bit of stuff acts according to the necessity of its nature producing a chaotic whirl. Chance and necessity together evolve patterns of "fit" among bits of matter, and such configurations make the sea of stuff more mirrorlike by activating their tendencies towards greater harmony. The evolutionary process results in a world that is full of many and various evils, from which we rightly morally

12. C. E. Rolt, *The World's Redemption* (London: Longmans, Green, 1913), 13, 14–16, 24–27, 37, 56–83, 92–93, 181–83. Parenthetical page citations in the following two subsections refer to this work.

recoil, although it also contains emerging elements of harmony and beauty in imitation of God.

On this scheme, God does not have the power to *coerce* primal chaos into organization, but God's being what God is and the tendencies in primal stuff being what they are, the primal stuff will evolve towards an ever greater collective imitation of God. Thus, for Rolt, God's power (like that of an exemplar) lies in being what God is and in ever patient waiting (93–94).

> The truth merely remains true, and in this calm assurance it quietly reposes until at last the raging forces of discord and strife stumble on some aspect of its being, and, having done so, cannot but manifest its presence henceforth by the formation which they now possess. (85; see also 88)

> Instead of bending anything against its nature, He can but wait until it finds its own true nature in Him. (87)

> The still heaven looks down upon the seething mass, but no reflection of its tranquil mass is given back again, for this angry chaos of battling forces can afford no mirror to refract it. But serenely the calm heaven waits in the silent patience of its own eternity, until presently the fury of the waters begins little by little to abate. (93)

If Rolt's modifications stopped here, his resultant position would make God aloof from the rough and tumble of the realm of becoming, where the pain and suffering occur.

3.2. Divine Goodness as Suffering Love

Rolt cancels this implication with a further Christianization of the model. Not only does he identify Divine Goodness with perfect love (a medieval commonplace); he interprets the power of perfect love as power to endure suffering, love Whose perfection lies not in the mere capacity of suffering but requires its actual endurance. Drawing metaphors from personal language, Rolt speaks of the tendencies on which primal stuff initially acts as tendencies to "self-assertion," those on which it later acts with tendencies toward cooperation and "self-sacrifice" for the sake of the universe and, so, of greater Godlikeness (85–86, 88–89). Further, he contrasts two types of conquest: the *coercion* model on which the victor compels his/her opponent to surrender and/or forcibly prevents any further exercise of the opponent's power; and the *absorption* model on which there is so much to the victor that without striking out or hitting back at the opponent, s/he can absorb all the opponent's blows without losing integrity.

Rolt claims that in Christ, Divine love defeats evil (now identified with coercive self-assertion) the second way, by absorbing all its blows without losing integrity. Moreover, there is an explanation of how this is possible: Divine love just *is* the power to endure suffering; actually enduring suffering perfects it; absorbing by suffering all of evil's blows brings Divine love to full perfection. Therefore, so far from destroying or dis-integrating Divine love, evil's assaults occasion the perfection of Divine love (186–88, 227–28, 245, 247, 251–52). Thus, for Rolt,

> The whole process of evolution is itself one mighty redemption wrought out by the meek suffering of a perfect love which, strong in that strength which seems like weakness, can bear the assaults of all its foes unmoved, unconquered and unchanged and by its own inherent patience draw, even from the things which seek to crush it into nothing, the elements of its own eternal victory.(251–52)

On this scheme, it is "a mistake to regard the Passion as a temporary defeat which was only reversed by the Resurrection." Rather the absorption model allows us to relocate Divine victory in the passion itself (35). It can already be a *final* victory, inasmuch as Christ, made immeasurably sensitive by a perfect capacity for love, endured infinite agony of body and mind, indeed, "all that has ever been" and presumably ever will be endured (228–31, 245–46). For Rolt, Christ had to suffer, not "as a debt paid by God's mercy to His justice," but because accepting the benefits of life in this world incurs some collective responsibility to suffer, while sympathetic suffering discharges this obligation and forges a sense of kinship with the human race (227, 229–30). Likewise, full solidarity with the world's sufferings at the point of their "sharpest terror" required Christ temporarily to forego the sense of His Father's presence that was with Him through His ministry (248). Rolt concludes that because Divine love thus suffers, God is not aloof and all created suffering is holy (249).

If solidarity in suffering perfects Divine love, creation evolves on towards perfection insofar as it becomes evermore Godlike. If, for material creation, this means the ever-increasing activation of cooperative tendencies, for created persons it means growing in our capacity to love as God does. For Rolt (as for patristic and medieval soteriology), Christ is our exemplar and teacher on a human scale. When we refuse to respond to evil's blows with coercive force, but instead absorb them with suffering love, we become more Godlike. Rolt believes we are empowered to do this without losing integrity by Divine love suffering with us. When this presence "of an almighty and unconquerable Being Whose power consists in the burning intensity of eternal and infinite love" (61) is consciously experienced, it furnishes an inner core of joy and strength, a "true happiness" that is "the transfiguration of sorrow rather than its abolition"(58–59, 242–43). He seems to hold that this is true even in the presence of what I have called horrendous evils: "[The experience of Divine love] has caused a passionate conviction that beneath the sufferings or the sins of that apparently ruined life there lay something of imperishable value for the sake of which it was worthwhile that the anguish or the degradation should be borne"(59–60). At the same time, such experience of Divine love, deepens human affections so as to render them "more sensitive" to being "pierced by the suffering or the wrong-doing" of other humans, thus "making the soul more capable of pain" while removing the accompanying "bitterness" (59, 229–31). Rolt also seems to suggest that our patient endurance, absorbing the blows of others, could—like God's—have some redemptive effect on those who strike us, that is, our posture of suffering without returning the blow would draw them away from self-assertion towards harmony with God's purposes, but Rolt does not further explain how this works.

3.3. Threshing the Harvest

Where providence and evil are concerned, Rolt's book is rich in provocative proposals. His Platonizing remodeling of God-creature relations does secure a metaphysically distinctive position for God as the universal exemplar Who (like Platonic forms) is ever more imitated but cannot be replaced or equaled, rivaled or surpassed. Relating science to religion, his scheme gestures toward an integration between evolutionary theory and teleology. Rolt meets the problem of suffering with two distinctive ideas— namely, Divine capacity to suffer and the absorption model of defeat—that suggest multiple ways for a noncoercive God to lend positive meaning to the suffering of personal creatures. Not only does Divine solidarity lend dignity to suffering by turning it into a dimension of Godlikeness, but also embracing suffering as a vocation, absorbing it without returning hostility, becomes a way of collaborating in God's work of redeeming the world. Nor will Rolt have reason to worry that in making actual suffering necessary to Divine perfection, he puts creation in the position of having to suffer for the sake of perfecting God. For his Platonizing reconstruction of the relation between God and creation treats the *existence* as well as the *nature* of material things as metaphysically necessary and hence not products of free and contingent Divine choice. Material nature dictates an evolutionary process in which created suffering is metaphysically necessary. Metaphysically necessary Divine suffering makes God and creation a matched pair.

Painting his picture in bold strokes, however, Rolt is inattentive to analytical details. How, for instance, are we to cash his "political" contrast between coercive force and weakness relative to the more metaphysical notions of active versus passive efficient causal power? If coercion involves the former, it seems doubtful whether power to suffer can be exhausted by the latter. If it is spirits who have power to suffer, it seems they would also have active powers to think and will. In any event, it seems doubtful whether any *thing,* much less a spirit, could be exhausted by passive powers (compare this to Aquinas's identification of prime matter with pure potency and his consequent denial that it is an individual [*hoc aliquid*]). Wouldn't God's role as universal exemplar demand some positive feature(s) over and above passivity? Also implausible is the suggestion that power to suffer exhausts love. Would it not also involve some active (cognitive and affective) appreciation of an active will to be united with the beloved, an active purposing of the world's redemption? Turning in another direction, the metaphysics of Rolt's Christology is left unclear. What analysis does he presuppose to interpret the idea that God suffers in Christ? Moreover, we may wonder whether Rolt's Platonizing reconstruction, together with his emphasis on capacity to suffer, does not inherit the vices of its virtues in evacuating the Godhead of power over whether any creation shall *be* and/or power ever to *make* it obey!

4. A Process Theological Portrait

Charles Hartshorne and David Griffin also decry the picture of God as an omnipotent tyrant arbitrarily wielding power to determine what all creatures do.[13] Painting over it, they substitute a metaphysical portrait that takes its inspiration from Alfred North Whitehead's *Process and Reality.*

4.1. A Free Society

Hartshorne and Griffin agree that God, as a being a greater one than which cannot be conceived, must have perfect power, the greatest power it is conceivable for a being to have. How much that is cannot be decided in a metaphysical vacuum, however, without considering the nature of any other beings there may be. Following Whitehead, they insist that it is impossible for any actual being to be completely determined by some other

13. David Griffin, *God, Power, and Evil* (Philadelphia: Westminster Press, 1976); Charles Hartshorne, *Omnipotence and Other Theological Mistakes* (Albany: State University of New York Press, 1984), 6, 12–14, 16, 58, 67, 75–83. Parenthetical page citations throughout section 4 refer to Hartshorne's *Omnipotence and Other Theological Mistakes.*

being, because every actual being by nature is—that is, both has and exercises power to be—at least partially self-determining.[14] If each creature is thus "free" in a sense incompatible with causal determinism, nature cannot be the closed causal nexus of Kant, Schleiermacher, La place, and Bultmann; rather, it must, Hartshorne concludes, include some chance (3, 16–17, 20–22, 67).

At the same time, Hartshorne's God is not Tillich's Ground-of-Being, Being-Itself beyond all beings, but rather *the* being in which all creatures live and move and have their being, *the* being essential to all, universally relevant, unique in status, the subject to whom all individuals are infallibly known and upon whom they essentially depend (31–32, 47). Appealing to the analogy of mind-body relations within humans, Hartshorne styles God as the World Soul Who persuades creatures into the organic unity of His body (94).

Griffin elaborates on the essential partial self-determination of creatures along Whiteheadian lines. On the one hand, every actual being is an event or occasion, so that the basic elements of the universe other than God lack temporal extension, while macro-objects and continuants are constructs, constituted by more or less coordinated bundles. On the other hand, Grif-

---

14. Like Hartshorne's, Griffin's text is littered with inferences from

> (P1) God *has power* to completely determine the condition of another actual being,

to

> (C1) The being whose condition is completely determined by God (or some being other than itself) has no power for self-determination (or has no power at all),

which looks blatantly invalid, because it seems to confuse *having power* with *exercising power*. It does not follow from the fact that I have the power to eat the whole of the last cookie that you do not also have the power to eat it; rather it is not the case that both of us can exercise that power. In fact, I believe there is an ambiguity in

> (T2) Every actual being by nature is at least partially self-determining,

which—in Griffin's mind—means not simply that

> (T2′) Every actual being by nature *has power* at least partially to self-determine its condition,

but

> (T2″) Every actual being *by nature exercises power* at least partially to self-determine its condition (Griffin, *God, Power, and Evil*, 268–70)

and therefore

> (C2) It is impossible for one being to have and/or exercise the power completely to determine another.

fin is a pan-psychist, insofar as each actual being is at first *a subject* of experience, whose data are impressed upon it by the previous states of the universe, and whose task is to integrate these data (an activity called concrescence). The Divine ideas make an impression on the subject and suggest an optimal direction of integration; but by nature subjects are partially self-determining with respect to the integration of these data. In particular, subjects *positively* prehend data when they choose to include it in the integration, *negatively* prehend data when they choose to marginalize it. Its integrating activity complete, the actual occasion becomes *an object* for successive actual beings who are *subjects* confronted with the task of integrating different data.[15]

4.2. The Uniqueness of God's Role

Similarly, Hartshorne explains, God is *a subject* of experience, but unlike creatures, God is the *universal subject*, who as a perfect knower has a perfect grasp of all occasions. God's integrative goal is to fit the various occasions together in such a way as (relative to any given point) maximize the beauty of the whole world. This involves the appropriate appreciation (positive prehension) of each for exactly what it is. Moreover, because the past remains real, the appreciation is permanent. God forever remembers, is ever reintegrating each actual occasion into the ever-increasing society of the world as a whole (37–38, 110).

At the same time, God is the *universal object* of experience insofar as God's conception of the most beautiful integration is among the data fed into each occasion, although because of their differing cognitive capacities, different occasions grasp God's suggestions with varying degrees of clarity (110–11). Because not only humans but all creatures are essentially partially self-determining, God cannot fully determine any creature, but can only exercise persuasion, apparently via the Divine idea(s) being included among—as a suggested organizing principle for—the data to be integrated by each occasion. This influence does not impose the Divine plan, not only because created occasions grasp it only imperfectly, but because—once again—each is partially self-determining. To the extent that it is successful, Divine good management explains cosmic order that limits the scope of freedom and chance to avoid meaningless chaos without reducing creatures' creative scope to zero (18, 38). Indeed, Hartshorne can say, God as world-soul is the individual integrity of the world, without Whose management and organizing efforts, it would be a mess of myriad creatures.[16]

15. Griffin, *God, Power, and Evil*, 278, 280–81, 283.

16. Hartshorne, *Omnipotence and Other Theological Mistakes*, 59–60. Oddly, given the vehemence of his rhetoric against tyranny, Hartshorne does occasionally speak of God's "ruling over" the components of the world and "quasi-determining" them insofar as God subjects them to laws (ibid.).

4.3. The Power of Persuasion

Hartshorne takes some trouble to explain why Divine ideas should have any appeal at all. First, Hartshorne reminds us, intrinsic value motivates (81). Which intrinsic value? The mind-body composite that God *is*. Sometimes Hartshorne identifies this valuable with the beauty of the world which every creature enjoys and to which each makes unique contributions (25, 81); other times, as insurpassable love, which inspires worship (14, 81). For Hartshorne, such apparently nonequivalent descriptions are connected. On the one hand, Divine love is construed cognitively in terms of the accurate appreciation of each occasion, and benevolently in terms of Divine will to surround it with the most fitting possible circumstances (81). On the other hand, Hartshorne follows Whitehead in taking his general model of cognition not from vision but from touch or feeling. Thus, Divine omniscience includes perfect empathetic capacity, which involves God in feeling whatever created occasions feel—not only the joys and delights, but also the pain and suffering (14, 27, 31). The love of God that accurately and permanently appreciates our worth inspires love (37–38); the love of a fellow sufferer who understands, inspires love in return (14). This being so, the thought that God will feel whatever joys or sorrows we cause to ourselves or others is likewise a great motivator (28, 81).

4.4. Norms of Integration, Global Goods

Griffin gives the norms of integration more explicit attention. He lays down twin, frankly aesthetic dimensions that are in tension with each other: harmony and intensity as intrinsically good; discord and triviality as intrinsically bad/evil. Greater variety increases intensity but disrupts harmony and requires a fresh and more subtle strategy of integration. He posits a positive correlation between the capacity for intrinsic goodness and degree of freedom because the capacity for enjoying intrinsic goodness just *is* the capacity to integrate ever greater variety harmoniously. At the same time, there is a positive correlation between the capacity for intrinsic goodness and the capacity for intrinsic evil insofar as increased freedom means increased creative or destructive impact on self and others.[17]

Griffin draws these value-theory assumptions together to offer a global explanation of the existence of evil in terms of God's luring partially self-determining creatures into arrangements of higher-level intensity. Perfect Goodness is in the clear in exposing everyone to the greater risks of disharmony, however, because the Divine subject is Itself prepared to suffer all

17. Griffin, 292, 295. Cf. Hartshorne, *Omnipotence and Other Theological Mistakes,* 85.

possible consequences, and because God works continually to overcome evil with good (by always furnishing ideal aims for the next state of the world).[18]

4.5. Goodness *to Individuals?*

Within the process scheme, horrendous evil would involve a massive "download" of painful data beyond the individual's capacity for integration. Given limited Divine power to set things right, would not unsurpassable love hesitate to lure creation into intensity levels productive of horrendous by-products? Would not doing so limit Divine *goodness to* created persons within the context of their individual lives?

Hartshorne insists the process picture recognizes a number of ways God is *good to* metaphysically basic individual occasions and even to those sub-societies commonsensically identified as human persons. For whatever the feeling tone of their actual existence, whatever their failed attempts at integration, God *honors* every actual being in multiple ways: by forever remembering and appreciating it for what it is, for continually seeking its ideal integration into the whole, and by enduring all of its suffering (121–22).

At the same time, Hartshorne boasts the resourcefulness of process metaphysics in de-emphasizing this dimension. For the worries about Divine *goodness to* created persons and the overall positive meaning of their lives are urgent on the assumption that they as continuant substances are somehow metaphysically fundamental and so—given that they are *personal* substances—are appropriate objects of special consideration over and above the value of the world as a whole. But process metaphysics is pan-psychic, turns every actual occasion into a momentary self. Moreover, it reduces created substance continuants to "societies of occasions" (108–9). This means that an individual's self-love of his/her own person (that is, "ordinary-sense" person conceived of as having temporal extension) and concern for his/her own personal history (the overall meaning of his/her life) involves a kind of altruism of the "I-now" towards the other occasions in the bundle. In Hartshorne's mind, this introduces a kind of arbitrariness into concern for subsocieties of occasions less than the whole. By contrast, Deity represents the highest form of inclusion of others in the self and the highest form of self being included in others (110). Global focus, on the beauty of the whole, the hylomorphic composite whose dominant member is God, is nonarbitrary. Accordingly, Hartshorne construes "the first and great commandment" (to love God with all one's heart, soul, mind, and strength) to

18. Griffin, 306–9.

imply that only God deserves special consideration and that others are to be loved only insofar as they are included in God (105–7, 121).

4.6. Processing the Insights

This process theological approach brings out of its storehouse what is old and what is new. Taking its cue from classical free will approaches, it generalizes and reinforces them by awarding freedom to *every* actual being other than God and by trimming the scope of Divine power down to the power of persuasion. In a way akin to Rolt's, it remodels Divine causality along the lines of exemplar causality insofar as its God exercises influence mainly if not entirely through Divine ideas. Like best-of-all-possible-worlds accounts, Griffin's and Hartshorne's line spotlights aesthetic value. Not only God but every actual occasion is an artist-subject, who exists to perform the task of integrating its data in such a way as to maximize harmonious intensity. God's intrinsic value consists in cosmic beauty; the value of other actual occasions is a function of their contribution to the beauty of the world as a whole. Particularly striking is the insistence on the Platonic linkage between love and beauty—the claim that Divine aesthetic appreciation and aesthetic enhancement of creatures is a dimension of God's love for them; creatures' efforts to cooperate with God's ideas, and thereby contribute their best to cosmic beauty, is a way for them to love God back. Also notable in process theology are its promotion of feeling as a way of knowing, its understanding of the cognitive partly in terms of empathetic capacity, and its startling conclusion that Divine omniscience makes God a participant in all the sufferings of the world. Of equal importance is the notion that God works continually—both during our lives and after our deaths—to give our lives new and fuller meanings far beyond what we could orchestrate for ourselves.

Metaphysically, some points stand in need of further clarification. What precisely is the sense in which all actual occasions are *in* God? They cannot be merely objects of the universal subject, because it is only as subjects that they exercise their freedom. If they are thought to be the world-soul's body, more needs to be said about the manner of their relation. Again, folk psychology regards the integration of psychic data as a process. If the God of classical theology is allowed to make all calculations, see all connections "all at once" in the "now of eternity," is it either intelligible or plausible to describe the activity of instantaneous occasions this way?

Theologically, process thought's claim that God cannot exist without some creatures or other can seem a radical compromise of Divine transcendence. Likewise, its deployment of political models is peculiar. For if it begins with democratic objections to cosmic tyranny, it ends by demanding that individuals—both metaphysically basic occasions and those larger bundles to which ordinary-sense personal continuants are reduced—value themselves only insofar as they are parts of cosmic society. Hartshorne even scolds that the universe does not owe individuals anything, that we do not deserve more than we get (121). Given that some individual occasions and person-constituting bundles experience evils of horrendous proportions, this looks like the Stoic demand to love God, admire the universe that crushes you. Also, for those individuals or bundles who fail at the integrative task, God's permanent memory and appreciation of them for what they are—in themselves, ruinously ugly—will scarcely seem a favor. Rather, so far as aesthetics are concerned, Divine honor paid to them would consist in God's global integration of them to enhance Divine beauty. Yet, this is a benefit that would come too late for many participants in horrors subjectively to appropriate, because for Hartshorne the immortality of occasions and of ordinary-sense personal bundles is only objective (as objects of Divine thought), while progressive reintegrations into Divine beauty would be won after their subjectivity had come to an end.

5. Horror-Defeating Power

My own reflections about Divine power and agency are driven by a third systematic consideration: God must be not only the source and sustainer of being and goodness, but also the defeater of horrors. My question thus becomes, *what would it take for Divine power and agency to be able to guarantee created persons lives that are great goods to them on the whole, and to defeat their participation in horrors not just globally, but within the context of their individual lives?*

5.1. Personhood (Agency That Acts by Thought and Choice)

My insistence on this criterion already reflects a distinctive metaphysical bias. In the *Coherence of Theism*, Richard Swinburne points out how philosophers divide over whether what there is is personal at bottom or impersonal.[19] Influenced by Platonizing hierarchies, Tillich would distinguish two forms of "impersonalism"—between materialism that makes the fundamental stuff of the universe (matter and the void, electrical ooze) less than personal, and some brands of idealism that posit the One or the Absolute, which is more than personal. I reject both kinds of impersonalism, and

19. Richard Swinburne, *The Coherence of Theism* (Oxford: Clarendon Press, 1979), 22–50.

maintain, with Swinburne, that persons—that is, agents who act by thought and will—are metaphysically fundamental. If materialist programs to reduce to or eliminate mind in favor of matter were true, or if ordinary-sense persons were Humean bundles of perceptions or Hartshornean societies of occasions, there would be a metaphysical basis for de-emphasizing the category of horrendous evils the way Hartshorne ultimately does.[20]

My philosophical instinct to make human personality fundamental is matched by a drive, like Swinburne's, to join the mainstream of Christian theological tradition in regarding Divine agency as personal—that is, at bottom, agency that acts by thought and will. Discussion in sections 1 and 2 above is intended to confront and undermine the charge that personhood in this sense is necessarily leveling, that it would automatically shrink God down to anthropomorphic giant-size.

Once freed from this down-sizing disadvantage, Divine personhood offers systematic advantages where the problem of horrendous evils is concerned. For horror-defeating power is meaning-restoring power, and meaning-making is personal activity par excellence! Recall (from Chapter 2 above) that my definition of the horrendous in terms of its capacity prima facie to devour the positive meaning of participants' lives, was advanced as *objective* (so that it would be possible for individuals to think their lives not worth living and yet be wrong) and at the same time *person-relative* (in the twin sense that one may be able to withstand what will crush another and that persons' own estimates of whether their own lives are worthwhile is to be given very serious weight). We may thus distinguish between *objective* and *recognized* meaning, so that relation to some great enough good might objectively defeat evil within the context of an individual's life without their knowing about those connections. Again, there is a difference between *seeing* connections and *valuing* them. A traveling salesman may recognize the breakup of his marriage as a side effect of long hours on the road that enriched his company, but he will not find consolation in this and make this positive significance his own unless he is a company man. So, too, there is a difference between meanings being recognized and appropriated *by others* and their being recognized and appropriated *by the individual him/herself.* The soldier scout who wishes to serve his unit, who steps on a land mine and is blown to smithereens, does not live to recognize how his accident saved dozens of lives, even though he may be posthumously decorated and his family justly proud of his heroism. Similarly, the creatures of

---

20. Not that one would be *forced* to do so. For reductive programs differ from eliminative ones in allowing the conceptual framework to be reduced a level of legitimacy; and this legitimacy could be sufficient to give bite to the problems raised within it.

Hartshorne's God do not survive to appreciate their successive and widening contributions to Divine beauty. Further (expanding on what was said in Chapter 2), I assume that for an individual's life to be a great good *to him/her* on the whole, it is not enough for good to balance off or defeat evil *objectively speaking*. The individual involved must him/herself also recognize and appropriate at least some of those positive meanings. Even curmudgeons take satisfactions in their appropriate relations to goods, even if they do not readily admit it.

If Divine agency is personal, God, too, is a meaning-maker, indeed, mainstream Biblical religion contends, the One Who decisively settles the meaning of history (Rev. 5–6). It is then straightforward to credit God with superlative imagination needed to make sense of horrors that stump us, and to think of the meaning-making God as also the Teacher Who coaches us to recognize and appropriate objective meanings already (Divinely) given, Who heals and helps us to make new meanings ourselves. To be sure, a Tillichian might claim that given the built-in tendencies of human nature, the omnipresence of the nonpersonal Ground of Being would suffice—given enough time—to spark creative personal integration. But surely the prospect of Divinely fostered meanings and individualized syllabi are less of a stretch if Divine agency is personal, too.

5.2. Incommensurate Goodness

Classical theology advertises God as a being greater than any other conceivable being, as supreme or infinite goodness. Rolt and Hartshorne also cast God in the role of paradigm or exemplar goodness, which is essential to the goodness or well-being of all else. *Pace* Mill, I suggest that Divine metaphysical goodness is essential to horror-defeating power, not because it changes the subject by setting aside the question of God's *goodness to* created persons, but because it furnishes the currency for God to be *good to* each and all, no matter what their antemortem experience. For what is good *for* a person is for him/her to be appropriately related to great enough goods. Consequently, one way to be good to persons is so to relate them. If horrors are so personally ruinous that no package of merely created goods could defeat them, the problem of horrendous evil cannot be solved unless God is a great enough good to make the difference. Nor is it plausible to suppose (in semi-Pelagian fashion) that Divine Goodness is a large finite good, just the right amount to "top up" created packages that fall short by a finite margin. Many participants in horrors die, having passed through antemortem careers of virtually unrelieved misery. By contrast, if Divine Goodness is infinite, if intimate relation to It is thus incommensurately good for created persons, then we have identified a good big enough to defeat horrors in every case.

5.3. The Capacity to Suffer

Classical theology understands the incommensurate Good to account for the goodness of things, to be the standard of goodness for creatures and/or the rightful object of unqualified love. It also understands the incommensurate Good to be immutable and impassible. But when classical theologians turn to the problem of evil, they focus on the problem of sin and give suffering short shrift, quickly categorizing it as educational or numbering it among the punitive consequences of sin (see Chapter 3 above). Against classical theology's argument—that suffering involves changes and if God is perfect, any change would be a change for the worse—Rolt and Hartshorne reply that some essential Divine perfections themselves involve change. For Rolt, love essentially involves suffering with those who suffer. For Hartshorne, omniscience includes empathetic capacity and so means that God feels the feelings of everything else. Both vividly portray how Divine compassion keeps God from being aloof and opens ways for suffering (even horrendous suffering) to be caught up into the participants' relationship with God. Thus, when it comes to defeating horrors, Divine passibility seems prima facie to afford certain systematic advantages (see Chapter 8 below).

5.4. Omnipotence

Nevertheless, it seems to me, if God had only the passive and persuasive powers allowed by Rolt and Hartshorne, no one in the universe would have enough power to solve the problem of horrendous evils on the terms I have required.[21] Many participants in horrors do not recognize or appropriate the positive meanings in their lives (for example, those furnished by Divine compassion and appreciation) before they die; many indeed are driven mad by their experiences. Therefore, if such individuals are to have lives that are great goods *to them* on the whole, God must be able to preserve them in life after their death, to place them (á la Hick) in new and nourishing environments where they can profit from Divine instruction on how to inte-

---

21. Paul Fiddes agrees, aiming to characterize "a God who suffers eminently and yet is still God" (*The Creative Suffering of God* [Oxford: Clarendon Press, 1988], 3, 61–62, 100–109, 110). So does Richard Creel, who stands on the other side of the impassibility issue. For Creel, although God has no obligation to suffer with us, God does have an obligation to redeem our suffering (*Divine Impassibility: An Essay in Philosophical Theology* [Cambridge: Cambridge University Press, 1986], 147–49, 155–56).

grate their participation in horrors into wholes with positive meanings. In my judgment, Rolt's account of how individuals might be empowered by Divine compassion to enter upon their own vocations of suffering love, fails to address the case of persons who are psychologically too wrecked for such spiritual exercises, and so fails to assign God enough power to defeat horrors in every case. Hartshorne's account suffers from similar limitations.

For my part, I follow classical theology in crediting God with power to create things other than God *ex nihilo,* as well as power to reduce them to nothing. Horror-defeating power will surely include power to produce *supra*natural effects—those that lie outside, go beyond any that created natural powers could produce. Reversing horrors would also seem to require power to substitute for nature (for example, in restoring bodies to prime working condition) and to override natural causes (for example, to keep resurrected bodies from decaying and dying, minds from becoming forgetful again). And so, *pace* Tillich, I count it an advantage of personal agency that—unlike Aristotelian fire and stones—it is able to do one thing (such as substitute and override) as opposed to another. Also, I deliberately contradict process metaphysics which makes it metaphysically impossible that one agent should altogether substitute for or "coerce" another. I do not agree that the mere possession of so much power would automatically turn God into a tyrant. Rather, despotism would be a function of Divine *policy* for the use of power, while experience confirms that created agents are (at most) rarely interfered with. Moreover, I take it to be an implication of the distinctiveness of God's ontological niche that creatures are dependent on God, not only for their coming into but also for their continuing in being; likewise, all created agents are dependent upon Divine concurrence in the exercise of their causal powers. This means that much of Divine action in relation to the created world, so far from competing with created agents, is actually *agency enabling.* Only where Divine agency is leveled, can it seem that created agency deserves the "hands-off" respect that parents owe to their late adolescent or adult children. In any event, I do not see how total noninterference that leaves created agents implicated in undefeated horrors, could be a sign of Divine respect (see Chapter 3 above).

5.5 Incompatible Desiderata?

It may be objected, however, that my hybrid portrait of horror-defeating power falls into metaphysical incoherence with its suggestion that incommensurate goodness suffers. For classical theologians—in positing God as the unitary explanation of being and goodness—reason from the axiom that only what is self-explanatory can be the ultimate explanation to the conclusion that God is whatever God is *per se* and so is incapable of being causally affected from without. At the same time, they understand suffering and feeling to be *passions,* which involve passive power to be acted upon by something else. Since the ontological gap is thus partially "cashed" in terms of a causal one-way street, how can I maintain that Divine goodness is incommensurate and yet suffers?

Rolt and Hartshorne are ahead of me in arguing that God can suffer and still occupy a distinctive ontological niche. My alternative is to claim that Divine omnipotence combines with Divine aseity with respect to being and essential perfections, to make the good that God *is* incommensurate with creatures. Clearly these features are enough to circumscribe the range of effects that creatures can have upon God. Even if there is causal interaction between God and creatures, it will be metaphysically impossible for them to jeopardize Divine existence or perfection, and it will remain within Divine power to prevent them from acting on God whenever It wants.

[5]

Purity and Defilement

1. At-one-ment, Problem Refocussed

Problems of evil vary in focus (as I have discussed in Chapter 1). Where contemporary analytic philosophers of religion have concentrated on whether God and evil are logically compossible, Christian theology (whose consistency is at issue) focuses on sin and redemption. Christians normally assume the following:

(1) Personal creatures were created for the purpose of happy intimacy (at-one-ment) with God and each other.

(2) Sin is an obstacle to such at-one-ment.

(3) In Christ, God "makes atonement" by overcoming the obstacle of sin.

Soteriology (the doctrine of salvation) studies how's and why's of (3). Its answers are a function of how sin in (2) is conceived. Where free fall approaches locate the root obstacle to at-one-ment in created free actions contrary to God's will (see Chapter 3), and so in what humans *do*, my contrary proposal finds the fundamental difficulty in a metaphysical devaluation of humankind in relation to Divinity, and so in what both God and humans *are*. Moreover, I want to suggest that this philosophical thesis is a good translation of Biblical and traditional declarations that God is holy while creatures are unclean. For aid in making this connection, I turn first to the phenomenology of religion, in particular to Rudolf Otto's long famous *Idea of the Holy*, and then to social anthropology, through an extensive examination and application of Mary Douglas's insights in her fascinating book *Purity and Danger*.

2. Religious Experience, "Size Gap" Made Vivid

In *The Idea of the Holy*, Rudolf Otto offers a rational reconstruction of our supposed derivation of the idea of God ("the Holy" or "the numen") from religious experience.[1] Otto's approach is particularly apt for our purposes, because its results describe the Holy and human relationship to the Holy at one and the same time. Accordingly, Otto's search for the genetic roots of the idea of the Holy promises at the same time to identify the source of our models of Divine-human relationship and its impediments (41–49).

2.1. Reading the Feelings

(i) Otto identifies the paradigm religious experience, which content-wise is *of* God (the Holy, the numen), in which God is presented as something other than the self, and which is attended by a full range of feeling accompaniments (8–11). By analogy, one might identify a paradigm experience of a tiger as a visual experience in which the tiger is presented to me as something other than myself, and which is accompanied by a wide range of feelings, such as terror, awe, and admiration. (ii) Continuing with the analogy, my experience provides me with two sources of tiger descriptions. Most obviously, I can read off a characterization of the tiger from its visual appearance (such as it being huge in size and having orange and black stripes, long claws, and sharp teeth). In addition, I can infer features of the tiger from the feeling accompaniments, according to the following pattern: 'Feeling ϕ accompanies my experience of x; therefore I experience x as the logically appropriate object of feeling ϕ'. For example, terror accompanies my vision of the tiger chasing me; therefore I ex-

1. Rudolf Otto, *Idea of the Holy* (New York: Oxford University Press, 1958), 8–11. I am particularly indebted in this section to Nelson Pike, who regularly used to begin his courses on the nature and attributes of God with a unit on Otto. For years, I have followed Pike's practice (as well as many interpretive details) in my own teaching. Parenthetical in-text page references in section 2 of this chapter refer to Otto's *Idea of the Holy*.

perience the tiger as a logically appropriate object of terror—as terrifying and terrible! Where ordinary objects are concerned, information from the one source can be checked against and/or corrected by that from the other. For example, I may be terrified of ladybugs, but they (as harmless to human well-being) are not logically appropriate objects of terror; or a detective may have a feeling that something is wrong, although everything looks fine.

Otto insists, however, that because God (the Holy, the numen) is so different from and so much bigger than we are, we cannot read off a characterization of God from the "visual" content of religious experience; instead, we can characterize God *only* as the logically appropriate object of the feelings that normally accompany paradigm religious experiences that are content-wise of Him. For present purposes, we need not accept this strong thesis, that religious feelings are our only route to God characterizations. We can profit from Otto's remarks so long as we concede the weaker claim that religious feelings *contribute* to the content of our idea in the way he describes.

(iii) According to Otto, our efforts thus to articulate our idea of the Holy are further complicated by the fact that such religious feelings are *sui generis* and only analogically related to those that accompany our experience of ordinary objects (consider, for example, the contrast between our fear of loose tigers and our dread of graveyard ghosts on Halloween). This means we will have to proceed by comparison and contrast and must be alert to the fact that feeling vocabulary will often be used analogically.

(iv) Finally, Otto hypothesizes that, in addition to reason and the five senses, humans are endowed with a special faculty for religious experience, a faculty for having experiences in which God is presented as something other than the self and for having a wide range of feeling accompaniments (112–16, 136–42). Moreover, such religious feelings can be triggered in different degrees by situations other than paradigm religious experience (by telling ghost stories, for example, or watching horror movies). Thus, Otto expects most (if not all) of his readers to have had the feelings to which he refers in his reconstruction.

2.2. The Holy Portrayed

Drawing on various religious texts including the Bible, Otto identifies and classifies religious feelings and infers the consequent God characterizations as follows:

Feeling Experience of Myself	*Characterization of God/Holy/Numen*

A. Tremendum

1. Fear, dread	1. Aweful, eerie, weird, dreadful
2. Creature-feeling	2. Powerful, plenitude of being
3. Radically threatened	3. Living, urgent, active

B. Mysterium

1. Angst, stupor	1. Wholly other
2. Attraction	2. *Fascinans*

C. Augustus

1. Profaneness, uncleanness	1. August, holy

(A) First, God is experienced as a worthy object of trembling and terror. (A1) paradigm religious experiences, Otto claims, would be accompanied with something like my fear of a loose tiger, but different from it in the direction of my reactions to graveyard ghosts on Halloween. Stories of ghosts and active corpses make flesh creep and blood run cold; they seem eerie, uncanny, and weird (13–17). Biblical examples include God's smoking fire pot covenant with Abraham in Gen. 15:7–12. Abraham splits and arranges the animals for the ratification ceremony and shoos the birds away all day long. Then, "as the sun was going down, a deep sleep fell on Abraham; and lo, a dread and great darkness fell upon him" (Gen. 15:12) and "behold, a smoking fire pot and flaming torch passed between these pieces. On that day the Lord made a covenant with Abraham, saying, 'To your descendants I give this land . . .' " (Gen. 15: 17–18).

(A2) paradigm religious experiences would be accompanied by creature-feeling, the sense of being radically weak and impotent in relation to something overwhelmingly efficacious; of being (in Anselm's words) "almost nothing" in relation to an infinite ocean of being (Damascene's image). In Biblical language, it is the experience of hearts melting, of strength draining out, of being utterly undone at the very sight of the other (8–11, 20–21). In (A3) paradigm religious experience, I would not only experience myself as utterly unable to affect what has an overwhelming capacity to affect me; I would experience myself as on the verge of being ruined, done in, or annihilated, and accordingly experience the Holy as living, urgent, active (23–24). Thus, the voice of the Lord is said to shake the wilderness (Ps. 29:8), to make the oak trees writhe, and to strip the forests bare (Ps. 29:9); His presence, to make mountains skip like rams and little hills like young sheep (Ps. 114: 4, 6) and to cause seas and rivers to flee (Ps. 114:3, 5). Again, in preparation for the Sinai summit, God warns Moses that the people must consecrate themselves and not touch the mountain, lest the Lord "break out against them" (Exod. 19:12–15, 21–24) as He later did against Uzzah who reached forth his hand to steady the ark (2 Sam. 6:1–11). When the time came for the Sinai meeting, the people were so terrified at the thunder and lightning, the trumpet blasts, and smoking mountain that they insisted on dealing with God only through intermediaries like Moses (Exod. 20:18–20).

(B) Otto's second category, the *Mysterium,* breaks down into two parts. On the one hand, in paradigm religious experience, I would experience (B1) great anxiety, I would feel stupefied, at a loss for words. Thus, when God finally grants Job a hearing, Job stammers, "Behold, I am of small account; what shall I answer thee? I lay my hand on my mouth. I have spoken once, and I will not answer; twice, but I will proceed no further." (Job 40: 3–5) And, seeing Jesus transfigured, Peter suggests three tents "not knowing what he said" (Luke 9:33). Otto infers that one experiences God as wholly other, utterly unique and unlike the ordinary objects of our experience (25–26, 29, 179–86). On the other hand, (B2) I would feel powerfully attracted to the Holy (31–32). For instance, the psalmist writes, "As a deer longs for the water-brooks, so longs my soul for you, O God. My soul is athirst for God, athirst for the living God; when shall I come to appear before the presence of God?" (Ps. 42: 1–2) Or again, "O God, you are my God; eagerly I seek you; my soul thirsts for you, my flesh faints for you, as in a barren and dry land where there is no water." (Ps. 63:1) And, "How dear to me is your dwelling, O Lord of hosts! My soul has a desire and longing for the courts of the Lord; my heart and my flesh rejoice in the living God." (Ps. 84:1) Accordingly, the Holy is experienced as fascinating and enticing.

(C) Finally, Otto claims that in paradigm religious experience, I would experience myself as profane, unclean, sinful. Thus, when Isaiah sees the Lord in the temple, he cries, "Woe is me! For I am lost; for I am a man of unclean lips, and I dwell in the midst of a people of unclean lips; for my eyes have seen the King, the Lord of hosts!" (Isa. 6:5) Likewise, faced with God, Job gasps, "I had heard of thee by the hearing of the ear, but now my eye sees thee; therefore I despise myself and repent in dust and ashes." (Job 42:5–6) And Peter, seeing the miraculous draught of fishes, falls down before Jesus, saying, "Depart from me, for I am a sinful man, O Lord." (Luke 5:8) Conversely, God is experienced as pure and holy (50–57).

Drawing Otto's conclusions together, we see that feelings in category (B1) reveal God to us as "separate" in the sense of being radically unlike anything else in our experience. Those in category (A) tell us that this Wholly Other is radically dangerous to the health of beings of our kind, while category (C) introduces a normative element: it is not just that God is "very, very big" while creatures are good but "very, very small"; rather the decided normative priority lies on the side of God. Nevertheless, as Otto himself insists, all of these characterizations are premoral (50–59). The devaluations of creatures in (A2) and (C1) have nothing to do with the unique conditions or behavior of individuals; but pertain to individuals qua members of a certain kind. (A2) simply expresses the ontological incommensurability between God and creatures, while (C1) is a relative devaluation consequent upon it. On Otto's analysis, then, the notion of sin would be, in its genetic origin, premoral. Creatures are to be characterized as sinful or unclean, because the radical incommensurability of Divine and created natures obstructs relations between God and creatures, and the problem lies, not in any flaw in the Divine nature, but in the radical limitation and finitude of created natures in comparison to God.[2]

2.3. Moralizing Reservations

Even if we agree that Otto's focus on religious feeling catches something fundamental and *uralt* (that is, primal and primitive) that should not be lost sight of in our attempts to understand God and Divine-human relationships; even if we concede that part of the soul of religion is lost when theological concepts are entirely cut off from these feeling roots, we might consider Otto's reflections on genetic origins inconclusive. After all, so much Biblical attention to Divine-human relationships revolves around themes of covenant, commandments, obedience, and disobedience. And these latter notions seem prima facie congruent with the voluntaristic/moralistic commonplaces about sin. To undermine this objection, I turn now to the work of Mary Douglas, which provides a framework of ideas relative to which the Biblical structure of covenants and commandments emerges as a solution to the more fundamental problem of the incommensurability of Divine and created natures.

---

2. Commenting on the difference between moral devaluation and that involved in (A2) and (C1), Otto writes, "Mere morality is not the soil from which grows either the need of 'redemption' and deliverance or the need for that other unique good which is likewise altogether and specifically numinous in character, 'covering', and 'atonement'. There would perhaps be less disputing as to the warrant and value of these later in Christian doctrine *if dogmatic theology itself had not transferred them from their mystical sphere into that of rational ethics and attenuated them into moral concepts*" (53; my emphasis). Again, " 'Atonement' . . . is a 'sheltering' or 'covering', but a profound form of it . . . . Mere awe, mere need for shelter from the *tremendum,* has been elevated to the feeling that man in his 'profaneness' is not *worthy* to stand in the presence of the holy one, and that his own entire personal unworthiness might defile even holiness itself" (54).

3. Purity and Defilement, Sketching the Categories

The calculus of purity and defilement operates with two principal evaluative categories, one positive and one negative, which are applied not only to persons but also to places, things, and states of affairs. In her book *Purity and Danger,* Douglas offers a social-anthropological analysis of cleanliness metaphors and institutions in terms of twin ideas: that dirt is stuff out of order and that stuff out of order is both powerful and dangerous.[3]

Order and boundaries come in many varieties. Within society, social classes or castes, political, social, and familial roles give definition and create order. In the world at large, national boundaries, treaties, and international agreements give structure and definition to relations among nation-states. In nature, genus and species boundaries give structure and definition to plant and animal worlds.

Disorder is experienced as doubly dangerous: fundamentally, because order confers identity on individuals and groups by giving them definition—what compromises identity threatens existence (2–3, 36); and pragmatically, because order makes reality predictable and so enables individuals and groups to plot survival and prosperity strategies. At the same time, disorderly elements seem powerful, not only because they threaten to disrupt the old, but also because they symbolize creative potential for the new. Powers outside the order may bring superstructural blessing as well as curse and so may be objects of admiration as well as terror (109–13, 160–79). For example, Douglas remarks, the "numen" or "numenal" individuals (such as, witches, medicine men, pregnant women, ghosts, madmen, saints) are felt to be powerful, dangerous, and/or attractive, because they fall between the cracks of social, political, and/or natural categories (95–98).

Douglas explains that where group boundaries (whether social, political, or natural) are under assimilative pressure, communities tend to meet the threats to group identity by evolving codes and regulations that clarify and strengthen group definition. And such institutions often metaphorically express the problem and its resolution, by positing sharp distinctions between the clean and the polluted, whether with respect to natural or to social boundaries. Douglas sees "the abominations of Leviticus" in this light (49–57). Etymologically, 'holy' means separate, so that, in one sense, holiness involves the clear and distinct separation of one thing from another (49–51). Thus, animals are clean or unclean insofar as they perfectly

---

3. Mary Douglas, *Purity and Danger: An Analysis of Concepts of Pollution and Taboo* (London: Routledge and Kegan Paul, 1966), 2, 35–36, 49–50, 94–113, 160–61. Parenthetical in-text page citations in section 3 of this chapter refer to this work.

conform to or compromise the species boundaries of rudimentary zoology. Those which fall between the taxonomical cracks or blur the distinctions by participating partly in one category and partly in another are unclean (Lev. 11:3–7, 26–28). Similarly, swarming things are unclean, because in swarms motion is indeterminate, no more of one sort than another (Lev. 11:10–11, 29–38, 41–43).[4] Furthermore because 'holy' symbolizes the whole, complete, or perfect, things which are defective members of their kind (such as the lame, the blind, those with crushed limbs or sex organs [Lev. 21:17–21, 22:20–25; cf. Lev. 1:3, 10]) are unclean (51–53). And because holiness implies purity, being of the same kind all over and through and through, it follows that hybrids (such as mules [Lev. 19:19], mixtures (such as linsey-woolsey), and those with blotchy or blemished surfaces (partially leprous people, partially mildewed walls or cloth, [Lev. 13, 22:4]) are unclean. Because the human body is itself an image of society, bodily emissions symbolize ruptured group definition; hence, bodily discharges of whatever sort (including menstrual blood and semen [Lev. 12:1; 15; 22:4]) render one unclean (114–28).

Uncleanness is communicable by contact. For example, it passes from the ejaculating man or menstruating woman, to their clothes, to whatever they touch and to whoever touches them, even to what they spit on (Lev. 15:2–30). It is removable (if at all) by purification rituals: for example, the man by taking a bath and washing the clothes (Lev. 15:5–11), the woman by offering two birds for sacrifice (Lev. 15:29–30). Recovered lepers must be examined, must shave and bathe, and must offer sacrifices (Lev. 14). But pottery dishes touched by unclean persons must be broken (Lev. 15:12); mildewed cloth, burned if the mildew doesn't come out in the wash (Lev. 13:53–58). Moreover, these classifications have nothing to do with the beliefs or intentions of affected persons. Many subjects of uncleanness are impersonal. Uncleanness may be the known result of intentional action (as when spouses voluntarily have sexual relations), but disease is usually involuntary as are birth defects. Other contaminating conditions (such as forcible rape or mutilation) are imposed by others. And the one who unwittingly bumps into a menstruous woman or steps on a grave is unclean all the same.

4. Rules about sexuality are similar (Lev. 18:6–20): "Holiness means keeping distinct the categories of creation. It therefore involves correct definition, discrimination, and order. Under this head all the rules of sexual morality exemplify the holy. Incest and adultery (Lev. 18:6–20) are against holiness, in the simple sense of right order. Morality does not conflict with holiness, but holiness is more a matter of separating that which should be separated than of protecting the rights of husbands and brothers" (Douglas, *Purity and Danger*, 53).

4. Sin as Uncleanness

It is unclear to me whether Douglas intends a sociological reduction of religion generally, as of such institutions of purity and danger in particular. Happily, we need not (and I do not) embrace any reductive program to accept her generic thesis—that human perceptions and responses to others are profoundly shaped, both individually and collectively, by social context and institutions—or to profit from her more precise observations about how a thing's relation to social structure, or a group's position in its wider context, affect ascriptions of purity and pollution, danger and power. Adapting Douglas's ideas, I want now to press my contention that, at the most basic level, sin is uncleanness, an outgrowth of two metaphysical roots.

4.1. The Metaphysical Gap

Once again, Biblical imagery conveys how the "size gap" between God and creatures misfits us for each other's company. Divine knowledge and power swamp any created capacity (cf. Job 7:7–21). Compared to the heavens, humans are flimsy, temporary, vulnerable to attack from all kinds of things (Job 7:6–9; 14:1–2; 15:14–16; 35:5–8). But in relation to God, "the vast expanse of interstellar space, the planets in the courses," are metaphysically minuscule (Job 26:5–14; 40:14–24; 41:1–34). On the one hand, we have no more rightful place in God's household than worms and maggots do in ours (Job 24:4–6); nothing we could naturally be or do would make us suitable for Divine company. Because Divine and created natures are incommensurate, God will be unclassifiable relative to any merely human order (social, political, international) or to any human perception of natural order. Since we are unable to fit Him into any of our categories, we experience God as (B1) wholly other, and therefore as utterly unpredictable, as arbitrary power (A2), at once dangerous (A3) and attractive (B2). Yet, because God and creatures are so radically different in kind, and because roles not only confer identity but define relationships, it is difficult to see how God and humans ever could be "at one," occupying the same social world.

4.2. Metaphysical Straddling

Quite apart from comparison with the Divine, human nature seems unclean in itself, because—like linsey-woolsey—it is not simply of one kind or the other. Within the tradition, this heterogeneity of human nature has been variously conceptualized—human being involves soul and body, spirit as well as matter, is personal as well as animal; likewise, soul and body are sometimes two substances united only as, or more closely than, a pilot to its ship, but sometimes they make a hylomorphic compound. However much the great scholastics celebrated the human position at the metaphysical borderline, they also acknowledged the risk that each element could compromise the integrity of the other.[5] Traditional anthropologies agree, the material, corporeal, animal distracts mind's cognitive and evaluative attention, disrupts its balance, lures it into preferring lesser to greater goods. Because the material, corporeal, animal is perishable, it coopts mind to share its fears and anxieties, provokes it to desperate and futile survival strategies. At the same time, mind interferes with matter, trying to impose its agenda on the corporeal animal nature, reign in, harness the latter's instincts for "higher" things. Whether normative relations are understood in terms of elimination (as with ascetic aims to amputate bodily concerns) or subordination (where reason rules but gives animal needs a voice), theory and experience witness that these are difficult to achieve, that stable virtue is easily out of reach for most. Contemporary psychologies envision even more intense mind–body interaction (see Chapter 3, section 4).

4.3. Natural Uncleanness?

Human uncleanness is thus a consequence of twin metaphysical necessities. The metaphysical gap results from what the Divine essence and human nature *are,* quite apart from any exercise of either agency. This problem lies, not in any flaw or hostility in the Divine nature, but in the radical limitation and finitude of created natures in comparison with God. The human being straddles the spiritual and the material (both personal and animal kinds) and, thus dualistically conceived, is—in the words of Leviticus—neither of one kind nor another. The issue is not one of *individual* misbehavior or unique conditions, but pertains to humans insofar as they are members of humankind.

This double defilement does not *consist in* but is the *root of* human relationship difficulties and inappropriate behavior. Once again, because of the size gap nothing we could be or do could count—simply by virtue of what it is—as an appropriate move in relation to God, any more than a worm's wiggling to the right could be intrinsically more respectful of humans than its wiggling to the left.

Moreover, and independently, human heterogeneity makes it extremely difficult for us to "get our acts together" to move towards virtue, to con-

---

5. E.g., Aquinas, *Summa Contra Gentiles,* 2.68.6–12 [bk. 2, chap. 68, secs. 6–12]; and Bonaventure, *Breviloquium,* 2.10–11 [bk. 2, chaps. 10–11].

form to human-sized ideals, rules, and regulations reliably and with good motives. Aquinas appreciated these latter incongruities, when he posited that even in Eden, humans were supernaturally infused with a habit that inhibited natural corruption and the "supervirtue" of original justice that disposed Adam and Eve to exercise and restrain their powers in an appropriately coordinated way.[6] Crucial for present purposes, metaphysical straddling is the source of human contamination with horrors. If personality were not tied to an animal life cycle, if early childhood adaptations did not become so readily entrenched, adult human beings would not persist in operating out of such childish worldviews and the sins of the fathers and mothers would not descend to the third and fourth generations. If biology did not so easily dominate, even swallow psychology, we would not be vulnerable to degradation through disease and radical deprivation of material needs. If mind and body, personality and animality, were not so interactive and integrated, we could not by invading the body so deeply wound the soul.

5. Statutory Holiness, Size Gap Overcome?

5.1. Covenants as Cover

If what counts as dirt is order-relative, then one remedy for uncleanness would be an order that is new. Mere humans cannot cancel the alienating implications of the metaphysically necessary size gap, because the Reality of God explodes any categories we might fashion—God is too big to squeeze into any humanly contrived social role. But God can create a social order that networks God and humans together. God can assign Godself a role that clarifies expectations, makes interactions safer and more predictable. At the same time, the Divine social order invents roles for us. Just as human civil law confers value, turns paper worth a few cents into $100 bills, so Divine legislation establishes statutory definitions of what will count as a fitting or appropriate response by finite creatures to God.

When the Hebrew Bible formulates this solution in terms of Divinely initiated contracts, codes, and covenants, the point is not—on my reading— that God is taking on obligations to created individuals or nations, nor that actions are the primary obstacle to Divine-human at-one-ment. Rather God accomodates Himself to the human condition to assure us of Divine good will, despite the perils of the metaphysical size gap. How sure can

---

6. *Summa Theologica* 1–2.109.7 [first part of the second part, quest. 109, art. 7], cf. 1–2.85.6.

Abraham be that God will make him the father of many nations? How confident can Israel be that covenant keeping will bring prosperity? At least as certain as they could be when someone seals a contract (Gen. 15:7–16) or international treaty (Exod. 20; Deut. 5–8) with conditional curses; only more so, because Divine integrity is stronger than any oath, because the Word of God stands forever (cf. Mat. 5:33–37)!

More fundamentally, contracts, codes, and covenants are themselves a friendly Divine gesture (in the spirit of Psalm 119), insofar as they define the statutory category of created holiness. "You must be holy for I am holy!" (Lev. 19:2; 20:26; 22:31–33). God has Moses announce this to the people of Israel as a necessary condition for at-one-ment. So God imposes a suzerainty covenant with rules of various kinds. Because it is distinctive ("this law is not given to any other nation"), obedience separates Israel out from other peoples, makes her metaphorically holy, gives her identity as a unique and clear-cut specimen of "YHWH's kind of people" (see Lev. 19:2; 20:7, 24, 26; 22:31–33). Conversely, disobedience blurs the boundaries, runs in the direction of assimilation, eventually breaks the covenant, cancels the contract, exposes the people to wrath and unshielded contact with Divine power.

5.2. Limited At-one-ment?

Formally and in principle, a Divine social order overcomes the obstacle to at-one-ment posed by the metaphysical size gap. Yet, more often than not, the Hebrew Bible understands this solution to be exclusive. The explicit purpose of the holiness code is to separate Israel out from other nations, by imposing commands and prohibitions that will make her behavior *different* from theirs (Israel is forbidden to sacrifice pork or to flavor offerings with honey, because that is what the Canaanites do [Lev. 2:11–13]). The power of obedience to make Israel metaphorically holy depends on a contrast with others who are left out.

Even where "the chosen people" are concerned, the effectiveness of Hebrew Bible versions of this strategy is undermined by the consequences of metaphysical straddling. Israel's history spirals through cycles of commitment, followed by a slow then a rapid slackening of discipline, rampant disobedience calling down Divine wrath, exile, and dissolution (see Ps. 78, 80, 105, 106). The seer in pseudepigraphal 4 Ezra complains that God knows how within the human heart the evil desire (*yezer*) is stronger than the good and should be fully aware of how this makes consistent *collective* obedience virtually impossible. This human motivational structure turns the "gift" of Divine law into a "set-up": the clarity of expectations raises hopes for at-one-ment, which are rudely dashed by human inability to meet them (4 Ezra 3:20–22).

6. Divine Defilement, Interim Solution!

The God of the Bible is relentless. When metaphysical straddlers won't meet Him on holy ground, God takes the opposite approach of joining us in our defilement. Recall, after all, how Divine involvement with humans began with mudpies in Eden (Gen. 2:4–7)!

6.1. The Incarnation, Enmired Twice Over!

According to Christian doctrine, God the Son assumed our human nature. One person with two natures, isn't God Incarnate like splotchy walls or skin—neither merely human nor exclusively divine? What is by nature maggotlike, unfit to inhabit the same social world as God, is *a fortiori* unsuitable to be hypostatically united to Father, Son, or Holy Spirit.[7] This much contamination would apply no matter what created nature God assumed, even an angelic one. But if human nature is itself unclean, not simply one kind of thing or the other, the Word made flesh is doubly defiled!

6.2. Crucified and Cursed!

On the cross, Jesus takes our defilement to the third degree. For crucifixion is not (like the right slit to the throat) a *clean* death. The Issenheim altarpiece draws a vivid and realistic picture of how—in killing—crucifixion caricatures humanity, twists the body, wrecks psycho-spiritual balance, does its best not only to blemish but to degrade. With good reason, Christian tradition appropriates Isaiah's Servant Songs: "my servant" "was so marred, beyond human semblance, and his form beyond that of the sons of men" (Isa. 52:13–14); and "he had no form or comeliness that we should

7. Medieval Christian metaphysicians distinguished not only secondary substances or substance kinds (human being, donkey, etc.) from individual substance natures (this humanity versus that; this donkeyhood versus that); they also distinguished individual substance natures from substance individuals, *hypostases,* or supposits (e.g., Socrates versus Plato, Brownie versus Blackie, etc.). Following Boethius, many defined a technical sense of 'person' as 'the supposit of a rational nature'. While normal Aristotelian doctrine would say that a substance individual (such as Socrates) is necessarily identical with an individual substance nature (Socrates' humanity) and accordingly possesses only one such nature; Christians felt the doctrine of the Incarnation required them to say that one person (God the Son, or the Divine Word) necessarily supposits the Divine nature but contingently supposits an individual human nature. The Divine Word is said thereby to *assume* the individual human nature to which it is hypostatically united. This was a metaphysical interpretation of the Christological formula agreed upon at the Council of Chalcedon (451 C.E.). See Chapter 8 below.

look at him, and no beauty that we should desire him. He was despised and rejected by men; a man of sorrows and acquainted with grief " (Isa. 53:2–3).

Liturgically speaking, Golgotha's sacrifice was not pure but defiled by the agency (Jesus was crucified at *Gentile* hands), by the place (Gehenna, the garbage dump outside the city gates, a scene of rotting vegetables and corpses), and by the manner of offering (crucifixion). St. Paul applies Deuteronomy 21:23 to the crucifixion when he declares how "Christ . . . became curse for us—for it is written. 'Cursed be everyone who hangs on a tree' " (Gal. 3:33)—not only killed, but cut off from the people and from God. But if God in Christ crucified *becomes* curse, the power of curse is canceled: curse cannot exile us from God anymore. Likewise, if Christ is made sin for us (2 Cor. 5:21), sin loses its power to separate us from the love of God!

6.3. "Is That All There Is?"

Symbolically, this would have been enough for at-one-ment, but not for togetherness of a beatific kind. Phenomenologically, for humans, the metaphysical size gap and the condition of straddling often play themselves out in such a way that people feel abandoned by God, experience only Divine eclipse, find themselves angry and unwilling or unable to believe. Many are unable to get beyond their contamination and accusations, to surmount their despair of being able to find any meaning in their lives given what they've suffered and/or done. I shall argue later that Divine at-one-ment with human beings in such conditions would—if a fact—be able to ground beatific, intimate at-one-ment (see Chapters 6, 7, and 8 below). But for God's atoning work to be complete, won't we eventually all have to be clean?

7. Apocalyptic Reversal, New World Order

7.1. Contagious Holiness

The calculus of purity and defilement presupposes that cleanness is fragile and dirty is catching. Prima facie plausibility favors this axiom. After all, it takes hours to sparkle the kitchen, which is instantly messed by spilled milk or muddy shoes. Nevertheless, the oxymoron of Divine defilement challenges, the New Testament upsets, reverses the direction of contagion: it's holiness, not defilement, that's catching! The leper is cleansed by Jesus' touch and command (Mark 1:40–42; Matt. 8:1–4; Luke 5:12–16); hemorrhage halting power pours forth from Jesus when the bleeding woman touches His garment's hem (Mark 5:25–34; Matt. 9:18–22; Luke 8:43–48).

When Jesus touches the bier at Nain (Luke 7:11–17), or enters Lazarus's tomb (John 11:17, 38–44), creative power conquers destructive power from the margins, raises the dead to life. Table fellowship with tax collectors and sinners (Mark 2:13–17; Matt. 9:9–17; Luke 5:27–32; cf. Matt. 22:1–14; Luke 14:16–24; Luke 15:2) and foot washings by women who fell between the social cracks (Mark 14:3–9; Matt. 26:6–13; Luke 7:36–50) did not contaminate Jesus but ordered the people involved into the Reign of God. Equally explicit is Peter's post-Pentecost vision ("What God has cleansed, you must not call common!" [Acts 10:9–16]): space has been created, not only for nonkosher foods, but for Gentiles in God's all-inclusive Realm! In Roman Catholic theology the sacrifice of Christ becomes a spotless oblation, the blood of Jesus cleanses sinners (Rev. 1:5) and bleaches martyrs' robes (Rev. 7:14) because His holiness swallows up crucifixion defilement. Pregnant Mary is immaculate, not merely because bodily boundaries remain intact, but because she is God-bearer. Once again, as Douglas emphasizes, dirt is the correlative of order; shift the order, and the dirty becomes clean. The sparkling floor with a puddle of milk and mudprints could be the teenager's wreck of the housekeeper's handiwork; but it could also be some avant-garde artist's design. Crossbreeding produces hybrids; genetic mutations not only compromise existing kinds but evolve new ones.

7.2. Cashing the Metaphors

Stepping back, we see that it is not *heterogeneity* itself that is problematic. Biological organisms, by definition, have parts of different kinds. Beulah the cow would not be a perfect specimen of bovinity, if she did not have stomachs as well as ears, eyes as well as lungs. Organic bodies differ from junkyard heaps in that variety is organized into a functional unity: the living, healthy cow. What is troublesome is heterogeneity in the absence of adequate ordering power. Defilement arises because our human capacities are not up to the demands of individual and social integrity. We lack the imagination to invent organizational grids accurate to the structure of reality, partly because real world complexity exceeds our conceptual capacities. Also limited are human power and skill to organize the variety we recognize relative to the grids we conceive. Socially, we are inept—always oversimplifying, counting some in by cutting others out. Individually, we lack power to achieve harmonious integration of our several dimensions, of the personal with the animal, the psychological with the material. Unsubtle about boundaries, our identities tend to get diluted, our integrity compromised when we mix with others not of our own kind. If muliplex incompetence taints our attempts to grapple with creation, *a fortiori* our relations with God! If networking God into societies of our own devising shrinks God too small, moving into the region of the Divine threatens to blow our conceptual schemes, our self-images, to smithereens. If our attempts to see things from God's point of view inevitably fail, we also prove chronically unable to pull ourselves together to live within any Divinely established "courtesy" categories.

Thus, we really are defiled *relative to our human grids* and really are defiled *relative to the holiness code.* And Christ really is defiled relative to human grids and the holiness code as well. So long as we fix our gaze horizontally, uncleanness seems absolute. Nonconformity leaves gaps in social functions (Wild West towns were in trouble when the blacksmith couldn't or wouldn't make horseshoes). Refusal to enact canned social scripts also threatens to multiply variety beyond human organizational capacities. Where human governance loses its grip, chaos seems ever lurking in the wings.

7.3. Sanctifying At-one-ment

By contrast, the Christian God does not labor under any such handicaps. Jesus' ministry dramatizes how God's integrity is *inviolable,* no matter what company He keeps. Chalcedon renews the emphasis: in the Incarnation, when Divine and human natures are united in unity of person, the two natures are "preserved in their characteristics," remain altogether "unconfused."[8] Talk of contagious holiness is a way of saying that *when God smudges human boundaries, God in effect cancels the legitimacy of human grids in favor of Divinely established norms.* After all, it is stuff ordered God's way that God calls "good" (Gen. 1:3, 10, 12, 18, 21, 25, 31)! God, the "total cleanser," reclassifies our human nature, so that it is no longer a mulelike straddler but a distinctive kind of its own. According to Divine taxonomy, the basic reason why the human mind and body, the human psycho-biological organism has so much difficulty functioning is not that it is heterogeneous, but that—by itself—the duality isn't whole. A third factor was left out, whose job it is to midwife the integration: the Holy Spirit of God. St. Paul teaches how the Holy Spirit of God moves over the human psyche at its deepest core, at unconscious levels, even before we are conscious of anything (Rom. 8:23–27). Like the mother with the newborn infant, Holy Spirit's influence is omnipresent, nudging, sighing, murmuring, evoking our capacity to be

---

8. H. H. Denzinger, "Conc. Chalcedonense 451: Oecumenicum IV (contra Monophysitas)," in *Enchiridion Symbolorum et Definitionum* (Freiburg-in-Brisgaw: B. Herder, 1911), 65–67.

personal, spiritual beings. The Spirit protects us from the size gap's threat of metaphysical and psychological ruin, not with the "courtesy holiness" of covering rules, but with ever courteous pedagogy that graduates self-disclosures over a developmental cycle. Human beings are called to grow up into their full stature by getting to know the Spirit, more and more consciously, and intentionally cooperating with the Spirit, aiming to act always and only in partnership with the Spirit, until we can say with St. Paul, "I, not I, but Christ in me" (Gal. 2:19–20). Significantly but unsurprisingly, Christians celebrate this Divine (re?)definition of human nature into a trinity of body, mind, and Spirit, with all of its cleansing potential, in Holy Baptism, a ritual *rebirth* and *bath!*

Moreover, believers are baptized into community. The Realm of God can be all inclusive because Divine Goodness is infinite. No matter how badly humans fail to function, God can fill in, guarantee there will never be any shortage of essential needs. Likewise, because Divine organizational skills are incomparable, variety is not dangerous but delightful. For it will take an infinite array of finite creatures to compose optimal created collective portraits of God.

Again, Divine order is not static but dynamic and evolving. No matter what mess we make, God can clean it up, not only "the easy way" by eliminating it (the way the housekeeper mops up milk and mud, wrings out the mop, pours the water in the sewer), but by recontextualizing it into a more subtle plot (see Chapter 7 below). In the Realm of God, the worst that we can suffer, be, or do, is not finally ruinous because God invents a new organizational grid that endows us with amazing meaning (for example, gruesome degrading caricatures of human beings become instances of identification with God in Christ crucified).

8. Collecting the Insights

That the purity and defilement calculus is not fully congruent with morality is clear from the fact that their negative and positive value categories are not coextensional with one another. What one handles easily, the other finds difficult to compute. That is why in struggling with problems of evil, it is worth trying on different evaluative lenses to see how they affect the view. Where purity and defilement are concerned, three features loom large.

(1) Looking through the spectacles of purity and defilement, we see that the very feature that leads many to regard it as inferior to morality where

ordinary human interactions are concerned—namely, its insensitivity to agent knowledge, intention, or capacity to do or be otherwise—suits it for grasping the fundamental problem in Divine-human relations as well as for identifying the source and conceptualizing the trouble with horrors. For it concentrates our attention on mismatching kinds and misfitting individuals. The radical metaphysical disvaluation of human in relation to Divine being is the principal obstacle to beatific at-one-ment; whereas the metaphysical straddling of human nature dualistically conceived accounts not only for the difficulty of virtue, but for radical human vulnerability to horrors. Participation in horrors stains because it threatens to make us irremediably defective members of the personal kind.

(2) Through the lens of purity and defilement categories, we can see clearly how obstacles to Divine-human at-one-ment are irresolvable apart from superhuman powers to organize and to mend, to reclassify and to harmonize into an inclusive functional unity, both at the individual (psychological) and collective (sociological) levels. God alone has the creative imagination and persuasive power to organize utopian society. Human mind and body, personality and animality, have a chance at peaceful coexistence, even productive collaboration only when joined, guided and directed by the Holy Spirit of God. Concentration on moral categories drives Craig, Swinburne, and others to stress agent competence, indeed, to overestimate the capacity to subdue, with discipline, one's "lower" nature and to shoulder the responsibility to decide one's own destiny. By contrast, the lens of purity and defilement focuses the difficulties caused by metaphysical straddling, allows us to take seriously our experience of human agency confronted by horrors, and to replace a priori idealized models with a more empirical psychology.

(3) Focus on moral categories has lured philosophers into leveling Divine-human agency under the rubric "morally responsible person," into viewing God and rational creatures as "near enough" peers not only to be networked by mutual rights and obligations, but also to make urgent the concern that significant causal input from God might threaten creaturely autonomy.[9] By contrast, the purity and defilement calculus places the metaphysical size gap between Divine and created natures front and center. It combines with New Testament pictures of the sanctifying (holy-making) indwelling of Holy Spirit, to recall the point that where agencies are disproportionate, it is necessary to distinguish, among the effects of the "bigger" on the "smaller," those that are agency-obstructing or-manipulating from those

9. Cf. Swinburne, Stump, Craig; See also Chapter 3 above.

that are agency-enabling or-developing—in other words, those that supply necessary preconditions for the "smaller" agent to function at all.

Return to the mother's relation to her infant offspring. According to developmental psychologists, human infants can actualize their potentiality for personality only in a personal human environment. The infant organism is first enabled to organize the booming, buzzing confusion of its psychic field when it recognizes, (imprints on) the mother's face. Particular nurturing acts of the caretaker, holding, singing, babbling, caressing, feeding, changing, rocking, all contribute to a hospitable environment which engenders the trust and confidence the infant needs to take the risks involved in development. Its wholesome progress through the stages to maturity presuppose not only the nurturing *presence* of adults but also a plethora of particular acts. My suggestion is that what the mother does by way of training and controlling the child in its earliest stages is agency-developing and-enabling; it cannot count as manipulation until the child's agency is better formed.[10]

The metaphysical gap between God and creatures means that however mature adult human agency may seem in relation to other human beings, it never gets beyond (up to?) the infantile stage in relation to the Divine. Just as the mother's face and particular nurturing acts are enabling conditions of the infant's actually becoming a human person, so—Scripture and tradition suggest—the Holy Spirit of God is the personal environment that first pulls us into focus as spiritual beings capable of connecting with one another's spirits, even of romancing with God. Beyond that, the personal and nurturing presence of Holy Spirit is a necessary enabling condition for drawing us into vocational focus, thereby constituting our agency as disciples.

My contention is that once returned to the forefront, such metaphysical incommensurability combines with the mother-infant analogy to make room for particular Divine providence without jeopardizing the phenomena of created voluntary action. Just as developmental psychology understands the infant's emerging personality as an interactive product shaped by the characteristics and the many and varied responses of mother and child,

---

10. Julian of Norwich gives extensive development to the image of God, the Trinity, and/or Jesus as Mother to our infant or toddler, in her *Revelations of Divine Love,* trans. Clifton Wolters (London: Penguin Books, 1966). Nelson Pike analyzes this theme in his book *Mystic Union: An Essay in the Phenomenology of Mysticism* (Ithaca, N.Y.: Cornell University Press, 1992), 66–86. See also my "Julian of Norwich on the Tender Loving Care of Mother Jesus," in *Our Knowledge of God,* ed. K. J. Clark (Dordrecht: Kluwer Academic Publishers, 1992), 203–19.

so the formation of our identities as spiritual beings and disciples is a collaborative process involving give and take on both sides, but a process in
which the Holy Spirit functions as an agency-enabler and -developer rather
than an agency-obstructor or -manipulator.

Divine providence could once again be seen as both prospective—, for
example, as God creates each individual with a unique package of abilities
and gifts to equip them for a vocation in one or another of several areas—
and retrospective—as God reenvisions a range of possibilities for an individual in light of his/her past experience and choices, among other things
opens opportunities for participation in evils to be redeemed. Nor would
it follow from the fact that some humans die unconverted, without recognizing Divine presence, that the Divine Mother lets any out of Her nurturing arms. Rather, just as autistic children are unable to recognize the
parental love that surrounds them without anyone's being at fault, so, too,
some antemortem humans do not recognize God's nurturing embrace. And
just as some autistic children can be loved out of their shells by caretakers
who hold them for hour after hour, day after day, so also with horrors' most
devastated victims and most hardened perpetrators. Eventually, cognitive
and emotional scales will fall and everyone will recognize the omnipresent
tender loving care of God!

Symbolic Value: Honor and Shame

1. Values—Symbolic versus Concrete

In attempting a rational systematization of morality, nineteenth-century utilitarians reduced the good or bad *for* persons to pleasure and pain in much the same way as contemporary economic theory works with a for-the-sake-of-argument reduction to material goods and services. Further, the good or evil *of* persons was equated with a moral evaluation of their actions. Such oversimplified focus on concrete values has the prima facie appeal of tractability to calculation. Postpositivist value-theory skepticism also leads to emphasis on the *concrete*: most people agree that pleasure, physical and material well-being, is good for humans; *symbolic* values, possessed by actions, persons, or states of affairs by virtue of what they symbolize, are inextricably controversial. Most analytic philosophers debating the problem of evil over the last thirty years studied Bentham and Mill in history of ethics classes. While few of us consciously subscribe to their views, my hunch is that their concrete focus has exercised an unconscious effect—via our own desire for tractability—on the way we think about the problem of evil. In particular, they often lead to a for-the-sake-of-argument focus on the concrete evils of pain, lack of physical and material well-being (Pike's spoonful of bitter medicine, stomach ache, or painful operation; Rowe's slow death of the fawn in the forest fire), on the one hand, and the moral evaluation of actions and their consequences (Swinburne, Plantinga), on the other. Yet, arguably the worst evils and the best goods are symbolic. What makes evils horrendous is their power to *degrade* by being prima facie ruinous of personal meaning (see Chapter 2, section 6 above). Free fall approaches insist on Divine respect for the dignity of human nature even at the eternal expense of concrete well-being (see Chapter 3, section 6 above).

Historically, where Divine-human relations are concerned, symbolic value has been front and center for Biblical religion. Traditionally, both narrative plots and theological models have been shaped by the honor code, whose twin valuations wear their relevance to the problem of evil on their face. For the center of the honor/shame calculus is precisely the worth of persons, how much there is "to" them, whether or not they "have the stuff" to fill their roles. It is a matter of power, resourcefulness, and integrity. Social expressions of esteem are an important source of positive meaning in life. Conversely, denials challenge and erode our sense that life is worthwhile. This chapter attempts to retrieve the insights available through this interpretative lens.

2. The Honor Code and Its Social Frame

Before we can fully appreciate the relevance of honor and shame to the problem of evil, we will need a firmer grip on these notions themselves. Happily, help is at hand. Social anthropologists have found some contemporary small village cultures in Mediterranean society which still make honor and shame the central evaluative categories of their social organization. Fieldwork studies have combined with the examination of historical and literary documents from earlier times, to yield the following analysis of the categories of honor and shame and their social function.[1]

2.1. Honor and Shame

Once again, the category of honor centers, not on the evaluation of deeds, but on the sacred quality of persons.[2] Honor is double sided, including (i) the value of a person in his/her own eyes (his/her own *claim* to honor) and (ii) the value of a person as corroborated by society (the person's *reputation* and social right to pride or status).[3] Obviously, (ii) the social

1. The most important collection here is *Honour and Shame: The Values of Mediterranean Society*, ed. J. G. Peristiany (London: Weidenfeld and Nicolson, 1965). See also Bruce J. Malina (e.g., *The New Testament World: Insights from Cultural Anthropology* [Atlanta: John Knox Press, 1981], and John H. Elliott, "Patronage and Clientism in Early Christian Society," *Forum* 3, no. 4 (1987): 29–48.

2. Cf. Julian Pitt-Rivers, "Honour and Social Status," in *Honour and Shame,* ed. Peristiany, 19–77, esp. 47.

3. Pitt-Rivers, "Honour and Social Status," 21–22. Cf. Malina, *The New Testament World,* 25–50, esp. 26–28.

component of honor is relative both to social structures and ideals and to *public* perception of how well the individual measures up against them. Moreover, (i) the individual's claims to honor are from the beginning shaped (although not completely determined) by (ii) social estimates, for the simple reason that societies educate their members to fill relevant social roles and to evaluate themselves in terms of social norms. Thus, "the sentiment of honour inspires conduct which is honourable, the conduct receives recognition and establishes reputation, reputation is finally sanctified by the bestowal of honours. Honour *felt* becomes honour *claimed* becomes honour *paid*."[4] Through demonstrations of respect and the allowance of privilege, honor is *paid* to a person who *claims* it.

Two further, related distinctions are in order. We must make (iii) a distinction arising from an equivocation on 'value' or 'worth' between honor as virtue or excellence and honor of precedence, the latter being a function of de facto status and power to enforce compliance with it. These dimensions of honor break apart, most obviously, in the case of the tyrant or bully, or in the arrangements of unjust and oppressive societies generally.[5] (iv) The other distinction divides honor as to its origin, into *ascribed honor* and *acquired honor*, ascribed honor being a socially recognized claim to worth that comes to a person either through birth in a certain family or class or the like, or through delegation by a person who has the power to force acknowledgment of such claims (as when one is knighted by the queen), and *acquired honor* being a socially accepted status claim that is a function of the individual's performance in competitive social interactions.[6]

Sometimes a person's claim to status is so widely and thoroughly recognized that his/her honor is unimpeachable—whether because s/he has so much virtue or so much power to make people defer. In the latter case, might has a tendency to make right; in the former, attacks on the person's honor can only stain the offender, whereas the generous blind eye of the offended party magnifies (if possible) his/her own reputation.

Shame also is bivalent: (i) taken positively, it is sensitivity to communal norms and social reputation, both of which the shameless person ignores; (ii) taken negatively, it refers to the situation in which a person loses status or has his claim thereto publicly rejected (and so is put to shame, humiliated, or degraded). Where honor moves from the inside out (from a per-

---

4. Pitt-Rivers, "Honour and Social Status," 22.
5. Ibid., 23–24.
6. Malina, *The New Testament World,* 29–30.

son's claim to worth to public validation), negative shame moves from the outside in (from public rejection to individual recognition thereof).[7]

2.2. Transactions of Honor:

In principle, an affront places the honor of a person in jeopardy. In Mediterranean societies where the values of honor and shame predominate a code of honor prescribes what a person must do to maintain individual/collective honor in the face of such attacks. Since honor includes a component of social evaluation, publicity partly determines how much face stands to be lost or gained. Since what is at stake is relative personal worth, the honor-maintaining response to an affront is a function of the relative status of the parties involved.[8]

2.2.1. The Game of Challenge and Riposte. Public concessions of honor confer status and thereby privileged access to concrete goods. Because, at the small village level, the latter are in short supply, honor likewise becomes a limited good and so the object of competition. Among equals, an affront attempts to rob the affronted person of his/her honor; *satisfaction* is required if honor is to be maintained.[9] Honor is defended or lost according to the contestants' performance in the game of challenge and riposte, which has three stages.[10] First comes the *challenge*, or a claim to enter the social space of another, whether by word or deed. The challenge can be positive (as with a word of praise, a gift, a request for or promise of help) or negative (as with an insult, a physical affront, a threat accompanied or not by an attempt to carry it through). Next comes the *perception*, in which the individual (and onlookers) evaluate the action in terms of publicly accepted criteria, as to whether the action merely questions, attacks, or denies the individual's self-esteem. Then comes *the response*, which takes one of three forms: (a) *Positive rejection* disdains the challenger and his action, in effect humiliates him by denying him the status of equality prerequisite between players in the challenge-riposte game. If the original challenger is in fact an equal, he must avenge this insult to maintain his honor. On the other hand, if the person originally affronted was his superior, no further response is re-

7. Pitt-Rivers, "Honour and Social Status," 51–52. Cf. Malina, *The New Testament World*, 44–47.

8. Pitt-Rivers, "Honour and Social Status," 27, 31.

9. Malina, *The New Testament World*, 35–36.

10. Here I follow Malina, *The New Testament World*, 30–33. Cf. Pitt-Rivers, "Honour and Social Status," 25–26.

quired. (b) *Negative refusal* is simply no response, where the honor code requires one; it symbolizes cowardice or sloth in the person affronted and so dishonors him. (c) *Acceptance* of the challenge involves a corresponding action that constitutes a counterchallenge and potentially extends the game into a further round. The game of challenge-riposte is properly played only among equals. It is dishonorable to pick on someone who is not one's own size.[11] Honor does not require success, but only the attempt. The code makes each man the guardian of his own honor in contests with his equals, where it would be dishonorable to appeal to the courts, which exist to protect the weak against the strong.[12]

2.2.2. The Role of Intention. A person's honor is "committed" or "engaged" in a social interaction only through his sincere intentions. Failure to keep a promise is not dishonorable if he in effect "had his fingers crossed" when he made it. Not telling the truth to someone counts as lying only if that person is one to whom truth is owed (usually to kin but not to strangers). On the other hand, lack of steadfastness is dishonorable, because it symbolically desecrates what is—according to the honor code—sacred to a person—namely, his own true self. And to lie to someone on purpose is to attempt to humiliate him.[13] Unclarity as to intentions begets ambiguity in the game, and requires a person to judge whether the invasion of turf was, and will be deemed by others to be, "accidentally on purpose" or simply unintentional. Mistaking the latter for the former, exposes the respondent to the charge of touchiness; taking the former for the latter risks charges of laziness or cowardice.[14] The purpose of oaths is to remove the ambiguity as to a person's intentions, but oaths, too, are binding only if the oath-taker is sincere.[15]

2.2.3. Collective Honor. In societies organized by the honor code, a person's behavior reflects not only on his/her own honor, but also on that of the groups to which s/he belongs. Where natural groups such as family or nation are concerned (that is, collectivities of which one is a member willy-nilly), the honor of the group is symbolically invested in its head, who

11. See Pierre Bourdieu, "The Sentiment of Honour in Kabyle Society," in *Honor and Shame*, ed. Peristiany, 193–241, esp. 198, 199–200, 205–6.

12. Pitt-Rivers, "Honour and Social Status," 28, 29, 30; cf. Malina, *The New Testament World*, 35–36, 39.

13. Pitt-Rivers, "Honour and Social Status," 32, 33, 34.

14. Pitt-Rivers, "Honour and Social Status," 28; cf. Malina, *The New Testament World*, 37–38.

15. Pitt-Rivers, "Honour and Social Status," 34.

is charged with defending it and that of its members from external attack. Just as individual honor symbolizes the sacred worth of the person, so headship is a sacred role; the honor of its occupant, unimpeachable within the group.[16] Accordingly, the members owe the head obedience and respect of a kind that commits their individual honor unequivocally, so that, for example, disloyalty to and assaults on the king or the father (as in regicide or parricide) become irrevocable stains.[17] Participating as they do in the honor of the head, individual members have a stake in defending it (such as by rendering military service in time of war). But equally, the dishonorable behavior of one member (such as sexual impurity in women, unwillingness to respond to peer challenge among men) redounds onto the whole group. Further, the unavenged humiliation of members by a more powerful outsider, puts the head to shame by symbolizing his lack of power or will to maintain honor.[18]

Typically, where social institutions benefit the haves and cannot be counted upon to deliver a meaningful, social human existence for the havenots, institutional and legal arrangements become overlaid with patron-client relationships between social superiors and their inferiors. If the relation between monarch and subject is a patron-client relationship par excellence, other such arrangements are entered into voluntarily. Although extralegal, they are taken to be mutually binding and advertised as involving life-long solidarity. Patrons control access to first-order goods, such as land, jobs, goods, funds, citizenship, power, information, and so forth, and show favor to their clients (that is, they "play favorites" with their clients) by making such patronage available to them as needed. Clients return the favor by enhancing the prestige, reputation and honor of the patron in private and public life, offering daily early morning salutations, supporting him/her in political campaigns, supplying information when needed, refusing to testify against him/her in court, and constantly bearing public witness to their patron's benefactions. Such arrangements are quasi-familial and have the effect of subsuming institutional connections under an overarching network of kinship. One more role must be noted in this connection: namely, that of the broker, who manipulates his/her own second order good—a network of strategic contacts with those who control first-order goods—to put clients in touch with significant patrons, in exchange for services, information, good will, advertising, and honor. Social brokerage is a competitive business. Success requires the energetic broker to take initia-

16. Malina, *The New Testament World*, 42.
17. Pitt-Rivers, "Honour and Social Status," 36.
18. Malina, *The New Testament World*, 36, 39.

tives and risks in attracting customers, and to develop such wide-ranging and reliable links to those who control first-order goods that no other broker will be needed.[19]

3. Divine-Human Relations, Reconfigured

Once profiled, this model is easily recognizable in the conceptuality of the Bible and traditional theology.

3.1. Role Assignments

God is *the patron king*, personally self-sufficient and the ultimate proprietor of all resources (cf. Ps. 50: 7–13), the source of the being and well-being of everything else (cf. Gen. 1; Ps. 104). Beholden to none, the God of the Bible nevertheless takes the initiative to form patron-client relationships— calling Abraham, promising land and dynasty as numerous as the stars, summoning Moses, forming a people out of a motley crew of slaves, covenanting at Sinai with the giving and receiving of the Law, sending Jesus to announce Kingdom come, establishing a new covenant in His blood (Luke 22:20). God's chosen owe *the client's* duty—to magnify the patron's reputation by making Divine favors their boast, by rendering continual thanks and praise. Their side of the bargain includes exclusive loyalty, as well as general cooperation with Divine purpose, obedience to God's commands. Moreover, because Divine-human encounters can be intimidating—when God approaches, storm clouds gather, lightning flashes, the earth quakes, hills skip, mountains belch forth smoke and fire (Exod. 19; Ps. 114)—God regularly appoints mediators—Moses, Elijah, the prophets, Jesus—to *broker* Divine benefits and demands.

3.2. Problems of "Symbolic" Evil

According to the honor code, God has no *obligation* either to take on clients or to service them once acquired. Nevertheless, unless God's fingers are crossed, Divine covenants invest God's honor in the relationship, turn the behavior and condition of His clients into conventional signs of how much there is "to" God. Client disloyalty sends many slanderous messages: that Divine persons are too insubstantial to deserve respect; that God is too lazy about honor-maintenance to do anything about infidelity; that God is

---

19. Malina, "Patron and Client: The Analogy behind Synoptic Theology," *Forum* 4, no. 1 (1988): 2–32, esp. 3–5, 7–8, 10–12, 16; see also Elliott, "Patronage and Clientism in Early Christian Society," 39–48, esp. 42–43.

a bad judge of character, manifestly a fool to entrust His reputation to such clients. The poor condition of God's clients furnishes additional incentive for client unfaithfulness, broadcasts that God cannot be counted upon to deliver the goods, raises the questions whether He is unable or unwilling, whether God is a might-makes-right tyrant Who makes promises with no intention of keeping them, whether God has turned hostile, or whether He simply doesn't care. No matter which it is—patron or client—who appears to fall short of expectations, Divine honor is called into question.

3.2.1. Worthless Clients? The Bible bulges with examples of clients failing to hold up their side of the bargain, repeatedly proving they don't have what it takes to be loyal to God. Warnings of client incompetence were built right into the annual covenant renewal ritual as a presumption to be defeated by strengthened collective resolve (Josh. 24: 19–24). Yet, experience showed the twelve tribes weren't up to it. From the beginning, from the golden calf episode at Sinai, Israel tried to hedge its bets by worshipping other gods, whether in addition or instead. Over and over, God's chosen people show themselves unable either to trust or to keep His commandments (cf. Ps. 78, 106). In 4 Ezra, the seer, reeling after the second destruction of Jerusalem, accuses God of a "setup": surely the Creator knows how—in the human heart—the evil inclination is stronger than the good, thereby making perfect obedience impossible for a whole nation (4 Ezra 3:20–27). Prophets are commissioned to inveigh against rock-hearted and stiff-necked people who stop up their ears against the warnings. So, too, in the Christian New Testament, the Pharisees in general, Saul of Tarsus in particular, those most zealous to prepare the way for God's Messiah, drastically fail the test of discernment, mistaking the Holy Spirit's effects for the work of the devil. Jesus' journey towards Jerusalem culminating in His death puts the twelve to shame, while on the road, for failing to comprehend His passion predictions, while in Jerusalem, for betraying, denying, and/or fleeing the scene. Their behavior in Gethsemane, in the courtyard, and at Golgotha makes a mockery of their discipleship, dispels any illusions of integrity, shows there is not enough "to" them to persevere to the end.

3.2.2. Divine Patronage of Dubious Quality? Similarly, God's Bible-story clients fare badly more often than not. At the beginning of Exodus, God has not serviced His patron-client contract with Israel for four hundred years, with the result that Israel's children are slaves in Egypt under a pharaoh who did not know Joseph (Gen. 15: 13; Exod. 1:8). Later on, after a Davidic Golden Age of expansion and prosperity, Israel splits from Judah (1 Kings 12:1–20) only to be overrun by Assyria, some generations before Judah falls to Babylon (Jer. 24:1; 25:8–12), then to the Greeks, then—after brief self-rule under the Hasmoneans—to the Romans who eventually raze Jerusalem for the second time. Heavenly brokers are typically threatened with violent ends. Elijah is menaced by Jezebel and Ahab (1 Kings 17–19; 2 Kings 1:1–18). Jeremiah thrown into a cistern, sunk in mud up to his armpits (Jer. 38:6). Truthful speech against Herod's marriage cost John the Baptist his head (Matt. 14:1–12; Mark 6:14–29; Luke 9:7–9). Jesus dies a ritually cursed death, His enemies' mockery—"If you are the Son of God, come down from the cross" (Matt. 27:40); "He saved others; Himself He cannot save" (Matt. 27:42; Mark 15: 31)—echoed in His desertion by friends (Matt. 26:56; Mark 14:50). And Jesus predicts the same fate, daily cross-bearing, for His disciples. Such a track record makes reasonable, yea urgent, the questions, whether Divine patronage is a blessing or a curse, whether clients are not fools to "sign on."

Thus, both problems of symbolic evil are raised by the Bible itself!

4. Dimensions of Honor, Soteriologically Entrenched!

Traditionally, the honor code was an obvious model because of its prominence in ancient and medieval social evaluations. It also proved a fruitful model because of its power both to articulate and explore problems of symbolic evil. Its putative solutions do not take the form of logically possible *morally sufficient* reasons why God permits symbolic evils in the amounts and of the kinds and with the distribution such as we find in the actual world. Although the honor code does shed light on honorable patron motivations, it usually contents itself with some partial reasons why and supplements with explanations of how the Heavenly Patron might vindicate Divine and/or client honor despite the apparent ruin of God's reputation and in the face of client degradation and shame. Moreover and predictably, just as in modern times morality has spawned a variety of contrasting and contradictory responses to the problem(s) of evil, so the honor code was malleable, its implications charted from a variety of angles towards different and sometimes startling directions. From multitudes of examples, I here content myself with four.

4.1. Challenge and Riposte in the Exodus—Reputation Restored

Perhaps no more exquisite example of Biblical thinking steeped in the honor code can be found than Exodus 3–15, which narrates the central redemptive event of the Hebrew Bible as a story about how God "got glory over Pharaoh" (Exod. 14:4) through winning an extended game of challenge and riposte.

At the outset, God has "cornered the market" on the honor of virtue but lacks reputation: He is unknown to Pharaoh (Exod. 5:2) and even among Israel (Exod. 4:13–15). Conversely, so far as the story is concerned, Pharaoh is a stranger to virtue but enjoys full honor of precedence due to his de facto status and power. God initiates the challenge for the twin purposes of closing the gap between His worth and reputation (Exod. 8: 10–11; 9:14–17; 10: 1–2; 14:4) created by His four hundred year delay in avenging the insult of the enslavement of His people (Gen. 15:13–15) and to renew and cement the patron-client relationship between Him and Israel His "first born son" (Exod. 4:22–23; note the language of kinship here). Throughout, Pharaoh's resistance is robbed of its power to dishonor God in the eyes of the reader via the explanatory premiss that God has planned and controls the whole scenario from the beginning (Gen. 15:13–15): God is the one who hardens Pharaoh's heart (Exod. 4:21; 7:3–4, 13, 14, 22; 8:15, 19, 32; 9:7, 12, 34, 35; 10:27; 11:9–10) to give Himself more scope for multiplying signs and wonders (Exod. 7:3) and punitive responses (Exod. 7:4), the better to magnify His reputation (Exod. 9:14–17; 10:1–2).

When God calls Moses to be His second in the contest, He at first presents Himself as above the need for reputation by refusing to give Moses any proof of His status, "Say I AM WHO I AM sent you" (Exod. 3:13–14) but then relents by supplying a reference to Abraham, Isaac, and Jacob (Exod. 3:15) and by renewing His promise of patronage in the form of freedom, the land of milk and honey (Exod. 3:16–17), and Egyptian spoils (Exod. 3:21–22; cf. Gen. 15:14). Moreover, God gives Moses magical powers to certify him as broker of heavenly patronage (Exod. 4:1–9) and allows him a "second" in Aaron (Exod. 4: 10–17). Convinced by the magic, the people respond favorably to their first approach and believe (Exod. 4:28–31).

The First Round: God challenges Pharaoh by sending His seconds with a request for help in the form of a three-day leave of absence for the people to honor Him with sacrifice in the wilderness (Exod. 5:1, 3). At this stage, Moses and Aaron cannot help but appear greatly inferior to Pharaoh in status, insofar as they present themselves as heads of a slave people and representatives of an unknown God. Accordingly, Pharaoh punishes the impudence of their request by forcing the slaves to make bricks without the benefit of straw to hold them together (Exod. 5:5–21), causing not only Moses and Aaron but also God to lose face with the people, renewed promises of patronage notwithstanding (Exod. 6:1–9).

The Second Round: God instructs Moses to counterchallenge with a renewed request, promising to reverse the damage to their reputations (Exod. 7:1), reasserting His promise of national patronage (Exod. 7:1–5), and instructing them on the use of the magical powers (Exod. 7:8). Moses delivers the request to Pharaoh again (Exod. 7:6), and Pharaoh insults them by challenging their status as brokers with a demand for a miracle (Exod. 7:9). Through Aaron Moses wins the trial by ordeal in magic (Exod. 7:10–12), but Pharaoh insists on his superior status by disdaining their request (Exod. 7:13).

The Third Round: God counters with a reassertion of His superior status, punishing Pharaoh's impudence by turning the Nile into blood via the offices of Moses and Aaron (Exod. 7:14–21). Pharaoh's magicians interpret this as a challenge to their status as brokers of heavenly patronage and match the feat (Exod. 7:22). Since the ordeal by magic ends in a draw, Pharaoh finds no reason to think Moses and Aaron are peers by reason of association with superior heavenly powers and disdains the request again (Exod. 7:22–23). Nevertheless, the reputation of God and Moses and Aaron is beginning to rise in the eyes of the Egyptian people (Exod. 7:24).

The Fourth Round: This time God has Moses couple the request with the threat of a plague of frogs, a humiliation the deeper for its penetration into Pharaoh's private space, with frogs in his house and bed (Exod. 8:2–4). Aaron's production of the promised punitive plague (Exod. 8:5–6) at the same time constitutes a challenge to the stature of Pharaoh's magicians as brokers of heavenly powers and places them in a double bind: failure to respond discredits them further, but producing more frogs (Exod. 8:7) as they do serves only to worsen the plight of the Egyptian people and undermine their own and Pharaoh's reputation. At this point, Pharaoh shifts his strategy from disdain and insult to tricky bargaining, a move which—insofar as it is bargaining—already symbolizes that Pharaoh's estimate of his opposition has risen. On the other hand, insofar as Pharaoh would take himself to owe nothing to foreign slaves or their titular heads, trickery itself would not seem dishonorable. Accordingly, he makes a concession conditioned on a request for help (in frog removal), thereby placing Moses and Aaron in a double bind: noncompliance could undermine their reputation for heavenly brokerage; but granting the request risks exposing themselves to the ridicule of "falling for a trick." God's strategy—of stealing Pharaoh's reputation through the multiplication of signs and wonders—requires Moses and Aaron to take the first alternative, not by removing but by killing the frogs, so that the land was filled with stinking corpses (Exod. 8: 12–14), whereupon Pharaoh withdraws his concession (Exod. 8:15).

Fifth Round: God counters punitively by producing a plague of gnats through Moses and Aaron (Exod. 8:16–17). Once again, Pharaoh's magicians interpret this as a challenge to their heavenly brokerage, but this time they fail (Exod. 8:18) and concede the genuine brokerage to Moses and Aaron (Exod. 8:19). Despite this defeat of his seconds, Pharaoh reasserts his superior status by disdaining the request (Exod. 8:19).

Sixth Round: God counters through Moses and Aaron by threatening a punitive plague of flies that will penetrate into the private spaces of only Egyptians if Pharaoh doesn't accede to the request (Exod. 8:20–23). When the plague follows (Exod. 8:24), Pharaoh again descends to tricky bargaining, making first one partial conditional concession (Israel can sacrifice without leaving; Exodus 8:25), which Moses rejects (Exod. 8:26–27), and then another (they can go but not far away; Exodus 8:28), which Moses agrees to. But Moses blunts the dishonor of Pharaoh's trickery by promising another punitive response (Exod. 8:29–31). Once again, Pharaoh refuses the request.

Seventh Round: God responds with a punitive plague on only Egyptian livestock (Exod. 9:1–6), which Pharaoh verifies but disdains (Exod. 9:7).

Eighth Round: God responds again with a physical affront on the Egyptians by ordering Moses and Aaron to produce a punitive plague of boils (Exod. 9:8–10). Already put to shame in the fifth round, Pharaoh's magicians are decisively humiliated when the boils so disable them that they cannot even try to match the feat (Exod. 9:11). Nevertheless, Pharaoh reasserts his superior position by disdaining the request (Exod. 9:12).

Ninth Round: God sends Moses before Pharaoh with His counterclaim of superior status and his vow to get a worldwide reputation (Exod. 9:13–17) and warns He will send a punitive plague of hail on only Egyptians the next day (Exod. 9:18–19, 22–26). God's reputation among the Egyptians has spread beyond the magicians to half of Pharaoh's servants who heed the warning (Exod. 9:20). Once again, Pharaoh resorts to tricky bargaining, this time even pretending to repent (Exod. 9:27–28). Moses announces his awareness of Pharaoh's trickery but says he will get God to end the plague to prove that the earth belongs to the Lord (Exod. 9:29–30, 33). The rain and hail stops. Pharaoh refuses the request (Exod. 9:34–35).

Tenth Round: Through Moses and Aaron, God threatens a punitive plague of locusts that will invade Egyptian private space (Exod. 10:3–7). This time God's reputation with Pharaoh's servants is so great that they urge concession (Exod. 10:7), but Pharaoh reverts to the strategy of tricky bargaining. Once again he offers a partial conditional concession, but this time counters Moses' accusation of trickery with his own charge of "evil purpose"

(Exod. 10:10). Moses insists that when the Israelites go, all will go, and the promised plague ensues (Exod. 10:12–15). Pharaoh responds again with trickery, this time in the form of an insincere confession of sin and conditional concession (Exod. 10:16). Moses agrees and removes the locusts (Exod. 10: 18–19), whereupon Pharaoh reneges (Exod. 10:20).

Eleventh Round: God responds through Moses with a punitive plague of thick darkness that covers only the Egyptians (Exod. 10:21–23). Pharaoh repeats the strategy of tricky bargaining, offering a partial conditional concession (you and your children can leave but not your flocks; Exod. 10;24), which Moses refuses (Exod. 10:25–26). Pharaoh then reasserts his superior position by disdaining the request and issuing a counterthreat to kill Moses if he comes back (Exod. 10:28–29).

Twelfth Round: As God predicted, the signs and wonders occasioned by Pharaoh's intransigency up to this point have won God, His seconds, and Israel a significant reputation among the Egyptian people (Exod. 11:3; 12:35–36). Now God through Moses tells the people to reap their spoils from the Egyptians by "asking" them for their gold and jewelry (Exod. 11: 2). Moreover, through Moses God counters Pharaoh's threat to kill Moses, the titular head of God's first-born, with the announcement that He will kill the first-born of all Egyptian people and cattle (Exod. 11:4–8). When this plague is produced (Exod. 12:29–30), Pharaoh concedes and requests a blessing (Exod. 12:31–32); in addition, the Egyptian people urge the Israelites to leave (Exod. 12:33).

Thirteenth Round: When God leads His people out, He does not take them to Canaan by the most direct route for two reasons. First, the patron-client relationship is as yet too unstable to withstand the test of the wars that would have to accompany entry of already occupied territories (Exod. 13:17–18). Second, having decisively humiliated Pharaoh in the twelfth round, God has the people double back, in order to trick Pharaoh into occasioning his own destruction (Exod. 14:1–4). Once Israel has gone, Pharaoh and his servants regret the loss of their slave labor (Exod. 14:5) and decide on a chase (Exod. 14:6–10). Despite all that has happened, Pharaoh and his army still enjoy considerable reputation among the people of Israel, who repent of leaving when they see the Egyptians coming after them (Exod. 14:10–12). Having again lost face with the people, Moses nevertheless promises that God will provide, as He does with the Reed Sea crossing (Exod. 14:15–22) in which Pharaoh and his soldiers—so far from blessed— are drowned in the Reed Sea (Exod. 14:23–29). This dramatic servicing of the patron-client relationship through Moses did wonders for the reputation of both God and His broker: for "when Israel saw the great work which the Lord did against the Egyptians, the people feared the Lord; and they believed in the Lord and in his servant Moses" (Exod. 14:31).

Thus, the Exodus story shows how the gap between God's honor of virtue and reputation turns challenge-and-riposte (strictly and properly a transaction between peers) into an apt vehicle of Divine trickery, a tool of decisive mockery. The disguise of ignominy casts Divine challenge as outrageous chutzpah, lures Pharaoh into false confidence, sets the stage for God to "strut His stuff," finally expose how Pharaoh and his chariots—so far from peers—are as disposable as gnats in the hands of Divine power.

4.2. Clientship—Earthly Costs, Heavenly Rewards!

If the Exodus story spotlights the moment at which Divine rescue finally comes through, much of the New Testament gives considerable attention to the plight of clients and brokers *in medias res*. Honor code in mind, it sees Christians as caught in the middle of a power struggle between competing social systems, each of which claims definitive authority to evaluate personal worth. The world—whether pagan Roman society or the non-Christian Jewish religious establishment—has its criteria which are often incompatible with the demands of the Kingdom of God as proclaimed by Jesus Christ. Both Gospels and Epistles record (predict) how the "powers that be" will "put down" loyalty to Christ with shame and dishonor, persecution and death. If Christ dies a ritually cursed death that sets Him outside the people of God (Gal. 3:13; cf. Deut. 21: 23), disciples must take up their crosses daily (Matt. 16: 24–28; Mark 8:34–39; Luke 9:23–27; 15:27), brokers become the offscourings of the world (1 Cor. 4:13) to be faithful to their calling.

The argument for persevering at such cost reminds Christians that clients participate in the dignity of their head, while God is a patron of unsurpassable worth. Especially in view of God's policy of choosing those of low estate, there is no way they can acquire more honor than through loyalty to Him. At the same time, clients in principle delegate their own honor-maintenance to the patron and, so, must be willing to swallow insults should this prove to serve the patron's overall aims. Christians are thus to have a policy of nonretaliation—to turn the other cheek, walk the second mile (Matt. 5:38–41), love enemies and bless persecutors (Matt. 5:43–48). But the present honor of serving such a patron, and their public vindication on Judgment Day, when God will acknowledge them before all creation, should be consolation enough to see them through (Matt. 10:32–33; 16:27; Mark 8:38; Luke 9:26).

4.3. Insulting Clients

If Exodus 3–15 deals with affronts from enemies in whose well-being Divine honor is not invested, St. Anselm's *Cur Deus Homo* sees the drama of salvation in terms of God's strategy for vindicating Divine honor assaulted by *rebellious* clients. Anselm begins with Divine dignity, understands God as a being, one more worthy of honor than which cannot be conceived. God acquires clients by creating, by building into other natures an end or purpose, a that-for-which-they-were-made. Because all creatures owe their being and well-being to God as Creator, they owe it to God to be that for which they were made. God honors all creatures by making them somehow Godlike, generates a hierarchy on the basis of how much they resemble the Supreme Nature, indeed wants some creatures to be as Godlike as it would be possible for any creature to be. To this end, God endows rational creatures not only with reason to discern relative goodness and will to choose accordingly, but creates them with a motivational structure that allows them to be self-determining with respect to whether they uphold justice or desert justice in favor of their own apparent advantage. Moreover, God destines rational creatures for a happy immortality in the heavenly city, an eternity of intimate enjoyment of God.[20] God thereby awards rational creatures standing to honor and to insult, to choose for themselves which they will do.

Anselm equates sin with insult.[21] When rational creatures refuse to subordinate all of their thoughts, desires, and choices to God, they send the lying message that God is not, after all, so worthy of honor as to make the least disobedience maximally indecent. Since any insult to God is worse than countless worlds,[22] Anselm is confident, no sin is the kind of thing God could just "let pass."[23] God must contradict the lie by punishing the sinner unless satisfaction is made.[24] That is why Adam's race is disgraced by suffering the penalty of original sin, not only the obligation to make satisfaction

---

20. Citations of Anselm will be to the critical edition in six volumes of his *Opera Omnia*, ed. F. S. Schmitt (Edinburgh: Thomas Nelson & Sons, 1938–61). Citations will be to volume number, page, and line, as noted below. Anselm, *Cur Deus Homo*, bk. 2, chap. 1 (Schmitt 2:97.4–5, 9–14 [vol. 2, p. 97, lines 4–5, 9–14]; cf. *Monologion*, chap. 68 (Schmitt 1:78.21–79.9); *De casu diaboli*, chap. 14 (Schmitt 1:258.21–26); *De concordia* pt. 3, sec. 5 (Schmitt 2:269.21–33, 270.7–9); pt. 3, secs. 12–13 (Schmitt 2:284.9–286.8).

21. *Cur Deus Homo*, bk. 1, chaps. 11–14 (Schmitt 2:68.1–72.23).

22. *Cur Deus Homo*, bk. 1, chap. 2 (Schmitt 2:88.13–89.32); cf. *Cur Deus Homo*, bk. 2, chaps. 6–7 (Schmitt 2:101.1–102.22).

23. *Cur Deus Homo*, bk. 1, chap. 12 (Schmitt 2:69.11–18).

24. *Cur Deus Homo*, bk. 2, chaps. 14–15 (Schmitt 2:72.3–74.7); cf. *De casu diaboli*, chap. 17 (Schmitt 1:262.9–19).

but also damage to human nature which makes it impossible either to be happy or to be just.[25]

Yet, Anselm recognizes, matters are not so simple. For Divine honor cannot be vindicated if clients are allowed to thwart God's plan, and God's plan involves including some of Adam's race in heaven. It follows that to defend Divine honor, God must restore the dignity of Adam's race by enabling it to make satisfaction and by rehabilitating it for heaven. Since God alone can do or be anything immeasurably worthy, the only feasible way for commensurate satisfaction to be made, is for God to become a member of Adam's race, to die an unjust death. Because the God-man is Divine, He will thereby deserve immeasurable compensation, and because the God-man is a descendent of Adam, this can be credited to Adam's race as satisfaction for sin. So, too, God must remove the shame of damaged agency from other descendents of Adam, supply grace to enable them to render what they owe, by being what God created them to be.[26]

Thus, the aims of Anselm's God do not allow Him to remain aloof and merely punitive; given Adam's fall, God must enter creation by uniting a Divine person to human nature in hypostatic union (take a human nature from Adam's race to be its own),[27] in order that the dignity of human nature may be restored. Nevertheless, Anselm's God makes Himself no more vulnerable than necessary for satisfaction to be had. Christ's identification with us is metaphysical (insofar as He assumes a human nature) and biological (as a member of Adam's race), for the quasi-legal purpose of making satisfaction without the services of a middleman.[28] To achieve this end, His human nature has to be able to die if He chooses to. But Christ's human nature is not like ours with respect to ignorance[29] or unhappiness,[30] since—as Anselm sees it—these degrading conditions would not serve any purpose in vindicating Divine honor or restoring Adam's race!

4.4. Eager Incompetence, Client Shame

Julian of Norwich's parable of the lord and the servant sets the problem of sinful and suffering clients in a different light:

---

25. *De conceptu virginali et de originali peccato,* chap. 2 (Schmitt 2:141.12–15, 23–24); chap. 8 (Schmitt 2:150.1–4); chap. 29 (Schmitt 2:127.7–8).

26. *Cur Deus Homo,* bk. 2, chap. 11 (Schmitt 2:109.4–112.4); bk. 2, chap. 14 (Schmitt 2:113.21–115.4); bk. 2, chap. 16 (Schmitt 2:118.13–119.10).

27. *Cur Deus Homo,* bk. 2, chap. 10 (Schmitt 2:107.27–108.12).

28. *Cur Deus Homo,* bk. 1, chap. 5 (Schmitt 2:52.14–24).

29. *Cur Deus Homo,* bk. 2, chap. 13 (Schmitt 2:112.26–27).

30. *Cur Deus Homo,* bk. 2, chap. 17 (Schmitt 2:112.10–12).

I saw physically before me two people, a lord and his servant. And God showed me its spiritual meaning. The lord is sitting down quietly, relaxed and peaceful: the servant is standing by his lord, humble and ready to do his bidding. And then I saw the lord look at his servant with rare love and tenderness, and quietly send him to a certain place to fulfil his purpose. Not only does that servant go, but he starts off at once running with all speed, in his love to do what his master wanted. And without warning he falls headlong into a deep ditch, and injures himself very badly. And though he groans and moans and cries and struggles he is quite unable to get up or help himself in any way. To crown all, he could get no relief of any sort: he could not even turn his head to look at the lord who loved him, and who was so close to him. The sight of him would have been of real comfort, but he was temporarily so weak and bemused that he gave vent to his feelings as he suffered his pains.[31]

The fall is sin and is incurred in the course of trying to obey God's will. Thus, it is not a function of rebellion, which would make the sinner guilty, but of human *incompetence* to subordinate its lower sensory nature to its higher spiritual nature, the result of an incapacity—a "blindness,"[32] "weakness,"[33] and "ineffectiveness"[34]—that threatens autonomy and produces shame. Julian recognizes sin to be the origin of pain and suffering,[35] indeed the worst scourge a soul can suffer.[36] She even admits that some sins are so bad it is difficult to see how any good can come from them.[37]

Nevertheless, Julian insists, God's choice of such clients was witting (Our Creator knows how little there is to us) and deliberate (God purposes at-one-ment with us in mutual joy and delight as a dramatic manifestation of Divine love). God has elected us as His "dear lovely children"; when we sin, He considers the source and is not angry,[38] does not blame[39] but excuses.[40] For Julian saw no anger in God,[41] reckons anger to be opposed to peace,[42] incompatible with "the integrity of his love," "contrary to the nature of his

31. Julian of Norwich, *Revelations of Divine Love,* trans. Clifton Wolters (London: Penguin Books, 1966), chap. 11, p. 81.

32. *Revelations of Divine Love,* chap. 11, pp. 80–81; chap. 64, p. 178; chap. 66, pp. 181–82; chap. 72, p. 190.

33. *Revelations of Divine Love,* chap. 51, p. 144; chap. 64, p. 178; chap. 66, pp. 181–82.

34. *Revelations of Divine Love,* chap. 51, p. 144; chap. 62, p. 174.

35. *Revelations of Divine Love,* chap. 51, p. 141.

36. *Revelations of Divine Love,* chap. 39, p. 120; chap. 40, p. 122; chap. 63, p. 175; chap. 77, p. 199.

37. *Revelations of Divine Love,* chap. 32, p. 109.

38. *Revelations of Divine Love,* chap. 49, p. 137.

39. *Revelations of Divine Love,* chap. 27, p. 104; chap. 39, p. 121; chap. 45, p. 131.

40. *Revelations of Divine Love,* chap. 28, p. 105; chap. 52, p. 154.

41. *Revelations of Divine Love,* chap. 45, p. 131; chap. 46, p. 133; chap. 49, pp. 137–38.

42. *Revelations of Divine Love,* chap. 48, p. 136.

power, wisdom, and goodness."[43] God's resourcefulness is exhibited in the Divine capacity to overcome the metaphysical size gap, the degradation of sin and pain; despite all, to do a great deed on the Last Day that will make everything all right.

If the nature of this deed remains partly mysterious, Julian's revelations point us in a striking direction: ultimately, the problems of sin and suffering will not be solved by Divine moratorium on debt removing the burden of *guilt*, but by Divine courtesy canceling *shame*. Technically, "courtesy" is an elaborate etiquette governing royal courts and conventionally defining behaviors as symbolic of worth and valor. As in the parable of the lord and the servant, Julian retains the heraldic imagery, but construes it kenotically, reversing lordly and servant roles. Julian knows of no greater honor than this: that Our Lord God is a great king who treats us, his servants, with genuine and spontaneous, intimate and loving friendship.[44] He is not at all condescending,[45] but "utterly kind and unassuming."[46] Our Lord does not disdain to serve us[47] by becoming one of us. For Julian, "there can be no greater joy . . . than that he, the most supreme, mighty, noble, and worthy of all, should also be the most lowly, humble, friendly, and considerate."[48] The passion of Christ is a deed of knightly valor which Lord Jesus gladly undertook to honor His Lady, the soul, in hopes that she will be pleased with His feat. Thus, in her vision, Julian reports:

> our good Lord Jesus Christ said, "Are you well satisfied with my suffering for you?" "Yes, thank you, good Lord," I replied. "Yes, good Lord, bless you." And the kind Lord Jesus said, "If you are satisfied, I am satisfied too. It gives me great happiness and joy and, indeed, eternal delight ever to have suffered for you. If I could possibly have suffered more, I would have done so."[49]

Meditating on its magnitude, Julian estimates that "the union in him of Godhead with manhood strengthened the latter to suffer for love's sake more than the whole of mankind could suffer," and she uses His courtly desert to measure the extent of His voluntary humiliation.[50] As compared with other feats possible for Him (such as the creation of countless worlds),

43. *Revelations of Divine Love,* chap. 46, p. 133.
44. *Revelations of Divine Love,* chap. 5, p. 67; chap. 7, p. 72.
45. *Revelations of Divine Love,* chap. 7, p. 72.
46. *Revelations of Divine Love,* chap. 10, p. 79.
47. *Revelations of Divine Love,* chap. 6, p. 70.
48. *Revelations of Divine Love,* chap. 7, pp. 72–73.
49. *Revelations of Divine Love,* chap. 22, p. 96.
50. *Revelations of Divine Love,* chap. 20, p. 94.

Julian estimates His "willingness to die times without number" and yet "count it as nothing for love of us," "the greatest gesture our Lord God could make to the soul of man." She regards Christ's passion "a noble and most worthy deed worked out in time" to reveal eternal love.[51] Christ, our rescuing knight in shining armor, presents elect souls to the Father in worship, and his Father most gratefully receives us, his present, and in his courtesy gives us back to his Son, Jesus Christ."[52] Human souls thereby redeemed are the Son's "happiness"—a fact which brings joy to the Father and delight to the Holy Spirit.[53]

In this passing life, God expresses His royal friendship for us, by using great courtesy in correcting us:"he holds on to us so tenderly when we are in sin" and exposes our "foul" condition "by the gentle light of mercy and grace," lest we despair Our repentance is met with a "friendly welcome" as to loved ones released from prison.[54] Life in heaven will not begin with court flattery and thanks from the servants to the lord, but with the honor of divine gratitude to us:"Thank you for all your suffering, the suffering of your youth."[55] Moreover, since the disharmony of lower and higher natures was the worst punishment and hell an elect soul could endure, God will compensate tortured souls for their sins. God will regard the healed wounds of such souls as "honorable scars," and their sins will receive a "great, glorious, and honourable" reward. "So shall shame be turned to greater honour and joy."[56]

5. Harvesting the Insights

In my judgment, the honor code, with its calculus of honor and shame, is better equipped than morality to conceptualize the problems posed by horrendous evil. (1) *It is ideally suited to plumb the depths of what's wrong with horrors: namely their power to degrade by symbolizing that one is subhuman or worthless.* As noted before (in Chapter 2, section 6 above), their ruinous power is no ready function of moral rights and wrongs. Some horrors have natural causes. For pain and the lack of physical and material well-being have symbolic negative value over and above their concrete negative aspect, which can be bad enough. Most obviously, pain is a natural sign of death,

51. *Revelations of Divine Love,* chap. 22, pp. 96–97.
52. *Revelations of Divine Love,* chap. 55, p. 158.
53. *Revelations of Divine Love,* chap. 22, p. 97; chap. 23, pp. 98–99; chap. 55, p. 158.
54. *Revelations of Divine Love,* chap. 40, p. 121.
55. *Revelations of Divine Love,* chap. 14, p. 85.
56. *Revelations of Divine Love,* chap. 14, p. 85; chap. 39, pp. 120–21.

which it so often precedes and accompanies, and anxiety over death lies at
the root of many human ills. Beyond that, pain, disease, and bodily defi-
ciency degrade, by swallowing up personality in biology, by threatening to
reduce us to merely animal or vegetative states. Loss of arm or leg, eye or
breast shames us, by making us defective members of our kind. The horror
of existing as less than a person explains why some people regard Alzheimer's
disease or prolonged use of life-support systems a fate worse than death.
Continued pain over a long period of time can give rise to what Simone
Weil calls "affliction"—in which there is self-loathing proportional to one's
innocence in suffering. Pain and physical disorders are natural signs of such
degradation, and this is arguably their worst aspect. The morally innocent
participate in horrors both as victims and as perpetrators, while moral culpability cannot plumb the depths of what is wrong with causing horrors.
By contrast, the honor code focuses precisely on personal worth and its
recognition.

Moreover, (2) when used to model Divine-human relations, *the honor
code—better than modern morality—appreciates the limits and source of human dignity, given human nature's radical vulnerability to horrors* (see Chapter 3, section
4 above). Participation in horrors regularly (though not always) stalemates
human meaning-making capacities, often allows us to wreck our own and
other's psyches beyond the power of nature and human science to repair.
For many participants in horrors (like Aristotle's badly brought up individuals), antemortem virtue is no longer a option. The honor code, theologically applied, can concede humans some measure of natural dignity while
squarely confronting its fragility. Clients are needy by definition; their principal and most reliable source of dignity comes from their participation in
the patron's honor, from the viewpoint of Biblical religion, their share in
the glory of God. To be sure, the honor code allows the patron to make
"moral" performance or virtue a condition of their continued relationship.
But it does not require the patron to do so; it even makes the patron's ability to succeed with worthless clients one way to advertise resourcefulness.

(3) The honor code more accurately locates how human horror reflects
on God. According to Mackie's formulation, what evil calls into question is
God's existence. For many, the route to the incompatibility of God and evils
runs through unfulfilled Divine moral obligations. Yet, medieval philosophical theologians who believed they possessed sound (even a priori) arguments for God's existence and metaphysical perfection, and even thinkers
who so appreciated the ontological size gap as to deny any Divine obligations to creatures, continued to worry about the problem of sinful and suffering clients. The honor code explains how—obligations aside—the honor

of the wealthy (potential) patron is willy-nilly invested in the condition and behavior of the clients. When clients fare badly or rebel, the patron's *reputation* is jeopardized. The patron's apparent inaction requires explanation.

On the positive side, the symbolic values of honor and shame are helpful for theodicy, precisely because they are not a simple function of such concrete values as pleasure and pain, material and physical well- or ill-being. (4) *Honor is the currency of the powerless; it is what clients short on material goods can offer to patrons.* This means that even those who are utterly bereft of concrete valuables, may still have the dignity that comes with the power to benefit others, with maintaining and expressing loyalties to other persons and "higher things." Moreover, insofar as patron-client solidarity allows the latter to participate in the honor of the former, the power to praise and thank a Heavenly Patron is at the same time the power to give oneself a share in the honor of the Infinite and Eternal One, Blessed be He!

(5) Myopic focus on concrete values tempts both victim and onlooker to believe that there is no way for God to be good to a person while the pain, suffering, and material deprivation remain. *But honor is a good that can be conferred on people even while concrete benefits are still lacking.* Thus, the sense of Divine good-pleasure has empowered many a religious martyr to face physical suffering, hardships, and social humiliation even joyfully. The fact of Divine favor, of God's honoring the suffering and humiliated with His presence or by identifying with them—whether sympathetically (by suffering His own pain) or mystically (by literally sharing theirs)—even if unrecognized at the time of material deprivation and/or horrendous suffering, will appear retrospectively to have been a great benefit that adds depth of meaning even to the worst moments of one's life.

(6) Conversely, *honor is a good that can still be exchanged even when concrete needs have been fully supplied.* What else could lovers give each other in utopia, what can the Blessed Trinity offer one another, if not honor, mutual expressions of appreciation, praise, and thanksgiving for who the other is?

(7) The honor code by itself underdetermines a variety of issues in theodicy. In particular, it does not require the heavenly patron to invest His honor in being *good to* all created persons—that is, in seeing to it that each gets a life that is a great good to him/her on the whole, one in which any participation in horrors is not merely balanced off but defeated. It allows scenario's in which God invests Divine honor in some places rather than others (in Israel for example, rather than Egypt, Assyria, or Babylon), as well

as for conditional investments (such as the Sinai covenant with blessings for keeping God's law and curses for breaking it).

Nevertheless, *the honor code allows even universalists to accommodate the Biblical threat that Judgment Day will put us to shame*. For whatever else it means, Judgment symbolizes God's making plain and public the truth about Who God is, who we are, and the evaluative truth about what we have been and done. But God is a being a more excellent than which cannot be conceived, indeed a more excellent one than can be adequately conceived, metaphysically a being whose honor of virtue is necessary and unsurpassable; whereas we are almost nothing. How could any created person not hide his/her face when confronted with the fact that s/he is not even the kind of thing that could respond to God appropriately (any more than a ladybug is capable of an appropriate response to human beings)? No considerations of ignorance or weakness, no appeal to good intentions—all of which exculpate where the moral responsibility of action-oriented ethics is concerned—will do anything to lessen that shame. Added to this ontological shame will be the humiliation of not having done all we could within the conventional framework of what the client owes the patron, of not having rendered whole-hearted service or relentless praise. Then there will be the shame that arises from a clear perception of God's policies: for the average person, at not having trusted the One who is completely trustworthy; for the wicked, of having hated Unsurpassable Love.

Yet, equally, *the honor code allows universalists to explain how in the Judgment, we will recognize how ascriptive honor is the cure*. For God will convince us that His attitude towards us is not, never has been, and never will be a function of our metaphysical and moral limits. God will be seen to have honored the patriarchs by making them His friends, Israel through election and the giving of the Law, making them a nation by His going out and coming in with them, through all of their trials. According to the Christian point of view, the Maker of all things has honored the human race by becoming a member of it, honored all who suffer horrendous evils by identifying with them through His passion and death. Still more amazing, God will be seen to have honored even the perpetrators of horrors by identifying with their condition, becoming ritually cursed through His death on a tree, taking His stand with the cursed to cancel the power of curse forever! For Christians, the cross is an outward and visible sign that through such identification, God has nullified the power of horrendous evils to degrade. Catholic Christians affirm that throughout this mortal life, God honors those who receive holy communion by becoming really present under forms of bread

and wine. In the life to come, God will continue to honor us with the intimacy of His loving presence, and according to Julian of Norwich, with
His gratitude for our earthly service in weathering the trials of human life,
with public honors for all our wounds and battle scars. Each of us secure in
the sense of his/her enormous worth to God, we will spend eternity in acts
of mutual appreciation. Biblical religion teaches that honor and glory, praise
and adoration will be the currency of heaven.

[7]

Taste and See . . .

1. Segregating the Values

In Anglo-American analytic philosophical circles, there is widespread (if often implicit) agreement that moral values are as different in kind from those treated by aesthetics as from the ones codified in rules of etiquette! On this picture, no matter what aesthetic considerations may be advanced, they can always be trumped by appeals to human happiness, welfare, and equality.

This influential compartmentalization of moral and aesthetic has left its mark on our problem. Not only (as I have been complaining for chapters) has Divine perfect goodness been construed in terms of *moral* goodness, but attempts by Pike and Chisholm, to introduce aesthetic considerations into the discussion, have encountered significant resistance.[1] Recall (from Chapter 2 above) how both philosophers attempt to shift the burden of proof regarding the logical compossibility of God and evil off the believer's shoulders by appeal to the aesthetic relation of organic unity (Pike with his appeal to Leibnizian best-of-all-possible-worlds themes, Chisholm in his distinction of two aesthetic relations—balancing off and defeat). Penelhum renders a Scottish verdict of "not proven" on their reflections. For he rightly

---

1. Nelson Pike, "Hume on Evil," *Philosophical Review* 72 (1963): 180–97; Roderick Chisholm, "The Defeat of Good and Evil," *Proceedings of the American Philosophical Association* 42 (1968–69): 21–38.

insists that arguments from evil against the rationality of religious belief must understand 'perfectly good' and 'evil' the way the religious tradition in question does and that believers' values and valuables will shape and delimit available explanations of evil. For instance, he points out, since Christianity exalts the values of personal welfare, character, and loving relationships, it could not consistently regard the aesthetically pleasing delicate pink flush produced in the cheeks of the tubercular patient as God's principal reason for permitting the disease. Turning to Pike and Chisholm, Penelhum wonders whether the permission of evils aesthetically related to greater goods in the way they suggest, is really consistent with Divine goodness as the believer conceives of it. What if some evils were to be found that the believer's values would not allow to be defeated by their relation of organic unity to the cosmic whole?[2]

Penelhum closes with the question; for others, its answer is ready to hand. Ivan Karamazov contends that his examples of torture and child abuse cannot be rendered compossible with the moral value of justice by appeal to the aesthetics of cosmic harmony. Likewise, Stump deems such aesthetic considerations at best supplementary, insisting that every instance of suffering must contribute to the salvation of the victim, if Divine *goodness to* created persons is to be guaranteed.[3] Philip Quinn goes further, maintaining that aesthetic considerations of simplicity and variety are "utterly irrelevant" in assessing which possible world an omniscient, omnipotent, and perfectly good creator could make.[4] Aesthetic values would be central to a solution to the problem of generic ugliness: namely, of how an omnipotent, omniscient God of supremely good taste could coexist with a world containing negative aesthetic values. But the traditional problem of evil focuses on Divine morals, on God's *goodness to* persons, not Heaven's aesthetic sensibilities!

These authors illustrate a trend within analytic philosophy of religion (where defeaters of evil compossible with Divine goodness are concerned) to move from

> (T1) Some sorts of aesthetic goodness are *insufficient to* defeat the evil
>   of some sorts of personal suffering (for example, the delicate

---

2. Terence Penelhum, "Divine Goodness and the Problem of Evil," in *The Problem of Evil*, ed. Marilyn McCord Adams and Robert Merrihew Adams (Oxford: Oxford University Press, 1990), 72–74, 81–82.

3. Eleonore Stump, "The Problem of Evil," *Faith and Philosophy* 2 (1985): 417.

4. Philip L. Quinn, "God, Moral Perfection, and Possible Worlds," *God: The Contemporary Discussion*, ed. Frederick Sontag and M. Darrol Bryant (New York: Rose of Sharon Press, 1982), 197–215, esp. 203.

pink flushed cheeks are insufficient to defeat the ills of tuber-
culosis, a cosmic order of maximum-variety-with-maximum-
simplicity is insufficient to defeat the evil of child torture),

to

(T2) Some sorts of aesthetic goodness are *at most supplementary* to the
defeat of the evils of (some sorts of) personal suffering,

to

(T3) Aesthetic goods are *utterly irrelevant* to the defeat of evils in the
amounts and of the kinds found in this world.

Beneath the surface is the parallel slide from the observation that aesthetic
and moral goodness sometimes break apart (in that some instances of the
former do not exemplify the latter), through overgeneralization, to a full-
scale compartmentalization of aesthetic from moral value and from goodness to persons.

My point is not to charge individual authors with invalid inferences. Different authors advance distinguishable claims, doubtless for a variety of
historical and philosophical reasons. Among them, there is the enormous
influence of Kant, whose *Critique of Judgment* enforces a separation of aesthetics from science and morals, for reasons distinctive to his own philosophical system. Anglo-American philosophy has been shaped by its reactions to logical positivism, which attempted to evacuate all value claims of
cognitive content. In the panic to reestablish morality on a solid footing,
aesthetics often got left out in the cold. Like philosophy of science and philosophy of religion, aesthetics has been marginalized by its requirement of
special expertise, thereby shrinking the circle of qualified participants. From
the side of the art world, the art-for-art's-sake movement protested utilitar-
ian values of an industrialized society with the declaration that art is and
ought to be useless and irrelevant to anything else! Whatever the actual influences on individual authors, my point is rather a Humean one: that as
one reads the literature, passing from article to article, invited now to consent to (T1), later (T2), elsewhere (T3), one finds oneself carried along by
the sheer association of ideas to join the consensus that aesthetic values have
nothing important to contribute to the problem at hand. My hope in this
chapter is to sabotage this trend.

Certainly, tradition should disturb us. In wrestling with the problem of
evil, Augustine appeals to cosmic and Divine beauty, even recognizes Di-

vine justice as one of its dimensions;[5] Leibniz notoriously leads with the aesthetic when he commends maximum variety with maximum simplicity as criterial for the best of all possible worlds; and Jonathan Edwards contends that beauty is the principal attribute, not only of God, but of being generally.[6] Without exercising itself over Divine good taste, the Bible does invite us to *taste and see* God's goodness (Ps. 34:8)! Moreover, if unity, proportion, and fit are numbered among aesthetic excellences, I have chosen to focus on the category of horrendous evils precisely because of their radical disproportion relative to human meaning-making capacities, because they furnish prima facie reason to doubt whether anyone could fit them into a life that would be worth living (see Chapter 2). I have traced the root of human vulnerability to horrors in the incongruity of welding spirit and matter, in the misfitting of personality and animality together in the same nature (see Chapter 5). But these hints can't be taken much further without a closer look at the category of the aesthetic itself.

2. Aesthetics Overviewed

If beauty and ugliness, the graceful and the grotesque, have been with us "since Eden," the term 'aesthetics' was coined only in the eighteenth century by Alexander Baumgarten, who defined it narrowly as an autonomous science of sensory knowing. Subsequent thinkers have reshaped the field in different ways. Perhaps because of its apparent subject matter—Plato denied the muse-inspired arts any governing rational principles, while Kant defined an aesthetic idea as an intuition of creative imagination for which no adequate concept can be found—aesthetics has yet to stabilize its own self-understanding even to the degree found in other areas of philosophy. Happily, a summary overview will be enough to orient us for the task at hand.[7]

5. Augustine, *On Free Choice of Will*, II.xi. 120–29; III.ix.85–103. Augustine, *Confessions* (in *Augustine of Hippo: Selected Writings*, trans. Mary T. Clark [New York: Paulist Press, 1984], 144) 10:27: "Late have I loved you, O Beauty, so ancient and so new . . ." See also Augustine, "Letter 147," in Clark, 22.

6. Cf. Roland Andre Delattre, *Beauty and Sensibility in the Thought of Jonathan Edwards: An Essay in Aesthetics and Theological Ethics* (New Haven: Yale University Press, 1968).

7. In gathering this synopsis, I have relied eclectically on a number of sources: *A Companion to Aesthetics*, ed. David Cooper (Oxford: Basil Blackwell, 1992); Frank Burch Brown, *Religious Aesthetics: A Theological Study of Making and Meaning* (Princeton: Princeton University Press, 1989); Richard Harries, *Art and the Beauty of God: A Christian Understanding* (London: Mowbray, 1993); John Hospers, "Aesthetics, Problems of," *The Encyclopedia of Philosophy* (New York: Macmillan, 1967), 1:35–56; James Alfred Martin Jr., *Beauty and Holiness: The Dialogue between Aesthetics and Religion* (Princeton: Princeton University Press, 1990); Mary Mothershill, *Beauty Restored* (Oxford: Oxford University Press, 1984); Patrick Sherry, *Spirit and Beauty: An Introduction to Theological Aesthetics* (Oxford: Clarendon Press, 1992); Nicholas Wolterstorff, *Art in Action: Toward a Christian Aesthetic* (Grand Rapids, Mich.: Eerdmans, 1980).

Let us begin ostensively, with a fairly catholic list of aesthetic properties, first helping ourselves to the distinction between *sensuous* values (such as light, colors, textures, sounds) and formal values (such as the arrangement of the aforementioned values in paintings, sculptures, and musical compositions so that they are balanced, tightly knit or loosely woven, graceful or clumsy, ironic, one-dimensional, and so forth). Assuming that there are nonphysical spiritual realities, a parallel distinction should be posited for them. We may proceed to distinguish pure *value* properties (such as being beautiful or sublime, ugly or dreary); *emotion* properties (such as being sad or joyful, somber or angry); *behavioral* properties (such as being bouncy, daring, frenzied or sluggish); *evocative* qualities (such as being powerful, boring, amusing, uplifting); *representational* features (such as being true-to-life, distorted, realistic); and even *historical* properties (such as being original, bold, conservative, derivative).

Within patristic and medieval Christian circles, beauty was the center of explicit attention; its characterization was molded by metaphysical and epistemological assumptions transposed from Greek philosophy. Aquinas thought three things were required for beauty—integrity or perfection, proper proportion, and clarity or light, where the first two find their natural measure in the nature of the thing.[8] Likewise, because this trio of features bears a natural proportion to human cognitive and affective faculties, contemplation of the beautiful produces pleasure in the beholder. Eighteenth-and nineteenth-century discussions fixed on the contrast between the beautiful (which they made a function of the formal properties proportioned to our cognitive and affective faculties) and the sublime (which they associated with what is vast in expanse or power, mysterious and obscure, of indefinite form, beyond our capacities adequately to represent or conceptually to domesticate). The latter (clearly a conceptual ancestor of Otto's idea of the Holy; see chapter 5) was said to evoke anxiety, fear, awe, even terror, but in a delightful way (as with "audience emotions" where there is no real and present danger).

Focusing especially on sensuous and formal features, many identify aesthetic properties as logically appropriate objects of *disinterested contemplation*, where objects are regarded *for their own sakes*. Kant understood indifference to mean abstraction from the existence (as opposed to the appearance) of the object, as well as from considerations of morality and practical utility. The twentieth-century art-for-art's-sake movement went further to insist that art must be antirepresentational, altogether divorced from symbolic content and human emotions.

8. Aquinas, *Summa Theologica* 1.39.8; *Summa Theologica* 1–2.54.1; *De divinis nominibus*, chap. 4, lect. 5.

The majority begged to differ, seeing art as essentially connected with human emotions in a variety of alternative ways: whether as articulations of the artist's inchoate feelings, as evocative of audience emotions and productive of cathartic effects, or as metaphorically expressing emotions itself by virtue of its sensuous and formal features and quite apart from whether artist or audience actually experiences such emotions in creating or attending to the work. The majority report connects the aesthetic with some sort of symbolic function—whether by participating in, imitating, exemplifying, or otherwise denoting what is symbolized; or by serving as that through which we organize and express our world of meaning. Light gets included on lists of positive aesthetic qualities not just because it is attractive or pleasing, but also because it signals the function of art or nature to instruct, to manifest, disclose, reveal truth, or at least show how things look from certain points of view.

Naturally, my aims as a value-integrationist do not allow me to preserve neutrality with respect to all points of controversy. Obviously, they put me at odds with extreme versions of art-for-art's-sake, and lead me to endorse the contrary assumption that aesthetic values (both sensuous and formal) may be related to other goods either as constituents or, instrumentally, as means. All the same, my goals are compatible with regarding sensuous and formal features of art and nature as (often among other things) *logically appropriate objects* of aesthetic contemplation; indeed, they pose no difficulty for treating some such properties as intrinsically valuable or for regarding aesthetic contemplation of them as intrinsically good for the beholder. My own argument will also credit the aesthetic with symbolic function, and make use of the idea that meaning-making and the invention of integrative symbols are artistic activities.

3. The Bible's Drama, Aesthetically Conceived

Philosophers and artists are not the only value-segregationists. Certain strands of Christian piety have regarded aesthetics with a suspicion that runs in a vicious circle as both cause and effect of value-theory compartmentalization. Splitting art off from religion turns them into competitors, each demanding to be the organizing principle of human life. Besides threatening idolatry, preoccupation with the aesthetic can distract us from what God really cares about—not the outward forms, but inward obedience, love of God and neighbor, the heart's bias towards mercy and longing for justice.[9]

9. Both Nicholas Wolterstorff, in *Art in Action,* and Richard Harries, in *Art and the Beauty of God,* acknowledge that engagement of art can be idolatrous, while urging that it has an appropriate and enriching place within Christian life and worship.

Such dichotomizing approaches will find much to wrestle with in the Bible. St. Augustine's adolescent complaints to the contrary notwithstanding, the document itself contains many texts of considerable literary merit. If aesthetic value is so opposed to the true worship of God, why—when the Word of the Lord seizes a prophet—does it so often get expressed in beautiful poetry? More importantly, if it would be both anachronism and genre mistake to find an aesthetic theory in the Scriptures, it is easy to sample the Bible's use of aesthetic categories to describe Who God is and what God does. In fact, "the Creator God as artist" is such a traditional trope, that it should scarcely surprise one to discover aesthetic categories at work in the story of creation. Less often remarked in philosophical circles is how the Bible parallels creation and redemption (or re-creation), arguably including the former as a cosmic model of the latter, so that the aesthetics of creation and the aesthetics of redemption are the same. Three themes will give us a sample of how the Bible uses aesthetic categories to tell the story of how evil is overcome by the Goodness of God.

3.1. Ordering Chaos

In its current arrangement, the Bible opens with the *Priestly*-source account of creation, which adapts a Babylonian story in which the military hero god conquers a watery chaos monster and then turns architect dividing its body to construct the world.[10] In Genesis 1, the Divine artist creates by separating the light from the darkness (Gen. 1:4), the day from the night (Gen. 1:14–19), the waters from the sky (Gen. 1:7–8) and the dry land (Gen. 1:9–11); by differentiating plant and animal kinds and assigning the boundaries of their habitations and seasons (Gen. 1:11–13, 20–25). And then God hands it over to human beings to govern and to use (Gen. 1:26–31). Nor does Divine creativity confine itself to physical order. At the political level, God defines Israel out of the undifferentiated mass of humankind with the gift of the Law (not only the Decalogue, but the Holiness Code, and other detailed regulations partly recorded in Exodus, Leviticus, and Deuteronomy) to order life together. God's enforcement of the act-consequence principle (good for good, evil for evil) is not, in the first instance, an indication of heavenly bias towards retribution rather than mercy, but rather a

10. Nineteenth-century source criticism of the Biblical texts issued in the widely accepted hypothesis that the first six books of the Bible are a composite of four sources: the Yahwist (J) (ca. 950 B.C.E.) and the Elohist (E) (ca. 850–750 B.C.E.) sources were distinguished on the basis of the names they use for God, and together with the Priestly (P) (ca. 538–450 B.C.E.) source, are woven together in the books of Genesis, Exodus, Leviticus, Numbers, and Joshua; while the Deuteronomy (D) (7th century B.C.E.) source constitutes a book on its own, with some D additions in Joshua as well. Cf. Gerhard von Rad, *Genesis: A Commentary* (Philadelphia: Westminster Press, 1972).

hedge against moral chaos in the world, an assurance to human beings of a stable regime within which there is something we can do (that is, obey God's law) to avoid the worst. Thus, in contrast to non-Biblical versions of the flood story which make the liquidation of creation the result of divine caprice, Genesis 6–9 explains its near reversion to chaos in terms God's moral order in the face of human wickedness (Gen. 6:5–8, 11–12, 17–18; 7:1). Throughout Israel's history, in times of crisis, prayers go up for God to reassert Divine conquest of the chaos monster to prevent the nation from losing definition through foreign conquest (Ps. 74:10–23; Isa. 51:7–13; 54:7–10; cf. Ps. 104:6–9, 26; Job 41:1–11). Late in the day (probably after the Babylonian exile), the *Priestly*-source story advertises Torah observance as a hedge against dissolution by ethnic assimilation in a pluralistic society (cf. Chapter 5, section 4). Its liturgical structure makes the first week paradigm and symbol of how humans are to participate in (collaborate with) God's work, ordering the chaos of their inclinations and lives by keeping the Law. God's six-day work week closing with Sabbath observance, not only charts the route to salvation, but foretells its consummation in eternal Sabbath rest, a day that will never be swallowed up in night.[11]

3.2. The Light of Divine Countenance

Aesthetic theory generally counts light, radiance, brightness among the positive aesthetic qualities. According to the Bible, God is light (1 John 1:5), Divine activity sends forth transfiguring light into darkness and brings everything at last to a glorious consummation. "Let there be light!" is God's first Word in creation (Gen. 1:3). When the Spirit of God moves over formless void and darkness, God separates light from darkness (Gen. 1:4, 18), creates the "lesser lights"—sun, moon, stars—and makes light to rule over night (Gen. 1:14–18). At Sinai, YHWH's Glory so shone upon Moses whenever he talked with God that Moses' own face shone with reflected light and had to be covered with a veil (Gen. 1:29–35). God's light led the children of Israel through the wilderness and was veiled in cloud by day and blazing with fire by night (Num. 14:14); the light of Divine Law was a lamp to their path (Ps. 119:105). When Israel is restored, God's glory will so shine upon Zion that all nations will see the reflected light and stream through her gates to pay tribute (Isa. 60:1–3; 66:18–19).

For Christians, Jesus is the Divine Word through Whom all things were

11. Cf. Jon D. Levenson, *Creation and the Persistence of Evil* (San Francisco: Harper and Row, 1988). In this fascinating book, Levenson distinguishes multiple symbolic levels (cosmic, political, liturgical, personal) of these stories and works out their implication for the problem of evil in detail.

made (John 1:9; 3:19), the light of the world shining on in the darkness
(John 1:15; 8:12; 9:5; 13:46), enabling His disciples to walk in the light (John
8:12; 1 John 1:7), to work while it is day (John 9:4; 12:35–36), and to have
fellowship with God and one another (1 John 1:7). By contrast, His enemies love darkness rather than light because their deeds are evil (John
3:19–21). If the light of the Gospel is veiled to unbelievers, the light that
shone out in the darkness at creation now shines in the hearts of believers
"to give the light of the knowledge of the glory of God in the face of
Christ" (2 Cor. 4:3–4, 6). In the synoptic Gospels, dazzling brilliance at the
transfiguration (Matt. 17:2; Mark 9:3; Luke 9:29) and resurrection (Matt.
7:24; 28:2–3; Luke 24:4; cf. Mark 16:5) brackets passion darkness complete
with eclipsed sun (Matt. 27:45; Mark 15:33; Luke 23:44); whereas in John's
Gospel the cross itself is the glorification of the Son of Man (John 12:23,
31–36; 13:31–32). When the Reign of God is fully manifest, the Son of Man
will come in glory with all His angels and sit on His glorious throne (Matt.
25:31), and the righteous will shine like the sun (Matt. 13:43). In the New
Jerusalem, there will be neither sun nor night, because the glory of God will
be its light (Rev. 21:22–25).[12]

3.3 Irony and the Meaning of Evil

The Bible is short on explanations of why God permits evils and relatively long on how God makes good on them. The meaning of participation in evil varies with the contexts in which it is embedded—from a literary point of view, with the plots into which it is woven. Like life and
history, the Bible is full of plots. As the author of creation, God manipulates
plots to achieve Divine purposes. The Exodus story (see Chapter 6, section
4.1) crystallizes the perceived Divine preference for certain literary de-
vices—maximizing suspense and narrative tension with multiple "insurmountable" obstacles, slapstick humor, skin-of-the-teeth comic reversals.
The contrasting scenarios of apocalyptic theology (epitomized by the
canonical books of Daniel and Revelation, as well as the pseudepigraphal
Jewish writings of 1 Enoch and 4 Ezra) and synoptic Gospel passion narratives illustrate how differences in the aesthetic qualities of plot lines affect
their soteriological power.

Apocalyptic Soteriology: Apocalyptic theology offers us two one-dimensional collective characters: the righteous and the wicked. Likewise, its plot
recognizes two opposite conditions—one all good (powerful, flourishing,

---

12. Richard Harries makes a good deal of the imagery of light vs. darkness in *Art and the Beauty of God*, 81–88.

enjoying a monopoly on the goods) and the other all bad (powerless, hor-
rendously suffering, verging on destruction)—and two ages. Its plot line
moves from one age to the other via the intervention of a heavenly rescuer
who effects a simple reversal: First, in this present evil age, the wicked pros-
per and the righteous suffer. This will continue until the powers of darkness
have done their worst, which includes the very undoing of creation. Then,
the Son of Man will come with His angels, who usher the righteous into
heavenly bliss and consign the wicked to torture chambers either eternally
or until they wither away. According to this scenario, evil is not defeated,
but balanced off in a retributive ordering: the sufferings of the righteous are
canceled (without being seen to have contributed to any good) by heavenly joys, while the crimes of the wicked are balanced off by their torment
in hell and/or subsequent annihilation. The two collective actors swap positions, but do not change character. The wicked are not redeemed, nor
does suffering come to an end. Sharing as it does all the aesthetic defects
of a grade B Western, apocalyptic theology pays the price of limited plot
resolution.[13]

Lucan Passion Narrative: There is an element of the one-dimensional in
Luke's passion narrative, as well. For the evangelist represents the crucifixion as the decisive battle between two one-dimensional characters: God and
Satan (cf. Luke 4:1–13; 22:3, 53) Jesus is God's righteous chosen one (Luke
3:22, 9:35, 23:47); Judas (Luke 22:3), the Pharisees, the chief priests, and the
scribes (Luke 22:53) have become (temporarily) instruments of Satan. Nevertheless, the plot drips with tragi-comic irony, as every step the enemies of
Jesus take to bring His ministry to a definitive end (Luke 6:11; 11:53–54;
19:47–48; 22:2, 4–6) actually occurs according to the definite plan and foreknowledge of God (Acts 2:23) and forwards the plot, enabling Jesus to fulfil His vocation (Luke 9:22, 30–31, 44; 19:31–33; 24:6–7, 25–27, 44–47).
Judas' action of betraying Jesus into woe (Luke 22:3–5) in fact brings woe
on Judas by whom the Son of Man is betrayed (Luke 22:22; Acts 1:16–20).
The chief priests and scribes who hope to destroy His ministry by having
Him killed among the criminals, fulfil the prophecy that He should be
numbered among the transgressors (Isa. 53:12; Luke 22:37; 23:32). They who
denounce the kingship of Jesus before Pilate and accuse him of perverting
the nation (Luke 23:2) themselves pervert the nation by persuading the
people of God to reject their king (Luke 23:13–25). They who condemn

---

13. I have said this before, in "Separation and Reversal in Luke-Acts," in *Philosophy and
the Christian Faith,* ed. Thomas Morris (Notre Dame, Ind.: Notre Dame University Press,
1988), 92–117, esp. 93–94.

Jesus as a blasphemer (Luke 22:66–71; see also 5:21; 11:15) themselves blaspheme, echoing the devil's taunts (Luke 4:3, 9) ironically twisting God's own testimony concerning Jesus (Luke 3:22; 9:35; 23:35). The Jewish leaders would mock the kingship of *Jesus* by crucifying Him, but Pilate mocks *Jewish* kingship by crucifying Jesus as King of the Jews (Luke 23:38). Consistently, Jesus' enemies, in mocking, advertise the truths they reject: His captors' taunting "Prophesy!" (Luke 22:63–65), fulfils the most detailed of Jesus' passion predictions (Luke 19:32–33). The rulers of the people ironically mouth the truth that "he is the Christ of God, His Chosen One" (Luke 23:35). Pilate proclaims to all who pass by that Jesus is King of the Jews (Luke 23:38), and Jesus makes The Skull his royal court. Mounting the cross, His throne of judgment, Jesus continues to expose the thoughts of the hearts of many in Israel by evoking their reactions to Him (Luke 2:34–35), to exercise His authority to forgive sins (Luke 23:34, 39–43; see also 5:20–24; 7:48), His royal prerogative to open the gates of Paradise (Luke 23:43). And, of course, these regal acts receive the Divine seal of approval, in Jesus' resurrection and exaltation (Luke 24; Acts 2:22–24, 32–36; 3:26; 4:10–13; 13:30, 33). Yet, this plot does not rest content with a simple reversal of fates. The human enemies of God are not left one-dimensional: for the worst they do in the passion narrative in their role as instruments of the devil, is turned by God into a fresh opportunity for them to step out of this role, through repentance, a change of heart (Acts 2:23, 36–42; 3:17–26; 13:26–32)! On this more subtle (because highly ironic) scenario, not only can the disciples who follow Jesus to martyrdom look forward to the promised Divine vindication (Luke 9:23–26; 22:28–30), but those who consented to the death of Jesus and repent afterwards have the opportunity to enter into the covenant blessings with the consolation of recognizing the worst thing they ever did as making a positive contribution to God's plan to spread His glory to the ends of the earth.

4. Beauty Bountiful!

For Plato, paradigm value is one—a perfect integration of Justice, Truth, and Beauty. And while Plato's own commentary spent this insight on strident critiques of mythology and poetry and insisted on the subordination of art to considerations of Justice and Truth (*Republic* 2. 375A–403C), Christian Platonists learned a more positive lesson, happily taking for granted the integration of aesthetic with other values, and having no qualms about using aesthetic categories to house their theological remarks.

4.1. The Great Chain of Beauty

For Christian Platonists (such as Augustine, Anselm, and Bonaventure), God *is* Goodness Itself, once again, the perfect integration of Justice, Truth, and Beauty. For everything else, *to be* is to be somehow Godlike, to participate in, to imitate or reflect Beauty Itself. What is altogether unified in Divine simplicity, is divided and partial in creatures. Thus, if Divine simplicity is the limit case, beauty in creatures is a function of the unity of distinguishable components; of symmetry, harmony, and proportion; and of light. Because God cannot act contrary to Divine nature, Divine Wisdom makes each nature according to measure, weight, and number (cf. Wisd. of Sol. 7:25–82); Divine Justice endows each with powers proportioned to its natural function and end. Because every created nature is essentially a way of imitating the Divine, each is a natural sign of some aspect of God's glory. Because each is "almost nothing" in relation to the Infinite and Eternal, God creates the universe according to the principle of plenitude—maximum variety with maximum unity—to maximize its collective Godlikeness.

Imperfect likeness comes in degrees. Created natures form a hierarchy, a great chain of beauty, each ranked according to how similar it is to God. Rational creatures (angels and humans) are at the top, insofar as they share with God the capacity for a self-determined orientation to the Good. But insofar as they are creatures, this focus is underdetermined by their nature-constituting powers whose properly coordinated functioning requires stabilization through habits. Thus, in the best case, human souls are further decorated with naturally acquired cardinal virtues (prudence, courage, temperance, justice), infused theological virtues (faith, hope, and charity), as well as gifts of the Holy Spirit. Acting in accordance with these to strive into God with all its powers, the soul pulls itself into an ever more sharply focused image of God.

4.2. Christ as Center

Bonaventure uses the aesthetic symbol of the *medium* (middle/center/means) to sum up the meaning of Christ, as the One in Whom all things hold together (Col. 1:17). Bonaventure reasons that because perfect productive power entails a perfect product, because a perfect product would be of the same nature as its producer, and because natures (such as humanity and bovinity) cannot but produce individuals of those natures (Socrates, Beulah the cow), there must be a plurality of persons within the Godhead: the Father as unproduced producer, Christ the Son as perfect product and (with the Father) coproducer of the Spirit Who is unproducing but produced. Christ is thus the *medium* of the Trinity, like the Father in producing but like the Spirit in being produced. Within the Godhead, Christ is Divine Word, the Father's perfect self-expression and exemplar of all created natures. Christ is thus the *medium* of creation, in the sense of being the Exemplar through Whom all things were made (cf. John 1:1–2). Thus, all creatures are Godlike by being like the Son to Whom they owe their form and structure; and humans are the image of the Image!

Taking a page from Pseudo-Dionysius, Bonaventure contends that self-diffusing Divine Goodness has a tendency—other things being equal—to pour into other things as much goodness as they can hold. So God has endowed created being with the remarkable capacity to be united to a Divine person, in such a way that the created nature in question becomes the Divine person's own. Just as humanity belongs to Socrates and Divinity to God the Son essentially, so a created nature could (through an exercise of Divine power) belong to a Divine person contingently. Among created natures, humankind stands at the *medium*, straddling the ontological border between matter and spirit. Accordingly, it is highly fitting and decorous for God the Son, *medium* of the Trinity and exemplar *medium* between God and creation, to actualize creation's highest potentiality by uniting Himself to it at its *medium*, by taking a human nature for His own.

When sin mars the image of God within our human nature, makes us as deformed and repulsive as Francis's lepers, Christ is the *medium* of salvation. His Incarnate career takes its shape (humility, poverty, obedience, and brotherly love) from the requirements of our reform. Christ crucified is both an outward and visible sign of the caricature into which sin has contorted us and a symbol of the soul's transformation through Christlike disciplines which "crucify the flesh and its desires." Spiritually, the soul journeys into cruciformity, finds its destination in the arms of the crucified, where like is known by like, knows even as it is known. Thus, if Bonaventure draws on positive aesthetic values to characterize Christ's role within the Godhead and in creation, the symbol of Christ crucified is bivalent, integrating negative into positive aesthetic values in the redemption and consummation.[14]

14. The easiest access to these ideas in Bonaventure is to be found in his *Itinerarium Mentis in Deum and Lignum Vitae,* both of which are translated by Ewert Cousins in *Bonaventure: The Soul's Journey into God; The Tree of Life; The Life of St. Francis* (New York: Paulist Press, 1978); and in Bonaventure's *Collations on the Six Days,* First Collation, trans. José de Vinck (Paterson, N.J.: St. Anthony Guild Press, 1970), 5:5–19. For a wonderful presentation of Bonaventure's Christology that takes account of his whole corpus, see Zachary Hayes, O.F.M., *The Hidden Center: Spirituality and Speculative Christology in St. Bonaventure* (New York: Paulist Press, 1981). For an examination of Bonaventure's ideas under an alternative aesthetic theme—namely, the coincidence of opposites—see Ewert H. Cousins, *Bonaventure and the Coincidence of Opposites: The Theology of Bonaventure* (Chicago: Franciscan Herald Press, 1978).

5. Aesthetic Valuables as Currency for Divine *Goodness*
to Created Persons

These brief but highly suggestive samplings show how the Bible and one important (Platonizing) strand of Christian tradition did not hesitate to use aesthetic categories, even when articulating the central events of salvation history—creation, redemption, and consummation. Appropriating some of their ideas, I turn now to show their relevance to the problem of horrendous evils. In this section, I want to make explicit how aesthetic valuables are implicated in ways for God to be *good to* created persons; in the final section, I shall return to the category of horrors.

5.1. *Aesthetic Goods as Necessary: Cosmic Order,*
Survival, and Sanity

Cosmic order is one aesthetic property that looms large both in the Bible and the Christian tradition, and in more recent best-of-all-possible-worlds approaches. Of course, Pierce has taught us that 'cosmic order' is a slippery notion because it is trivial: given any batch of things however situated, some (mathematical) order or other obtains between them. Thus, he insists, any distinction of order from chaos involves a necessary reference to the interests, aims, and tastes of persons. Leibniz himself anticipated this point, but followed Christian Platonists in pointing to the nontrivial property of maximum variety with maximum unity.[15] At any rate, so long as we include God among the persons whose purposes and tastes are at issue, I have no need to debate this point. My argument rests on the observation that the cosmos exhibits a different nontrivial order, one of a sort beneficial to humankind. For evidence, I turn to the commonplace.

Evolutionists tell us that human survival depends on some sort of commensurability (they would say "adaptation") between human capacities and the environments in which we live. In particular, human survival depends on our having a picture of the way the world is that is informative enough to enable us to cope with it. This match does not require that the "objective" world really be ordered by regularities simple and stable enough for human beings to grasp and use to predict and gain some measure of control over it. It is not even necessary that humans be able to work up to an accurate picture of the "objective" structure of things by successive approximations. Rather, a phenomenalist understanding of the correspondence will do. Human survival *instrumentally* requires a world whose structural

15. Leibniz, *Discourse on Metaphysics,* secs. 5–6.

properties and regularities can be modeled well enough by (and are in that
sense proportioned to) human cognitive capacities to enable human beings
to make reliable predictions; conversely, it depends upon human beings
having *a taste* for theories that thus model the world.

Besides the collective human capacity for both folk and academic science, developmental psychologists insist that human personality and sanity
depend on the individual psyche's functioning as an effective theory maker
in relation to the data of its psychic field. They imagine that the infant starts
with a booming buzzing confusion and (unconsciously) gropes with all of
its powers to find some organizing principle that will reduce the variety of
its data to a manageable simplicity. The earliest of these begin the differen-
tiation of the self from the "subjective" world. Because the child's capacities
are meager, its first theories are easily overthrown; as its powers increase, its
models become more durable as they approach an adult conception by successive approximations. Experiencing the world as ordered in a way that is
congruent enough with reality is *constitutive* of human sanity. Experiencing
the world as chaotic, or losing one's taste for orderings that match up with
the "objective" world, is part of what it is to be insane. The purity and defilement calculus (see Chapter 5) enforces this aesthetic norm at the *social*
level: no more diversity and complexity in social categories than humans
can keep organized.

Returning to the problem of evil, my point is that such structural properties as the world really has are *aesthetic* properties. Moreover, if developmental psychologists are right to posit a bias in the human psyche towards
managing variety with simplicity, and if (as has been traditionally assumed)
the latter is a positive aesthetic value, human beings have a taste for model-
ing the world with aesthetic goods. Consequently, God's producing a world
whose "objective" aesthetic properties are so proportioned as to be able
fruitfully to be modeled by human beings in terms of aesthetic goods is one
way God has of benefiting and hence of being good to human beings. For
by doing so, God supplies conditions instrumentally necessary for human
survival, conditions partially constitutive of human personality and sanity.

5.2. *Aesthetic Goods as Ingredients in a Good Life*

I have insisted that God's *goodness to* created persons involves His guaranteeing to each a life that is a great good to him/her on the whole. But
what makes for a good life? Once more, I turn to the commonplace.

5.2.1. "The Good Things of Life." First, and most obviously, a good life
includes satisfying relations to at least some of "the good things of life."

Many would include sensory pleasures in their number: delight in pleasant colors, sounds, and flavors; the comfort or excitement of textures and feels. Most would count the exercise of creative capacities—to paint, sing, dance; to understand and nurture people; to make intellectual breakthroughs— among the intrinsically worthwhile. Again, most everyone values (although perhaps too few enjoy) intimate personal relationships, characterized by mutual love, support, and appreciation. Importantly for our purposes, aesthetic enjoyments not only make the list, but are integrated into its other members as well. For example, the enjoyment of sensuous values is often aesthetic in its appreciation of the intensity of a color, the gracefulness and balance of a shape or contour, the delicacy of a rose, the subtle balance and blending of flavors in a dish. So, too, aesthetic appreciation of the formal structure and arrangement of complex wholes—whether in nature, paintings, symphonies, or mathematical proofs—makes a positive contribution to life experiences. Less often remarked nowadays (but see Plato's *Symposium*) is the fact that the joy of personal relationship also has its aesthetic dimensions, and that not only in the aesthetic contemplation of bodily beauty. There is also the sensuous sweetness and tenderness of personal presence; the beauty of personality found in grace, elegance, gentle simplicity, wit, and charm. Moral virtue also enhances the soul's beauty, involving as it does a two-tiered aesthetic skill: to balance and harmonize its own competing drives, interests, and functions within; and to produce acts that are not only generically good (as, perhaps, alms-giving in place of theft) but fit the circumstances (that is, at an appropriate time, place, in relation to suitable persons and ends). The history of a personal relationship is a story with its own formal aesthetic properties; which ones they are greatly affects the value the relationship contributes to the lives of the persons involved (see section 5.2.4 below).

Cast in the language of some philosophers, satisfying relationships to intrinsic goods are themselves intrinsically good; and in many ordinary cases, the aesthetic contemplation of aesthetic value is among their constituents.

5.2.2. The Meaning and Purpose of Life. Sometimes, a quite temporary but satisfying relationship to some great enough good (as in doing a dramatic heroic act or composing a great symphony) will be enough to make a person feel (and others agree) that his/her otherwise miserable, unproductive, and shapeless life was worth living. But usually it makes a difference how the bitter and the sweet are distributed and balanced over the whole course of a life. Moreover, a good life is expected to be one that has "meaning" and "purpose." This fact reflects the interaction of two common

human instincts. First, our generalized psychological drive to impose a simplifying order on data can be seen in the urge to find some simplifying gen-
eralizations or patterns structuring the experiences of our own or other
persons' lives. In addition, we human beings commonly exhibit a drive to
self-transcendence, to relate ourselves to something beyond ourselves, typically to something larger or in some sense more valuable or more permanent. Our life experiences can become organically related, our lives as
wholes organized around some goal or ideal at which we ourselves aim.
This may be conscious (as when one offers one's life in service of one's
country, or bends one's energies to the cause of social justice or the ideal of
world peace, or devotes oneself to the conquest of disease, to advancing the
frontiers of science, to art, to the family, or even to proving a difficult the-
orem). Or it may be unconscious (as when one repeatedly contrives to become just like or exactly opposite to Daddy). Alternatively, our lives may be
molded and expended by the individual or collective schemes of others,
consciously (as with the soldier in the dictator's army, or the salesman of a
large company) or unconsciously (as when we become specimens of a certain culture). When all else fails, many find comfort in relating themselves
to nature, in recognizing themselves as instances of a natural kind of long-
standing, their disease and death as causal products of natural regularities.

5.2.3. Internal versus External Points of View. As already noted (in
Chapter 4, section 5.2), the value of a person's life may be assessed from the
inside (in relation to that person's own goals, ideals, and choices) and from
the outside (in relation to the aims, tastes, values, and preferences of others).
Not surprisingly, such assessments may disagree. Hitler may have seen positive value in the lives of his soldiers, who expended their energies and died
as cogs in the war machines of *der Führer's* mythological designs. Doubtless
many of them put a higher premium on the civilian goals of home, family,
and nonmilitary career; others felt their lives contaminated beyond cleansing by their participation in the Holocaust. Conversely, the hermit or monk
who abandons the world in search of God, or the yuppy pressing his limits
towards his first million, or the starlet thirsting for fame may view each
other's life styles as foolish wastes.

My notion is that for a person's life to be a great good to him/her on the
whole, the external point of view (even if it is God's) is not sufficient. Rather
the person him/herself must value, and actually enjoy, his/her relations to
enough goods and to goods that are great enough. A lifetime supply of
chocolate will not benefit the choc-allergic, nor regular concert attendance
the deaf. (Once again, the curmudgeon is a counterexample to the claim that

an individual's judgments about the worthwhileness of his/her own life are incorrigible.) Similarly, if a person's life is to have positive meaning for him/her, that person must not forever see his/her life as expended only or principally for ends or ideals to which s/he is at best indifferent and at worst despises. Presumably, no human person will ever recognize, much less consciously value, all of the overarching patterns under which his/her life experiences are subsumed. A person's life will have positive value for him/her only if s/he eventually recognizes some patterns organizing some chunks of his/her experiences around goals, ideals, relationships that s/he values.

5.2.4. Form and Structure as Ingredients of a Good Life. Returning to our theme, the structure and arrangement of experiences in a life, the patterns of distribution of goods or ills, the relations of those experiences to self-transcendent goals or ideals are alike aesthetic properties. Which formal aesthetic properties are partially constitutive of a person's life makes a dramatic difference to how good or meaningful that person's life is. Contrast, for example, a life with an idyllic childhood and a miserable adulthood with one in which moderate goods and ills are sprinkled through the whole. Again, isolated evils (such as the loss of property in an earthquake) can be far more tolerable than others organically related to important aspects of one's life (for example, parental abuse of children). On the other hand, a mere Chisholmian balancing off of evils with good (the pain of a stubbed toe with the pleasure of a beautiful sunset) cannot endow the evils with the meaning of making a positive contribution to any great enough goods. Further, insofar as unity, integrity, harmony, and relevance are valuable aesthetic properties in a life, they will differentially value similar acts, experiences, character traits, and so forth, depending on the life context. For example, sensory enjoyments (which are good considered in themselves) obstruct the desert father's quest for purity of heart that wills one thing, while the latter's ascetic renunciations sound a dissonant chord within a life that aims at the Golden Mean. Exchanging Harris tweed for Indian peasant garb would (almost always) be irrelevant to vicarage life in rural England; but for Gandhi in India it was an act of integrity and solidarity. The cultivation of intellectual sophistication and managerial skills would have spoiled the simplicity and charisma of St. Francis, but they were fitting in St. Bonaventure who found his vocation in organizing the Franciscan order and integrating its work into university life. The above-noted contrast between apocalyptic theology and synoptic passion narratives (in section 3.3) furnishes a theological illustration of the difference aesthetic organization can make to the value of a person's life (as to the world as a whole).

5.3. Beauty Beatific!

So far, I have commented on how formal aesthetic properties are partially constitutive of moral virtues and morally virtuous acts and, with the Platonizing tradition affirmed, how distributive and retributive justice are but species of aesthetic order.[16] Also, I have noted how aesthetic enjoyment of aesthetic goods is not only to be numbered among the intrinsic goods, but also is partially constitutive of sensory pleasures and the enjoyment of persons in intimate relationship. Finally, I have called attention to commonplaces about how the aesthetic properties of the cosmos as a whole and of an individual's life history dramatically affect a person's survival and sanity, the goodness and meaning of his/her life. It follows that furnishing a person with satisfying relationships to aesthetic goods is one way to benefit a person, and so one way for God to be *good to* us. It is available, only to persons who have access to a store of aesthetic valuables and the capacity to make them accessible to others. The ability to contribute to the positive meaning of a person's life by overcoming evil with good is in part a function of aesthetic imagination, of the capacity to weave evils into complex goods through subtle irony and reversal. Given the horrendous evils God permits, God must have extraordinary aesthetic imagination to overcome them.

Further I suggest that—so far as the first approach is concerned—God is in an advantageous position. I join Christian Platonists in taking Divine perfection, the Good that God is, to include beauty; and I take the sizegap to imply that Divine beauty is immeasurable and incommensurate with any and all created goods or ills. Further, I assume that aesthetic contemplation that appreciates the object for its own sake, can itself be intrinsically valuable; in particular, that contemplation of unsurpassable beauty is itself immeasurably good for the beholder. It would follow that any such contemplation of Divine Beauty not only balances off but engulfs participation in horrendous evils.

Aesthetic contemplation of created beauty for its own sake is—I have insisted—one of the good things in life. Extra assumptions redouble its contribution to life's meaning by virtue of its symbolic value. Christian Platonists hold that created beauties are likenesses, naturally significant signs of the Divine. Nor do they think of this as two distinct things related by efficient causality and resemblance, on analogy with President Clinton and a photograph of him, where the picture comes between Clinton and the viewer in order to represent Clinton to the viewer (in the manner of Lock-

16. Cf. St. Augustine, *De libero arbitrio,* II.120–29; III.85–103.

ean ideas). For Christian Platonists, the created nature is not so independent of and distinct from the Divine essence, but rather participates in the reality it signifies. Accordingly, they speak of the exemplar as being *in* what participates in it in such a way as to be manifested thereby. Thus, one who contemplates the created beauty may pass through it to see Divine Beauty Itself, whether or not the beholder recognizes Divine Beauty as what s/he is seeing. Alternatively, one might simply hold—as Patrick Sherry does—that Divine Beauty is something to which we have (often unwitting but) direct access whenever we experience the beauty of nature and other persons here below (Ps. 19:1).[17] Either way, antemortem experiences of created beauty would gain added meaning by virtue of their integration into our relationship with God (see Chapter 8).

6. The Aesthetics of the Horrendous

From the outset, I have (implicitly or explicitly) made use of multiple aesthetic categories in formulating the problem of horrendous evils. In focusing on *the positive meaning of individual human lives*, I have been treating individual human lives as having an aesthetic dimension and understanding them to be bearers of symbolic content. Following the analogies of developmental psychology, I have put persons in the role of artists working to shape the materials of their lives into wholes of positive significance; so that upbringing, religious education, and psychotherapy become (among other things) art schools, enabling us to embrace this task with skill and strength, creativity and imagination. I have insisted that God must be a meaning-maker of extraordinary resourcefulness, from our beginnings a constant but often unrecognized teacher and collaborator, able to help us pick up and rearrange the pieces to make something new (see Chapter 4, section 5; Chapter 5, sections 6.2–6.3; and this chapter, sections 3.3 and 5.1–2 above).

Moreover, I have identified what is horrendous about horrors by appeal to the aesthetic categories of *disproportion* and *incongruity* (see Chapter 2, section 6; Chapter 3, section 6.4; Chapter 5, sections 3–6). Like light too bright for the eyes, horrendous evils overwhelm human meaning-making capacities, prima facie stumping us, furnishing strong reason to believe that lives marred by horrors can never again be unified and integrated into wholes with positive meaning. Put otherwise, participation in horrors leaves us

17. Patrick Sherry, *Spirit and Beauty*, 59–84.

feeling in the position of postmodern artists, who juxtapose the incongruous without any unifying framework, so much the better to send the despairing message that no underlying meanings are to be found.

Since Chapter 2, I have joined Ivan Karamazov's protest against *global* aesthetic solutions that rest content with defeating horrors via their organic relation to the "higher harmonies" of cosmic wholes—as if human participation in horrors could be put on a par with the bilious green in Monet's depiction of Rouen cathedral or discordant notes in Stravinsky's *Rite of Spring*. What I conclude (tipping my Platonizing hand) is not (like Quinn, Stump, and Penelhum; see section 1 above) that aesthetic considerations are irrelevant, marginal, or of dubious propriety, but that it is wrong to make the global context the primary, much less the only frame of evaluation when it comes to horror's challenge to the Goodness of God. Because I am convinced that paradigm value is one and that Divine *Goodness to* created persons is at least in part a function of endowing their lives with valuable aesthetic features (see sections 4–5 above), I have forwarded, as criterial for solving the problem of horrendous evils, the idea that God guarantee to created persons lives that are great goods to them on the whole (in which goods at least overbalance evils by a wide margin) and in which any participation in horrors is defeated within the context of the individual's life. The wreck of persons *is* different from the negative sensuous evaluations of colors or sounds, not because the former is a moral *rather than* an aesthetic matter, but because *personal* ruin is differently related to other value-dimensions. It is not enough for God to respond—like Monet or Stravinsky—by arranging the negatively valued part in such a way that it contributes to the positive value of the cosmic whole. God must *beautify* the person. Divine *goodness to* created persons is incompatible with God's playing the postmodern artist with respect to individual lives. A God Who permits horrors obviously cannot be specializing in idealized classical Greek sculptures. But at the very minimum, God must be a modern artist, ready, willing, and able to turn horror-torn individual careers into *Guernica's*, to house distortion within a unifying framework to produce wholes of outstanding merits, at least some of which can eventually be appreciated by the individual him/herself (see section 5.2).

Mention of Picasso's work brings to mind how distortion of nature can play a different symbolic function, one involved in the disclosive or revelatory aspect of art. We have already noted how Christian Platonists attribute this function to created things generally (section 5.3). In his dialogue *De Veritate*, Anselm takes this idea in a distinctive direction with his bold assertion that every action, by the very fact that it is done, signifies that it ought to *be*.[18] For him, the metaphysical framework of natural kinds with teleological structures that function as norms against which things here below are measured combines with global and generic metaphysical optimism—that to *be*, is either to be Goodness Itself or a way of being like it, that all genuine powers seek the Good—to create a presumption that things here below do as they ought by functioning smoothly. Against this background, he reasons, the fact that something is done makes the statement that it *ought* to be. Thus, when rational creatures act in accordance with justice, they *do* the truth; when they seek advantage at the expense of justice, they *lie*. Similarly, he might conclude that occurrent horrors declare that they ought to be and thereby lie.

More recent thinkers who (like John Dewey and Susanne Langer) recognize art as having symbolic function generally agree that symbols are polyvalent, indeed the more powerful they are, the wider variety of meanings they can organize and contain. Similarly, Nelson Goodman understands the language of art to be connected with its significata through complex chains of exemplification and denotation, both metaphorical and literal, with many intermediate stopping points. Again, polyvalency is what allows symbols to be transformative, as the viewer first enters the symbol via one reading, only to get trapped in its vortex and get gestalt-shifted into another meaning. The same symbol can have positive or negative significance for individuals because of personal history and context (such as the Union Jack which, in the 1940's stirred resentment of colonial oppression to Indian villagers but represented freedom and respect for human dignity to British soldiers fighting the Nazis). Most human beings stumped by their participation in horrors would find Anselm's metaphysical optimism both incredible and intolerable. The occurrence of horrors calls Anselm's global and generic metaphysical optimism into question; this is just another version of the problem of horrendous evil. Consequently, his confident assumption would not number among the background beliefs of most participants in horrors and, thus, would not be available to assign semantic content the way Anselm suggests.

On the contrary, I want to argue that horrors disclose truths, by drawing on the controversial but widely shared point of aesthetic theory—namely, that the semantic content of artistic symbols depends on various facts about the general nature of human subjectivity. If there is an objective standard of

---

18. Anselm, *De Veritate,* c.ix; S I.189. Cf. my "St. Anselm on Truth," *Documenti e Studi sulla Tradizione Filosofica Medievale,* 353–72.

what humans ought to be like in the metaphysics of natural kinds, this objective human nature builds certain subjective standards into our very organism. Psycho-biologically, we "imprint" on human beings. Our psychobiological drives give us an inchoate sense of human wholeness and flourishing, insofar as they strive towards them. The very animal structure of the human organism "knows" that metabolism is matched by catabolism, not only that death is inevitable but that we contain the seeds of our own demise. However unconscious and inarticulate this in-formation, it figures in the subjective background out of which we assign semantic contents. My suggestion is that relative to the objective standard of human nature, occurrent horrors testify to twin truths: that we as personal animals are highly vulnerable to horrors; and that because we are *persons*, horrors ought not to be. Just as Kant's beholders experience pleasure when viewing elegant forms, while their encounters with dark rugged mountains evoke anxious delight; so, too, all humans confronted with horrors are seized with revulsion and loathing, instinctively turn away, stop their ears, and veil their gaze. This is because (like Socrates eliciting geometry from the slave boy) actual occurrent horrors articulate and make explicit our natural knowledge that such things contradict our flourishing and that we are radically vulnerable to personal ruin.

The importance of cosmic aesthetic excellence—including the regularity of natural and psychological laws—is not that it defeats horrors (although, for all we know, they may be defeated on the global level; see Chapter 2). Rather, like the elegant composition of Picasso's *Guernica* or Grünewald's crucifixion, or the rhythms of color and stroke in Van Gogh's *Starry Night* or Francis Bacon's cadaverous forms, cosmic order houses horrors in a stable frame with the result that we can face them and hear the outrageous truths that they tell (see section 5.1). This truth-telling capacity endows horrors with a positive symbolic value that cannot be taken from them; like the blood of Abel, they cry out from the ground (Gen. 4:10)!

Part Three

RESOLUTION AND RELEVANCE

[8]

Resources to the Rescue

1. Making Good On the Horrors

My central thesis in this book is that horrendous evils require defeat by nothing less than the goodness of God. My strategy for showing how this can be done is to identify ways that created participation in horrors can be integrated into the participants' relation to God, where God is understood to be the incommensurate Good, and the relation to God is one that is overall incommensurately good *for the participant*. Our surveys in Part 2—of alternative models of Divine power and agency on the one hand, and neglected values on the other—are strewn with hints and suggestions. I want now to gather up these resources and join them with others to focus a variety of proposals for solving the logical problem of horrendous evil. A few methodological preliminaries will position us for this task.

1.1. Revisiting the Criteria

Let me first review the conditions laid down in earlier chapters for a successful solution. My suggestion (in Chapter 3) has been that to show God to be logically compossible with horrendous evils, it is not necessary to produce a logically possible morally sufficient reason why God does not prevent them. Indeed, I concluded the attempt is doubly misguided: first, because how bad horrors are finds its epistemic measure in our inability to think of plausible candidates for sufficient reasons why; second, because the pressure to provide such rationales anyway drives us to advance credible *par-*

tial reasons why as *total* explanations, thereby exacerbating the problem of evil by attributing perverse motives to God. At the same time, I conceded that God as person would act for reasons why, that possible partial reasons why are accessible to us, and that because we are persons it may be more satisfying to offer some partial reasons why rather than saying nothing at all.

In place of the futile search for sufficient reasons why, my strategy substitutes an effort to show how it is logically possible for God to be *good to* participants in horrors nonetheless. On my account (in Chapters 2 and 4), for God to be *good to* a created person, God must guarantee him/her a life that is a great good *to him/her* on the whole and one in which any participation in horrors is defeated within the context of his/her own life. Moreover, I have distinguished (in Chapter 4) between objective versus recognized and appropriated meanings, and insisted that for a person's life to be a great good to him/her on the whole, it is not enough that his/her life be objectively full of positive meaning or that these meanings be appreciated by others; s/he must recognize and appropriate meanings sufficient to render it worth living.

1.2. Symbolic versus Concrete Values?

The exploration (in Chapter 6) of the category of symbolic value prompts yet another distinction—between *balancing off (or defeat) by symbolic valuables versus balancing off (or defeat) by concrete valuables.* Unsurprisingly, these dimensions can break apart. It is plausible, for example, to suppose that since God is a good incommensurate with any creature, any relation of honoring or being honored by God confers incommensurate symbolic value on a creature—symbolic worth sufficient to balance off any and all of its concrete or symbolic evils, even participation in horrors. Thus, Christians with a high doctrine of Eucharistic presence tell how God immeasurably honors communicants, whether by "coming under their roofs" bodily under forms of bread and wine (as Roman Catholics and some Anglicans hold; cf. Matt. 8:8; Luke 7:6) or by raising faithful hearts to spiritual communion in heaven (as Calvinists say). Stoics attribute to us humans the remarkable capacity to endow concrete ruin with great positive significance by humbly submitting ourselves to the natural order and praising its Maker and ours.[1] Similarly, religious martyrs transform their tortured deaths from degrading occasions of victimization into acts of worship by offering themselves in sacrifice to God.

---

1. For an account of Stoic psychotherapy, in its ancient and modern classical forms, see Derk Pereboom, "Stoic Psychotherapy in Descartes and Spinoza," *Faith and Philosophy* 11 (1994): 592–625.

1.3. Contentious Standards?

My own estimate of what it would take to defend Divine *goodness to* created persons packs two further controversial assumptions into its baggage.

1.3.1. The Scope of Redemption. First, my criterion is universalist in insisting that God be good to each created person. Given the ruinous power
of horrors, I think (contrary to Hartshorne and Griffin) that it would be
cruel for God to create (allow to evolve) human beings with such radical
vulnerability to horrors, unless Divine power stood able, and Divine love
willing, to redeem. Given my estimate of the size gap between Divine and
created agency, and my sense that much of what God does in relation to us
is agency-enabling and thus could not count as coercion (Chapters 3 and
5), I do not share the worries of free will defenders about how God can
make sure to win human cooperation without violating our freedom. I
agree with them—since it is in any event empirically obvious—that created
agency has been allowed to "do its thing" to the point of producing one
horrendous mess after another. For that reason, I flatter the Creator with
enormous resourcefulness to enable human agency to work (Chapter 4),
not only to "grow it up" in the first place, but to rehabilitate it with new
environments and therapeutic exercises (for example, through the indwelling of Holy Spirit; see Chapter 5) sufficient to enable it to recognize
and appropriate positive meanings sufficient to defeat its own participation
in horrors. If this should mean God's causally determining some things to
prevent everlasting ruin, I see this as no more an insult to our dignity than
a mother's changing a baby's diaper is to the baby.

1.3.2. Concrete Satisfaction? Spiritual writers disagree about the role of
concrete well-being in Divine goodness to individuals. The stoically inclined and stout of heart might hold that God honors us simply by including us in creation and that this is objective, symbolic balancing off sufficient
for Divine goodness to each created person. Other Stoics maintain that Divine goodness to creatures is vouched safe by the additional gift of the
above-mentioned capacity for self-transcendence. Those who exercise it,
recognize and appropriate this meaning, even add to it by repaying the
honor. Some appear to hold that such Divine-human exchange of honors
is sufficient for symbolic defeat.[2]

2. For a discussion of these Stoic approaches, see Diogenes Allen, "Natural Evil and the
Love of God," *Religious Studies* 16 (1980): 439–56; reprinted in *The Problem of Evil,* ed. Marilyn McCord Adams and Robert Merrihew Adams (Oxford: Oxford University Press, 1990),
189–208.

In my judgment, such Stoic positions are deep and should be savored, to let the value of reciprocal honor sink in (see Chapter 6). My own contrary reading of the Christian tradition does not depend on the notion that God owes participants in horrors more than this. On the contrary, my estimate of the size gap between Divine and human personal agency drives me to deny that God has any obligations to creatures at all. I have, however, denied that God can honor human persons by assigning them vocations that permanently crush them. Moreover, Stoic therapy is elitist, insofar as it requires a Stoic education to develop virtues strong enough to weather participation in horrors. The Nazi death camps show how, in our world, horrors are not selective, visiting only the morally well prepared. My principal reason for thinking Divine goodness to created persons includes an eventual and permanent over balance of concrete well-being, however, is that this is what the Bible seems to promise—the land of milk and honey (Deut. 31:20), the Messianic banquet (Luke 5:33–34; 14:8, 15–24; 22:14-15; Rev. 19:1–9), rejoicing in God's presence (Exod. 24:9–11; Rev. 21:1–4) in the realms of light (Rev. 21:23–24).

While it is only fair for me to lay these cards on the table so that the reader will know what I am looking for, I hope in what follows to be fair another way: by including in my review scenarios with different estimates of what is sufficient for evils to be overcome.

1.4. Theoretical Economy versus Explanatory Power

Mackie's original target was theism, what Rowe later came to specify as "restricted standard theism," the unadorned assertion of (1) the existence of an omnipotent, omniscient, and perfectly good God (Chapter 1, section 1).[3] Splendid analytic philosopher that he was, Mackie doubtless prized economy, assumed that showing theism to be "positively irrational" would thereby eviscerate "expanded" theisms—Christianity, Judaism, and Islam—in the bargain. In response, I have argued (in Chapters 1 and 2) that Mackie's strategy gets caught in the snares of equivocation. It is now time to add that where theories stand in competition, even genuine economies must be weighed in the balance against explanatory power. All of the proposals I am about to review marshall troops of philosophical and theological assumptions by way of showing how God might overcome horrendous ruin. To the extent that they tell a coherent story, these expanded theisms arguably trump Mackie's false economy by exhibiting their explanatory resourcefulness.

---

3. William L. Rowe, "Evil and the Theistic Hypothesis: A Response to Wykstra," *International Journal for Philosophy of Religion* 16 (1984): 95–100.

2. Divine Suffering and Symbolic Defeat

Rolt and Hartshorne find it easy, at one level of abstraction, to explain *why* suffering occurs: namely, it is metaphysically inevitable, something God lacks power to prevent. Neither can consistently maintain that God will be *good to* created persons by guaranteeing each a life in which suffering is balanced off by concrete well-being. At the same time, each identifies several ways in which God confers positive meaning on the lives of suffering personal creatures.

For Rolt, exemplar goodness is suffering love, love which finds self-fulfillment through suffering. Because God suffers, created suffering has positive symbolic value as a dimension of Godlikeness. Because Divine suffering is paradigm, God functions as exemplar cause drawing creatures away from self-assertion to cooperation, in the case of personal creatures, to self-sacrifice. Insofar as this evolution occurs, created persons increase in dignity as they acquire a higher degree of Godlikeness. They win the honor of sharing God's work of suffering for the world's redemption by bringing an end to their own noncooperative self-assertion and by serving as created loci where suffering is defeated by absorption rather than coercion. Clearly, Rolt believes that those thus strengthened for imitative self-sacrifice will (ironically) find self-fulfillment through it, just as God does. Translating into my terminology, he would hold that imitative collaboration with God would constitute *objective, sometimes recognized and appropriated, symbolic defeat* of their suffering within the context of their individual lives. Unfortunately, this benefit is not universally available: for if Rolt's God suffers without losing integrity, what makes participation in horrors so bad is precisely that it is integrity destroying. And, once more, it is empirically obvious that many participants in horrors do not find a way to avail themselves of the Divine paradigm's strengthening presence.

Hartshorne's God is responsible for horrendous suffering to the degree that Divine ideas for cosmic integration reflect an allegedly justified preference for complexity over triviality. By way of compensation, Hartshorne's God awards creatures double honors. First, Hartshorne insists, because Divine perfection includes maximal empathetic capacity, God pays creatures the respect of *com*passion: God literally suffers with creatures by feeling everything they feel. Second, God pays creatures the respect of eternal appreciation that accurately estimates the value of each and continually seeks to give it new positive meanings by organizing it as a constitutive part of ever more valuable global wholes. For Hartshorne, this means that God loves and understands every creature. Translated into my terminology, he

probably believes that the honor of such Divine attention is sufficient to
constitute not only the objective, symbolic *balancing off,* but also the objective, symbolic *defeat* of created suffering, which—to the extent that it is
recognized and appropriated—motivates created cooperation with Divine
persuasion.

If both Rolt and Hartshorne resign themselves to the Stoic conclusion
that God cannot guarantee the concrete well-being of each created person,
both are determined to distance themselves from the Stoic ideal of personal
impassibility and detachment. Rolt and Hartshorne would find morally ob-
tuse objections that because suffering is intrinsically bad, the morally mature would not wish it on those who love them, that compassion could
have at most instrumental value, while in the case at hand, Divine suffering
would only multiply the misery without doing any good.[4] Rolt deems Divine suffering intrinsically valuable because he identifies it with paradigm
goodness; it is also instrumentally valuable insofar as it redeems the world—
that is, insofar as it draws creatures away from self-assertion towards cooperation by absorbing blows without striking back. Psychological commonplaces get at the intuitions behind Rolt's absorption theory. Most of us
know from experience how emotions (anger, fear, pain) can seem over-
powering, as if—were we consciously to expose ourselves to their full
force—our subjective worlds would come apart. We also know that such
feelings are easier to face in contexts of personal intimacy, where the burden is somehow shared. Switching roles, we sometimes experience how by
just being in the same room with someone who is hostile or anxious, we
also come to feel hostile or anxious—as if one way (not the only way) to
perceive the feeling is to have or share the feeling. Notice that for a friend
or therapist to have the feeling, it is not necessarily for them to *be* angry or
fearful or anxious; it is a matter of there being a sympathetic vibration in
the feeling core of friend or therapist, that enables them to perceive the
other person's emotions.[5] Such experiences of shared feelings, of bearing
one another's burdens, of having one's own load lightened, suggest that
sympathetic presence cures by absorbing energy from the emotional storm
so that it doesn't have to be contained, converted, or redirected. Given the
additional hypotheses that this process can operate at the unconscious level,
and that God is omnipresent with defenses down ready to empathize, Rolt's

4. Richard Creel repeatedly voices such objections and promotes the Stoic idea in chapter 8 of his book *Divine Impassibility: An Essay in Philosophical Theology* (Cambridge: Cambridge University Press, 1986), 140–58, esp. 155–58.

5. Richard Creel usefully makes a distinction like this in *Divine Impassibility,* 130–31. See
also sections 6.2–3 below.

picture of God's gradually weaning humans away from hostile self-assertion and toward cooperation becomes clearer; so does his notion that God's empathetic love might strengthen us to suffer: for insofar as God absorbs the destructive energy of our own anger, fear, and anxiety so that we don't have to manage them, we are freed to spend our resources suffering the emotions of others.

Both Rolt and Hartshorne recognize Divine suffering as a move in a personal relationship, as an expression of solidarity, of cost sharing in the expensive project of cosmic ordering, as a manifestation of Divine love. Because of God's privileged metaphysical position, it is only "meet and right" that God should take the initiative in sharing the pains and agonies of the world. Without going so far as to claim that love for the suffering *requires* the lover to suffer, my sympathies are with them in recognizing *com*passion as a powerful and appropriate way to express love, in my judgment, one not out of character for the Bible's God.

3. Suffering as a Vision into the Inner Life of God

An alternative suggestion for integrating horrendous suffering into the participant's relationship with God, is indifferent on the question of Divine passibility (perhaps also on the issue of Divine personality). It arises out of reflection on religious (indeed, mystical) experience, and consists of the hypothesis that suffering itself is a vision of God. To grasp the intuitive appeal of this idea, reach back to Chapter 5 for Rudolf Otto's notion that a paradigm religious experience of God triggers characteristic feeling accompaniments—fear, dread, radical dependence, terror, stupefying confusion, uncleanness, shame, fascination, and attraction. Otto himself recognizes that such feelings can be triggered by circumstances other than paradigm visions of God and that they can be had separately. Given Divine omnipresence and the size gap between God and creatures, would it be so implausible to propose that these feelings are themselves ways that human being perceives God? Simone Weil thought not when she compared *affliction*—a condition associated with long-term physical pain, which crushes the afflicted by destroying social relations and filling them with self-loathing, shame, and defilement almost in proportion to their innocence—to the painfully tight grip of a beloved's embrace (in this case God's). Nor is it surprising if many (perhaps all but the last) of these feelings should be brought on both by Divine presence and by horrendous suffering. For both are disproportioned to the human psyche and, as such, "mind-blowing," anxiety producing, incapacitating, and humiliating.

Were this hypothesis—that horrendous suffering itself is a vision into the inner life of God—true, it would follow that, alongside its horrendous aspect, horrendous suffering has a good aspect insofar as it is cognitive contact with the Divine. Simone Weil, recognizing (as she thought) the true character of affliction as Divine embrace, found experience of it to confer positive meaning, even in the absence of any hope of her affliction's being eventually balanced off by concrete well-being. Not only does she regard Divine embrace as an honor that would symbolically *balance off* the negative concrete and symbolic aspects of affliction, she also suggests that by virtue of this good aspect, affliction can be integrated into a relationship with God, the whole of which is sufficient for the objective, symbolic *defeat* of its horrendous aspect. Weil commends the subjective appropriation of this assessment as an occasion of self-transcendence in which the afflicted are in a position to love God for God's own sake, despite (perhaps in part because of) their own sense of degradation and even in the face of permanent *concrete* ruin.[6]

Alternatively, and in my view preferably, the notion that horrendous suffering has an objective good-making aspect (cognitive contact with the Divine) could also be combined with the assumptions that God preserves created persons alive after their death in wholesome environments, that their relationships with God resolve into beatific intimacy so that the "sufferings of this present life" are concretely balanced off. We could thereby arrive at the view that everyone will eventually be enabled to recognize any antemortem participation in horrors as other moments of intimacy with God and so, integrate them into the relationship that floods their lives with objective and (by then) recognized and appropriated positive meaning. Participation in horrors would still be defeated via its organic relation to the participant's relationship with God; the good-making aspect of horrors (cognitive contact with the Divine) would be significant, not as itself sufficient for defeat, but as the objective feature that constitutes the experience as part of the participant's relationship with God.

4. Divine Gratitude, Heavenly Bliss

If Simone Weil seeks meaning for affliction in our antemortem experiences, Julian of Norwich envisions a postmortem happy ending that could be a textbook case of Chisholmian defeat. As she sees it, God will usher us into heaven with the greeting, "Thank you for your suffering, the suffering

6. Diogenes Allen discusses Weil's position in "Natural Evil and the Love of God," 198–204.

of your youth!"[7] Because she reckons sin as the worst scourge a soul can endure,[8] she imagines that God will publicly compensate us for what we have undergone and that such Divine rewards will bring everlasting honor and unending joy.

Surely, God's expressed gratitude to us and eagerness to compensate us for our participation in horrors would integrate such participation into our relationships with God. Moreover, if God is the incommensurate good and beatific relationship with God is incommensurately good for human beings, then such Divine gestures constitute objective, symbolic defeat of horrendous evils within the context of the participant's life. Julian makes clear that many dimensions of this symbolic defeat are recognized and appropriated, not only by the participant, but also by the assembled heavenly multitude, including fellow human beings.[9] Finally, she is unequivocal that heaven is utopic in that not only symbolic but concrete well-being is eternally guaranteed.[10]

Julian's account combines a vivid appreciation of the size gap between God and creatures with an emphasis on God's delightful determination to pay human beings honors that they can't metaphysically deserve. There is, however, one honor that she omits: Julian's God does not pay created persons the respect of revealing any partial or total reasons why horrendous evils were allowed, the courtesy of disclosing what purpose they serve in the Divine plan. When Julian presses God about the problems of sin and reprobation, she receives twin assurances: that sin is necessary and that God will do a deed on the last day that will make everything all right.[11] Perhaps she believes that—because of the size gap—even in heaven, human nature at its postmortem best will lack the cognitive and emotional maturity necessary to grasp any of God's many reasons. No doubt, her religious experiences give her confidence that in heaven our incomprehension will not matter because the intimate presence of Divine Goodness will be so convincing, the overcoming of evil too evident. At another level, however, she may find one partial answer too obvious—namely, that God wanted to rejoice in human children, while vulnerability to participation in horrors is part of leading a merely human life (see Chapter 2).

While I myself want to harvest fruits from each of the above three stratagems, it is important to note that none of them is exclusively Christian.

7. Julian of Norwich, *Revelations of Divine Love,* trans. Clifton Wolters (London: Penguin Books, 1966), chap. 14, p. 85.

8. *Revelations of Divine Love,* chap. 39, p. 120; chap. 40, p. 122; chap. 63, p. 175; chap. 77, p. 199.

9. *Revelations of Divine Love,* chap. 14, pp. 85–86.

10. *Revelations of Divine Love,* chap. 21, p. 96; chap. 39, pp. 120–21.

11. *Revelations of Divine Love,* chap. 32, p. 110.

For example, versions of each would constitute satisfactory responses within Judaism as well. With the last two proposals, however, I seize the offensive against Mackie, to show how, when it comes to defeating horrendous evils, the central doctrines of Christian theology—Christology and the Trinity— have considerable explanatory power.

5. Chalecedonian Christology—A Christian Solution to the Problem of Horrors

Within the circle of Christian theology, my own Christological approach makes certain distinctive choices. (1) Over the centuries, there have been many philosophical accounts of the claim "God was in Christ reconciling the world to Himself." Insofar as contemporary Protestant theology has been dominated by German thinkers, its formulations tend to be shaped by Hegel and other post-Kantian idealists. The other main influence is, of course, process philosophy. Relative to these, my own position reaches back to that other period of analytic philosophy and might be counted neoscholastic insofar as it embraces medieval philosophical interpretations of the so-called Chalcedonian definition. Recall, the problem for the Fathers at Chalcedon in 451 C.E. was to define the relation of Divine and human natures in Christ.[12] On the one hand, they claimed that each nature was in Christ *complete* and *without confusion*. In particular, they maintained, the human nature of Christ includes not only a human body but a fully human soul with a finite consciousness: as the Sixth Ecumenical Council at Constantinople (680–81) was later to make explicit, a finite will distinct from the Divine.[13] On the other hand, the Fathers insisted that these two natures were united in one person, where the term 'person' is not understood in the contemporary ordinary sense as an individual center of thought and volition, but in a technical sense as an individual supposit of a rational substance nature. Thus, their claim was not—contrary to Apollinarius—that there was but one center of consciousness in Christ. Rather, where other substance individuals (such as Socrates) supposit (instantiate) only one natural kind (for example, human nature), the Divine Word, the Second Person of the Trinity (in the technical sense), supposits the Divine nature eternally and necessarily and also a particular human nature temporally and contingently. (2) For present purposes, I am interested in that part of the work of Christ that sheds light on Divine defeat of horrendous evils

12. H. H. Denzinger, "Conc. Chalcedonense 451: Oecumenicum IV (contra Monophysitas)," in *Enchiridion Symbolorum et Definitionum* (Freiberg-in-Brisgaw: B. Herder, 1911), 65–67.

13. H. H. Denzinger, "Conc. Constantinopolitanum III 680–681: Oecumenicum VI (contra Monotheletas)," in *Enchiridion Symbolorum et Definitionum,* 129.

in the lives of all participants (victims as well as perpetrators). In this connection, Anselm's satisfaction theory will be less helpful than Julian of Norwich's themes of at-one-ment and identification (see Chapter 6).

5.1. Partial Reasons Why: Divine Commitment to Material Creation

Returning to our question—how can God be seen to love human nature, to be good to each individual human person He creates, when He has
set us in a world like ours?—the first part of my answer is that God *loves*
material creation, and this love finds its focus in human nature three ways.
First, like any good parent with its offspring, God wants as far as possible,
for creatures to be like God and yet still possess their own integrity. And so
God creates physico-chemical processes, with energy and dynamic power
to interact, produce new things within a framework of order and stability.
Beyond that, God wants creation not only to move and change, but to live.
And so God makes plants and animals with a capacity for self-replication
and self-sustenance. Moreover, God endows life with perception, so that it
can take and interact with the world from its own point of view. Finally,
God endows animal nature with personality, with self-consciousness, with
the capacity for relationship, with the ability to give and receive love. Thus,
human nature is the culmination and crown of God's efforts to make material creation—while yet material—more and more like God.

Second, love seeks union with its object. Classical theology insists God
and creatures are united by a real relation of dependence of the creature on
God. Divine love drives beyond such metaphysical necessities for more. But
God and material creation make an unmatched pair: for God is infinite, creation, finite; hence they are ontologically incommensurate (see Chapter 4).
God is Spirit, matter, something of a fundamentally different kind (see
Chapter 5). So, much as a pet owner domesticating its animal, God seeks to
cross the gap between God and God's beloved, by lifting the material up
into the spiritual, first by animating it, endowing it with perception and appetite, then by personalizing it. Human nature thus stands at the frontier of
material creation, the point at which God can enter into loving intimacy
with it. God specially prizes human nature, because here the material creation takes an independent point of view on what God has made. It interests God to learn what we will think of it and how we will value it.

Yet, God was not content to join Godself to material creation in relations
of loving intimacy with created persons. God's desire for it was so great, that
God decided to enter it Godself, to unite a particular human nature to the
Divine person as God's very own nature, to become a human being. Incarnation is the culmination of a series of things Divine love does to unite it-

self with material creation. (Note: strictly speaking, the result would not have to be precisely Chalcedonian. If the Divine essence, or another of the Divine persons, or each of them could assume human nature, those would constitute alternative ways for God to unite material creation to Godself.)[14]

5.2. Identification: The "How" of Horrors Defeated

According to the account I am proposing, Divine love chooses to identify with material creation by assuming a particular human nature, by becoming a particular human being, because it is in human nature that the cost of joining spirit to matter, personality to animality is most keenly (because most self-consciously) felt, most prominently in human vulnerability to horrors. God Incarnate led a merely human life, saw the world from a finite human consciousness that did not have access to Divine omniscience. God Incarnate learned obedience through suffering (Heb. 5:7–8), working God's way through our developmental struggles. In God's merely human personality, God gave Godself to persons of unstable loyalties who deserted and betrayed Him. In the crucifixion, God identified with all human beings who participate in actual horrors—not only with the victims (of which He was one), but also with the perpetrators. For although Christ never performed any blasphemous acts in His human nature, nevertheless, His death by crucifixion made Him ritually cursed (Deut. 21:23; Gal. 3:13), and so symbolically a blasphemer. Thus, God in Christ crucified is God casting His lot with the cursed and blaspheming (and hence the perpetrators of horrors) as well.

God in Christ crucified cancels the curse of human vulnerability to horrors. For the very horrors, participation in which threatened to undo the positive value of created personality, now become secure points of identification with the crucified God. To paraphrase St. Paul, neither the very worst humans can suffer, nor the most abominable things we can do can separate us from the love of God in Christ Jesus (Rom. 8:31–39). Once again, I do not say that participation in horrors thereby loses its horrendous aspect: on the contrary, they remain by definition prima facie ruinous to the participant's life. Nevertheless, I do claim that because our eventual postmortem beatific intimacy with God is an incommensurate good for human persons, Divine identification with human participation in horrors confers a posi-

---

14. Ockham speculated that it was logically possible for the Divine essence or each of the Divine persons to assume a human nature; cf. my article "Relations, Subsistence, and Inherence, or Was Ockham a Nestorian in Christology?" *Nous* 16 (1982): 62–75; and my other article "The Metaphysics of the Incarnation in Some Fourteenth-Century Franciscans," in *Essays Honoring Allan B. Wolter,* ed. Girard Etzkorn (St. Bonaventure, N.Y.: Franciscan Institute Publications, 1985), 21–57.

tive aspect on such experiences by integrating them into the participant's relationship with God (see section 3 above). Retrospectively, I believe, from the vantage point of heavenly beatitude, human victims of horrors will recognize those experiences as points of identification with the crucified God, and not wish them away from their life histories. God's becoming a blasphemy and a curse for us will enable human perpetrators of horrors to accept and forgive themselves. For they will see, first of all, that these acts did not separate them from the love of the God who thus identified with them on the cross (see Chapter 5). They will also be reassured by the knowledge that God has compensated their victims (once again through Divine identification and beatific relationship). Finally, they will be amazed and comforted by Divine resourcefulness, not only to engulf and defeat, but to force horrors to make positive contributions to God's redemptive plan. (As noted in Chapter 7, the prototype for such Divine reversals is, of course, the synoptic Passion narratives, in which everything Jesus' enemies do to demonstrate that He cannot be Messiah, including bringing Him to a ritually cursed death, actually plays into His hands and enables Him to fulfil that vocation.) Hence, God's identification with human participation in horrors, enables God to defeat their evil aspect within the course of the individual participant's life.

Note, my view does not make participation in horrors necessary for the individual's incommensurate good. A horror-free life that ended in beatific intimacy with God would also be one in which the individual enjoyed incommensurate good. My contention is rather that by virtue of endowing horrors with a good aspect, Divine identification makes the victim's experience of horrors so meaningful that one would not retrospectively wish it away, enables the perpetrator to accept his/her participation in horrors as part of a good and worthwhile life. Nor is participation in horrors merely instrumentally related to the beatific end, as God's necessary or chosen means for educating one into beatitude. As a point of identification with God it is *partially constitutive* of the relationship that makes one's life overwhelmingly worth living and, so, is meaningful apart from any putative causal or educational consequences. Moreover, unlike Hick's soul-making theodicy, which allows individual participation in horrors to contribute to the mysterious aspect of the world, but delays individual participation in the good to some later point when the educational process has taken better hold (see Chapter 3), my approach makes present participation in horrors *already* meaningful because they are partially constitutive of the most meaningful relationship of all. My claim is that the Incarnation *already* endows participation in horrors with a good aspect that makes way for their objec-

tive, symbolic defeat, even if participants do not yet recognize or appropriate this dimension of meaning (say, because they are non-Christians or
atheists). If postmortem, the individual is ushered into a relation of beatific
intimacy with God and comes to recognize how past participation in horrors is thus defeated, and if his/her concrete well-being is guaranteed forever afterward so that concrete ills are balanced off, then God will have
been good to that individual despite participation in horrors. Theologically,
my concern is obvious: to insure that each person's earthly antemortem career has deep positive significance for her/him.

Once again, let me emphasize how Chalcedonian Christology (or its
metaphysically near relatives) is key here. If what does the soteriological job
of meaning-making is God's identification with human beings and God's
participation in horrors, this value cannot be obtained by sending someone
else, however exalted. It is *God's* becoming a human being, experiencing the
human condition from the inside, from the viewpoint of a finite consciousness, that integrates the experience into an incommensurately valuable relationship.

6. Passibility in the Divine Nature?

Of the proposals reviewed thus far, only the first and fourth appeal to Divine suffering as an instrument of the defeat of horrendous evil, and they
do so in different ways. Rolt and Hartshorne locate the suffering preeminently in the Divine nature, indeed make it not only metaphysically necessary but self-fulfilling for God as a loving and omniscient being. As developed so far, my Christological approach shifts metaphysical frameworks and
posits Divine participation in horrors by virtue of God's assumed human
nature. Thus, like the second and third strategies, marshalling the resources
of Chalcedon preserves neutrality where the impassibility of the Divine nature is concerned. Put otherwise, because each of the second through
fourth proposals is logically independent of the impassibility of the Divine
nature, each could consistently be combined either with this thesis or with
its denial.

6.1. Diametric Oppositions

The time is ripe to pause briefly over the problems and advantages of this
idea. The doctrine of Divine impassibility takes its inspiration from the *political* model of the self-sufficient patron able not only to flourish but to
wield unobstructable power from behind the walls of his impregnable
fortress (see Chapter 6). On its *metaphysical* interpretation, this picture
spawned what I have called the classical explanatory model, with its corol-

lary that the ultimate explainer must be pure actuality and so lack any capacity to be causally acted upon or affected by any alien power. Stoics took
this portrait to signify an *ethical* ideal of self-sufficient peace of mind so detached from externals as to be incapable of emotional disturbance. Classical
theology took the first to imply the second (at least where Divine happiness is concerned), because it understood the having of emotions (*passiones*)
to involve genuine causal passivity (being acted upon by something else).
Hence, Anselm, Maimonides, and Aquinas offer reductive analyses of Biblical talk of Divine emotions: God does not literally *feel* mercy (etymologically, *misericordia* means 'have a miserable heart') or anger, but only produces
effects of the sort that merciful or angry human rulers would produce.[15]
Coming from the other side, Rolt also grants that God's suffering love involves His being causally affected, while Hartshorne seems to agree that
empathetic omniscience involves the same. Philosophical theologians of
various stripes have begged to differ, rejecting any "causal theory of perception" where Divine cognitive psychology is concerned.[16] Berkeley's God
was supposed to perceive any and all ideas—presumably pains and feelings
as much as colors and flavors—without being causally affected by anything
else. In any event, I have already sketched (in Chapter 4) how the classical
explanatory model might be modified to permit the Divine essence to be
causally affected by creatures without giving passive power such prominence as Rolt and Hartshorne do.

So far as the Stoic ethical ideal is concerned, Rolt and Hartshorne simply counterchallenge with another one diametrically opposed to it. They
maintain that if benevolence might, love cannot be reduced to simply willing good for another. Rather, the capacity for love includes the capacity for
understanding and empathy. Rolt goes further virtually to exclude the possibility that actual love escapes suffering. It follows for him that because love
is God's nature, suffering love is paradigm goodness and thus intrinsically
valuable. It is also instrumentally valuable insofar as it drains off hostility and
strengthens creatures to cooperate with one another, even embrace their
sacrificial vocations to suffer with God. Likewise, without buying into their
metaphysical pictures, Julian of Norwich views Christ's desire to suffer for
human creatures positively, as an extravagant gesture in God's romance with
the human race. It is the currency of honor insofar as Christ undertakes

15. Anselm, *Proslogion,* chaps. 7–8, in *Opera Omnia,* ed. F. S. Schmitt (Edinburgh: Thomas
Nelson & Sons, 1938–61) 1.105.9–106.14 (vol. 1, p. 105, line 9, through p. 106, line 14). Maimonides, *The Guide for the Perplexed,* trans. M. Friedlander (New York: Dover, 1956), chaps.
50–58, 67–83. Aquinas, *Summa Theologica* 1.25.3 (part 1, quest. 25, art. 3), ad 2um.
16. Cf. Marilyn McCord Adams, *William Ockham* (Notre Dame, Ind.: University of Notre
Dame Press, 1987), 1115–50, esp. 1117–30.

crucifixion as the most difficult deed of knightly valor conceivable in His suit to win the soul's love. It shouts out solidarity, when "fairest Lord Jesus" submits to caricature by crucifixion to maintain the family resemblance, to make sure God and humans are still images of one another even after Adam's bruising fall (see Chapter 6). Again, *com*passion affects the character of collaborative enterprise, especially if (as I suggest in section 5) God's project of "wedding heaven to earth and earth to heaven" requires us to play a central and costly role. There is a relationship difference between the general who stays back at headquarters or who watches the battle from a hilltop high above and the commander who gets down in the trenches to take the fire with his soldiers.

Nevertheless, talk of God's suffering with us can be fast and loose, some think, even sentimental.[17] And, leaving classical explanatory models and Stoic ethics to one side, issues of intelligibility still remain. For Hartshorne not only declares that Divine omniscience feels all our feelings; he tries to comfort us with the notion that "God suffers what we suffer." Moreover, he appears to treat these two claims as equivalent. Two recent commentators have begged to differ.

6.2. Divine Will, How Thwartable?

Paul Fiddes warns that feeling what we feel will not guarantee Divine suffering, because suffering requires that the inner feeling is relevantly against one's will or appetite and so involves a measure of causal constraint.[18] Berkeley's God, Who feels all our feelings without being causally affected in any way, would not—on Fiddes's analysis—suffer thereby. Divine suffering is a possibility only on the assumption of other agencies operating independently enough of the Divine will as to be able to oppose it. Fiddes believes only free creatures fill this bill, and so opts for the process picture according to which all creatures are "free" in the sense of being self-determined to a degree. He reasons that what happens by natural necessity would not qualify where God freely and wittingly created things of that nature.[19]

Granting Fiddes's intuitive contention that suffering has to be relevantly against the sufferer's will or appetite, classical medieval metaphysics would contest his further inference that only free creatures could oppose God in

---

17. Rowan Williams seems to lodge this criticism against me in "Reply: Redeeming Sorrows," in *Religion and Morality,* ed. D. Z. Phillips (New York: St. Martin's Press), 132–48.
18. Paul Fiddes, *The Creative Suffering of God* (Oxford: Clarendon Press, 1988), 48–76.
19. Ibid., 207–57.

the requisite degree. Classical medieval metaphysics was virtually unanimous that the constitution of created natures (what it is to be fire or horse or human), as opposed to their real or thought *existence,* was metaphysically necessary and independent of anyone's will, human or Divine. Not even omnipotence included the power to make fire a natural coolant.[20] More importantly for present purposes, not even God could place human beings in a world like this without their being radically vulnerable to horrors. It seems to me that the metaphysically necessary constitution of created natures is something God has to work with and around in deciding whether and which sorts of things to produce in what circumstances. And this sort of independence of God's will constrains Divine plans in a sense robust enough to occasion frustration and grief.

6.3. *Suffering What* We *Suffer?*

Richard Creel raises the different objection that even if God feels all of our feelings, it will not follow that God *has the same emotions* as we have.[21] Consider a child who is terrified of having her teeth filled. In an effort to comfort and reassure, the parent schedules back-to-back appointments, so that the child can watch her mother safely undergo the ordeal before getting in the chair herself. Even if we grant for the sake of argument that the mother's sensory feelings are the same as the child's, their emotions will differ. When the dentist looms over the child with huge hypodermic in hand, panic may take over, driving the mother's example out of mind or making it appear a clever ruse. So far as the child is concerned, the needle's bite, the skull-vibrating drill may be meek preludes to unknown and gruesome tortures, stretching out for eternity or ending in death. By contrast, the adult has power to halt the procedure and knowledge to place the episode in a wider benevolent context, both of which enable the mother to submit with reasonable equanimity, at most wincing at a few twinges. Were this not so, watching the mother would not fortify but only frighten the child further. The mother must react to the same sensations with different emotions if she is to teach her daughter that dentistry is not really dangerous to one's health!

So, too, and all the more so, where God and human participants in horrendous evils are concerned. (i) Because there is a limit to how much finite minds can hold, it is possible for pain, dread, terror, anxiety, shame, or rage to crowd everything else out of our awareness. By contrast, even if God

---

20. Adams, *William Ockham,* 1065–83; and Adams, "Ockham on Truth," *Medioevo* 16 (1990): 143–72.

21. Creel, *Divine Impassibility,* 130–31.

feels our negative feelings, Divine consciousness would contain so much else—such as joy and delight in Divine perfections, in the love of one Divine person for another, in cosmic goodness—that our feelings would represent less than "a drop in the bucket" of Divine awareness. Even Hartshorne admits the affective tone of the Divine mind could not reasonably be dominated by our feelings. Finite imagination has limited capacity to manage complexity with simplicity, even keep its subjective bearings. The problem of horrendous evils gets its purchase from the fact that our meaning-making capacities are limited, indeed characteristically stumped by our participation in horrendous evils. Even on passibilist conceptions, however, it pertains to Divine perfection that the Divine mind cannot be "blown"; however silent, God cannot be the subject of dumbfounded confusion; in the Divine nature, God cannot lose cognitive grip.

Many meaning-threatening emotions involve beliefs and judgments that omniscient omnipotence could not share. Fear and dread, terror and anxiety often depend upon uncertainties and our inability to see developments in a wider context. Anger, fear, and anxiety respond to situations that damage our prospects for survival and flourishing beyond our powers to repair. Even for Rolt and Hartshorne, God's existence is metaphysically necessary; no matter how much suffering there is in creation, it belongs to God's nature to be able to respond to it in a creative and loving way. Thus, even if God feels whatever we feel, and has a comprehensive awareness of our beliefs, God cannot experience the Ottonian emotions that I have suggested might characterize participation in horrors (see Chapter 5, and section 3 of this chapter).

If the size gap makes it metaphysically impossible for God to have our emotions simply by virtue of feeling our feelings, Creel and Fiddes both press the point that we should not really want God to have all the same emotions.[22] If—like the child in the dentist's office—we want God to be present in our suffering in such a way as to cancel our sense of abandonment, we also need God to keep Divine composure in order to help us make good on the evils we experience. But in that case, it might seem, God's feeling our feelings would serve little purpose. For the surface appeal of Divine sympathy rests on analogies with human relationships, on the human cognitive limitation (see Chapter 2) that, for example, we can't fully know what it is like to lose a beloved child in a senseless accident if we haven't experienced it ourselves. People who have been through the same thing can sometimes comfort us with their understanding, as well as with

22. Ibid., 117–21, 155–56; Fiddes, *The Creative Suffering of God,* 32, 100–104, 107–9, 144–46.

the testimony of their very lives that this too can be humanly survived. If the size gap prevents Divine being from playing this role, how could passibility in the Divine nature make possible the relationship moves that allegedly deepen love and solidarity? If the hypothesis is both otherwise troublesome and useless for the purpose appointed (that is, for solving the problem of horrendous evils), should it not be dropped?

6.4. God-Sized Suffering?

In my judgment, such reasoning would move too fast. For it omits consideration of the idea that God—like the parent—might have His own (higher) way of responding to our plight. The father who signs the consent form for his son's open heart surgery may be angry at the necessity and grieved by the child's suffering, even though he understands what ills can be avoided and what greater goods can come from it. A mother may experience frustration, anger, grief at sibling conflicts, even when she knows that the fights will be short-lived and the relationships resolve into lasting friendships. Parents who watch their offspring make serious mistakes feel torn as the son or daughter is taken off to answer the consequences even when the young person is defiant and unrepentant. So too, with God, since even omnipotence is stuck with metaphysical necessities about the constitution of created natures and their (mis-)fits with one another. Even though God created personal animals on purpose with eyes open to their consequent vulnerability to horrors, even though God knows how to defeat participation in horrors by weaving it into many good and creative plots, He may be grieved, angry, and frustrated for us and with us while we participate in them. Even though horrors are metaphysically inevitable where humans are left to function without major miraculous interventions in a world like this, God may still wish with the force of Divine passion that we didn't have to pay that price. Despite Divine knowledge, power, and future plans, God could feel torn with anger and grief at the way we treat each other, perpetrate horror upon horror, amplifying through the social fabric, multiplying so that the sins of the fathers and mothers descend to third and fourth generation. No matter that Divine omniscience would recognize the size gap, that Divine wisdom would consider the source, God might also feel exasperated at our individual and collective inability to discern the benevolence of Divine intentions. Classical theology to the contrary notwithstanding, the Bible—on its most straightforward reading—tells us so.

6.5. Dividing the Labor

Unattracted as I am to Stoic ethical ideals (in no small part because they are elitist and beyond the reach of most participants in horrors) but drawn to the Franciscan thought that in soteriology God does not always follow Ockham's razor,[23] I prefer a version of my Christological hypothesis according to which God the Son suffers in *both* natures—in the Divine nature (not only feeling our feelings but also "God-sized" distress of the sorts just mentioned in section 6.4) and in the human nature (participation in horrors within the framework of a finite consciousness; cf. section 5.2 above). Divine consciousness is comprehensive and so is able to feel the feelings of all participants in horrors at every place and every time. Divine consciousness is knowledgeable enough and wise enough to respond to each appropriately, with perfect attention to nuance and detail. At the same time, the Divine mind is at once too vast and too stable to experience our participation in horrors in anything like the way we do. Here Christ's human nature compensates, enabling God the Son to experience this world, its joys and horrors, from a finite point of view. Divine and human natures in Christ thus make complementary contributions to God's solidarity with created suffering, with human participation in horrors here below. Let me add the Biblical footnote that such dual solidarity explains why it is "the Lamb that was slain" Who is worthy to open the meaning of history (Rev. 5:6–10).

Particularity is required for God the Son to "know from the inside" what it is like to be tied down to place and time and culture. For present purposes, its scandal remains that no single finite consciousness can experience each and every type of horror, and yet—among humans—no suffering can be adequately known and appreciated by those who have not undergone it themselves (see Chapter 2). Here I am inclined to be satisfied with what seems within reach: namely, that Christ, in His human nature, participates in a representative sample of horrors sufficient to guarantee His appreciation of the depth of their ruinous potential. Alternatively, one could envision multiple incarnations to fill out God's experience of just how bad horrendous sufferings can be. Jürgen Moltmann takes reflections about how much God suffers with us further still, with particular attention to a kind of suffering that has been relatively left out.

---

23. William Ockham, *Ordinatio*, bk. 1, dist. 14, quest. 2, in vol. 3 of *Opera Theologica*, ed. Girard J. Etzkorn (St. Bonaventure, N.Y.: St. Bonaventure University, 1977), 430, 432. Cf. Adams, *William Ockham*, 156–61.

7. Jürgen Moltmann: Crucified God, Trinitarian Solidarity

For Mackie, evil challenges the *existence* of God. For medievals, who take Divine existence and goodness to be logically secure or at least theoretically entrenched, the focus is on soteriology, the doctrine of how God redeems humans from evils. For Moltmann, working as he does with Biblical categories, suffering and injustice raise the question of the *righteousness* of God. Somebody may be "out there," but is it God or the devil?[24] Coming out of his experience, first as a young German prisoner and then as a citizen of Cold War Europe, Moltmann is particularly sensitive to how unjust social and political systems impoverish, oppress, and terrorize (4, 24, 62–63; cf. 11). With Auschwitz vividly in mind, he writes, "the question about God for me has been identical with the cry of victims for justice and the hunger of perpetrators for a way back from the path of death" (ix).

Moltmann is convinced that evil's challenge to Divine righteousness has to be met by God's suffering with us. He agrees with Rolt and Hartshorne against classical theology, that because love involves (the capacity for) compassion, Divine being would be impoverished by the inability to suffer and even by the inability to die (215–17, 227–28). Unlike Hartshorne, however, Moltmann's focus is Christological in that he centers Divine solidarity with the human condition in the Incarnation but, preeminently, in the cross of Christ: "God's passion . . . reveals itself in Christ's passion" (x, 49–50, 275).

Like Hick, Moltmann is clear that the scope of God's redemptive activity is universal. To testify against the injustice and oppression of exclusive human social arrangements, Christ identifies with the poor and oppressed—condemned as a blasphemer by the religious establishment and executed as a political criminal by Rome (130–34, 136, 140, 144–45). More difficult, God means to save perpetrators as well as victims, to rehabilitate not only oppressed but oppressors into functional citizens in the Realm of God (xi, 25, 178). By contrast with the script of apocalyptic theology where haves and have-nots simply change places, Moltmann's God aims neither at distributive justice nor just deserts (174; see also Chapter 7 above). Rather God can save everyone because (to take a page from Luther) Divine justice "makes just" or justifies (177).

So far, Moltmann travels the road of my Christological approach, in effect, insisting that universal defeat of horrors within the context of the par-

---

24. Jürgen Moltmann, *The Crucified God: The Cross of Christ as the Foundation and Criticism of Christian Theology* (Minneapolis: Fortress Press, 1993), 60, 174–75. Parenthetical page citations throughout the rest of this chapter refer to this work.

ticipants' lives requires Divine solidarity with the worst that humans can suffer, be, or do. His distinctive move reaches beyond Christology to claim that only a Trinitarian (at least, multipersonal) God could adequately identify with created misery. Humans not only suffer natural evils (pain, disease, bodily harm, death) and ills imposed by human society, but also *abandonment by God* (cf. 55, 276). Surely most participants in horrors experience their predicament that way, whether as atheists who are not conscious of any undergirding Divine presence, or as believers who cry to God in their troubles but find the heavens closed. Indeed, this silence of God—such apparent failure of the Divine to vindicate and rescue—seemed to many Jews in Auschwitz to belie God's covenant faithfulness, to falsify everything they had proclaimed God to be. Moltmann believes that for many this sense of abandonment breaks many backs that could otherwise bear up under the load. He concludes that Divine solidarity with our human predicament must include God's sharing our experience of abandonment by God (252).

Fixing, with Luther, on Jesus' dying words—his quoting of Psalm 22:1, "My God, my God, why have you forsaken me?" (Mark 15:34)—Moltmann makes it axiomatic that in His last gasp, Christ crucified took Himself to have been deserted by God (146–47, 149). And he expends further exegetical efforts to promote the conclusion that God was in Christ crucified in such a way as to make it true that on the cross *God* was abandoned by God (190–92). Moltmann rejects any maneuvers by classical theology to accommodate the latter claim by appealing to the two natures of Christ, in order to quarantine the sense of abandonment to Christ's human nature while leaving Christ's Divine consciousness as omniscient as ever.[25] Rather, he concludes, if God is to be abandoned by God, there must be some distinction within the Godhead itself between the Father who delivers the Son up to be crucified and the Son who feels abandoned (151–53, 243–44). Both Father and Son suffer, but differently: the Son suffers the pains of crucifixion and death; the Father does not suffer crucifixion but "suffers the death of the Son" by grieving in love (243). Moltmann's provocative conclusion is that crucifixion is first and foremost a disruptive event within the relationship of Father to Son! Nevertheless, if the actual event of crucifixion brings a subjective sense of alienation, the earthly career and passion of the Son is a matter of agreed policy among the Divine persons: the Father sends the Son, but the Son actively chooses

---

25. Ibid., 227, 231–35, 245–46. Thus, Moltmann does not seem to understand the Chalcedonian definition in a neoscholastic fashion, as I do in section 6 above. When I asked him (in October 1997) what his alternative metaphysics of Christology is, he replied simply, "Every German is a Hegelian and a Lutheran!"

to suffer in order to identify with the poor and oppressed, with those who feel abandoned by God (51, 244).

For Moltmann, the crucified God does not merely swell the ranks of the world's miserable, but rather functions as a symbol of transformation. Because God identifies with participants in horror, they are not abandoned after all. The initiative of Divine love to identify with what is other, confers value and includes the outcaste within the society of the Trinity (25, 27–28, 51). Moreover, because their history is taken up into the life of the Trinity, it is incorporated into "the future of God" and opened up to the new positive meanings that the Trinity will make for Itself. Once again, the scope of this project is universal—God's future actions will make good on horrors, not only for participants who survive to see the day, but for those who have long since been murdered and gassed (163, 175–76, 246, 255).

If such Trinitarian identification and future meaning-making are—in my terminology—the stuff of objective, symbolic defeat, what about the participants' *subjective* recognition and appropriation of positive significance? Moltmann finds Rolt instructive where human agency and capacity to believe in God have not been utterly disabled by life's experiences. The miserable who "feel [Christ's] solidarity with them," may be thus empowered to return the compliment—to give their misery positive meaning by turning it into an act of solidarity with Christ.(51) The socially privileged, who are thus complicit in the horrors of others, can identify themselves with Divine solidarity with what is alien by casting their lot with the poor and oppressed and by working for a new social order (253–54, 277). Recognizing that these spiritual exercises are not available to everybody, Moltmann reminds readers that the resurrection of Jesus was not a purely private affair, but a downpayment on the general resurrection, when this benefit will be shared with everyone, when the plot will resolve for each individually and for all collectively, into a universal solidarity among humans, between the Trinity and humankind (162,171,178). Speaking as he does of "eternal salvation, infinite joy, indestructible election and divine life," Moltmann apparently envisions a situation, not only of (in my terminology) *subjective appropriation of dimensions of symbolic defeat of horrors,* but also of *eternally secured concrete well-being.*

8. Presumptions and Possibilities:
A Methodological Correction

Nothing is free in philosophy. In presenting the above five scenarios as solutions to the logical problem of horrendous evils, am I trying to get something for nothing? It could be charged that I am. My advertised strat-

egy was to quarry the particulars of Biblical religions for ways God is
thought to make good on horrendous evil and to present them as logically
possible methods of Divine defeat. (In section 5, I factored into the bargain
some logically possible *partial* reasons why.) My focus on the special resources of expanded theisms has been overdetermined by my desire to
avoid the snares of equivocation, by my conviction that only religious
value-theories are rich enough to defeat horrendous evils, and by my desire to proceed aporetically and consider Mackie's argument as a puzzle that
forces one to burrow more deeply into the theoretical resources of the belief system in order to better understand how it works. If Mackie wanted
to shift attention from evidential to logical problems of evil in order to nail
theism into its coffin for good, many defenders stuck with the logical problem in the hope of winning epistemic advantage for themselves. Just as a pro-
fessor can readily think of many logically possible reasons a responsible student might have for turning in a late paper without knowing which if any
were the actual reasons, so too the actual mind of the Lord is hard to know
even though logically possible reasons why seem to be within epistemic
reach. In concentrating on the logical problem of horrendous evil, I have
also been attempting to exploit the explanatory power of expanded theisms
without assuming the obligation to convince atheologians of their truth.

Yet, to repeat, nothing is free in philosophy. Even within the supposed
parameters of religion-neutral value theory, this strategy proved problematic. Recall how in mounting his best-of-all-possible-worlds defense, Pike
ran up against the problem that 'the best of all possible worlds contains evils'
seems not to be a contingent proposition but rather the sort of proposition
that is necessary if true and otherwise incoherent or impossible. In such
cases, the epistemic gap between granting logical possibility and conceding
truth closes, so that one cannot expect to persuade the open-eyed to assent
the former when they are unwilling to accept the latter.

Pike is unusually candid in facing up to the complication this forces in
his argument (see Chapter 2): for all Pike knows, he has not succeeded in
presenting a logically possible morally sufficient reason; but for all Mackie
knows, Pike has! In fact, all of the approaches we have surveyed are loaded
with philosophical assumptions of comparable status. Plantinga, Swinburne,
Stump, Walls, Hartshorne, and Griffin all appeal to the metaphysically controversial notion of incompatibilist freedom; for Plantinga, this includes
even more contested views about counterfactuals of freedom.[26] Hick, Swin-

26. David Lewis (in "Evil for Freedom's Sake," *Philosophical Papers* 22, no. 3 [1993]: 149–72,
esp. 152, 156) gives ironic coverage to Plantinga's suggestion that defenses involve less theoretical controversy than theodicy, given the way Plantinga helps himself to such metaphysically loaded assumptions.

burne, Stump, and Walls presuppose that postmortem survival is metaphysically possible for humans, while Hartshorne seems to deny it. Against classical theology, Rolt and process theologians hold the existence of the material world to be metaphysically necessary and the Divine nature to be passible. My Christological approach appeals to substance-ontology, while process thinkers advance a metaphysics of events or occasions. Whether they seek for logically possible reasons why or logically possible explanations how, the writers I have discussed (myself included) don't seem to be able to tell a story that is rich enough to commend the logical compossibility of (1) and (2) (see Chapter 1, section 1) without deploying equally controversial metaphysical and value-theory assumptions—claims that would be necessary if true and otherwise incoherent or impossible. The result is that no one is in a position—*pace* Plantinga—to mount a demonstrative defense. The proposed solutions are thus *parochial,* at best strategies that might make sense within a given framework of philosophical assumptions—free-will approaches, for example, would be available to adherents of incompatibilist freedom, best-of-all-possible-worlds approaches to compatibilists and consequentialists.

One obvious way to limit the effects of parochialism is to economize by trimming such philosophical assumptions to a minimum, thereby making one's approach available within a wider range of philosophical positions. (This desire to secure wide acceptance was part of what drove defenders to agree to conduct the debate on religion-neutral value turf in the first place.) I cannot follow their lead because I am interested in an aporetic approach and because in the end I find "minimalist" proposals inadequate in the face of horrendous evils.

My alternative way of overcoming parochialism has been to consider a variety of contrasting positions and to probe the resources of each for showing how an omnipotent, omniscient, and perfectly good God could defeat horrors within the context of the participants' lives. Without being an exhaustive survey, the five proposals discussed above do run the gamut from classical to process to nineteenth and twentieth-century German philosophies. My strategy thus bears an analogy to that adopted by Alston in answering evidential arguments from evil.[27] Just as multiplication of reasons God might have had for permitting a given evil undercuts the presumption that the evil in question is pointless, so—I suggest—showing how a variety of philosophical frameworks would afford God the means for de-

27. William P. Alston, "The Inductive Argument from Evil and the Human Cognitive Condition," *Philosophical Perspectives* 5, Philosophy of Religion (1991): 26–67. Cf. Daniel Howard-Snyder, ed., *The Evidential Argument from Evil* (Bloomington: Indiana University Press, 1996).

feating horrors erodes any presumption that no philosophically coherent theory including both God and horrendous evil can be found.

Modally speaking, my claim to "solve" the logical problem of horrendous evil can thus be no stronger than Pike's at the end of his article. Happily this fits well enough with my general posture as a *skeptical realist* about philosophical theories. I am a *realist* about philosophical/theological theories in that I believe there are facts of the matter, independently of what we think, believe, or conceive of in our theories. I am a *skeptic*, however, because I believe that the defense of any well-formulated philosophical position will eventually involve premisses which are fundamentally controversial and so unable to command the assent of all reasonable persons. Given this outlook, I conceive of the task of philosophy as that of mapping the problems by formulating the alternative positions as fully as possible. This task will involve conceptual analysis and argumentation to clarify the interrelations among the various claims and the costs and benefits of alternative approaches. Each philosopher will have a certain set of intuitions that draw him/her in the direction of one premiss set or another, and s/he will have a particular commitment to develop that particular theoretical outlook so thoroughly and rigorously as to exhibit it as a viable competitor in the theoretical marketplace, where alternative frameworks will be assessed for clarity, coherence, simplicity, fruitfulness, and explanatory power. But demonstrative proofs and disproofs—for example, that idealism or incompatibilist freedom is true, that materialism or consequentialism are false—will not be in the offing.

Since the nature of reality and value is something we struggle towards via successive approximations, most humanly contrived theories can be expected to score better on some parameters than others. In this book, I have been arguing that allegedly more economical approaches to evil, those with supposedly less controversial assumptions (for example, Pike's best-of-all-possible-worlds and Plantinga's free will defense) pay compensating prices in explanatory power; while more expanded theisms are better able to explain how God can defeat horrors, precisely because of their richer assumptions. Once again, nothing is free in philosophy!

[9]

The Praxis of Evil

1. "Practical" or "Existential" Problems with Evil

Evil is a problem for everyone regardless of religious or philosophical orientation—the problem of how to cope in such a way as to survive and, if possible, flourish (hence a practical problem), of how—despite all—to win lives filled with positive meaning (and so an existential problem). Hope calls for the assumption that what we and others do, how we and others respond makes a difference. Common sense confirms that in many instances this is so.

When evil threatens, we can take measures to *prevent* it—by building safe roads, by taking care not to drop matches in dry forests, by boarding up the windows against hurricane winds, by passing laws to regulate food processing, by sending in peace-keeping forces and neutral negotiators to work out compromises before hostilities break out. In the midst of evil, we can try to *stop* it—like Dr. Salk, by working long hours in scientific laboratories to discover cures for crippling and fatal diseases; like Gandhi, Nelson Mandela, Archbishop Tutu, Latin American Jesuits, Malcolm X, and Martin Luther King, by organizing resistance to political oppression; like international aid agencies, furnishing money, equipment, and training to enable impoverished people to raise more successful crops; like peasant women forming cooperatives to market their crafts more effectively. When evil is a *fait accompli,* we can also try to *make good on* it. In some cases, we can *balance off* evil with good: court-awarded legal damages may balance off the wreck of our parked car, special tutoring programs, compensate for poor instruction in the lower grades, the pleasures of fine chocolate or gourmet risotto for the ordeal of root canal. More profoundly, we can *defeat* evils: With the help of her teacher, Helen Keller defeated the challenge of blindness and deafness to become an example of courage and dignity. Encouraged by Elijah Muhammad, Malcolm X turned his prison sentence into leisure for book learning, and combined his street-smarts with Black Muslim ideology to organize urban African Americans into constructive communities. Thousands of recovering alcoholics redeem hellish skid-row experiences by mentoring others in Alcoholics Anonymous. Folk wisdom joins popular psychology in assuring us that attitudes make a difference, counseling us to be optimistic (to see the glass as half-full not half empty), not to be unreasonably demanding (to "take the bitter with the sweet"), not to wallow in the victim role but to take responsibility, to confront evils as a challenge to be met with creative transformation. We know from experience how such significant praxis may be individual and private, or public and political;[1] how its focus is sometimes horizontal on human relations, but other times vertical involving personal or communal transactions with the Divine; how the actions taken and postures assumed may affect symbolic or concrete well-being.

Even where horrors are concerned, what we do can make a difference. Up to now, I have been stressing the intractability of horrors by identifying them in terms of the insufficiency of packages of merely created goods objectively to defeat them, as well as their power prima facie to stalemate human meaning-making efforts, to make it prima facie impossible for participants to integrate the materials of their lives into a whole filled with positive meaning. Nevertheless, even fragmented human beings, for whom personal integration seems an unreachable antemortem goal, may still be capable of acts that assert their dignity as persons and honor it in others. Throughout much of the story, the Bible's Job is frustrated in his efforts to make sense out of his multiple catastrophes. But in his blasphemous harangue (Job 3–31) he claims patriarchal standing—with Abraham, Isaac, and Jacob—to speak plainly. And his refusal to falsify the depth of his suffering

---

1. See Diogenes Allen, "Natural Evil and the Love of God," *Religious Studies* 16 (1980): 439–56. Allen tries to call analytic philosophers' attention to the fact that actions or spiritual exercises performed by the sufferer can transform the meaning that suffering has for them. His examples include Epictetus's Stoic therapy which sees one's suffering as a deterministic consequence of a rational creation; Basilea Schlink's acceptance of suffering as from the hand of a loving Father; and Simone Weil's experience of afflicition as the crushing embrace of a long-lost friend. See Chapter 8 above.

or the uprightness of his record, maintains loyalty to the truth as he sees it.[2] The Nazi's were partly successful in their efforts to degrade camp inmates, to reduce them to animals locked in a desperate Darwinian struggle for survival. Elie Wiesel tells how one son killed his father for a crumb of bread, only to be murdered in turn by starving onlookers. Wiesel confesses how he sometimes felt hindered by the burden of his own father, sometimes wished the old man dead. Yet, Wiesel also reports moments of self-transcendence, of food shared, health and life risked for others; of the Spirit's triumph over matter, as a violinist spending his last strength in service of Beauty, plays into the night of his death; of Yom Kippur prayers by which those who rebelled as much as those who devoutly accepted their fate, served notice that they were not cattle, but persons, a minion with standing to address and advise their Creator.[3] Wiesel does not see the latter acts as defeating the horrors of camp participation, much less of guaranteeing inmates lives as "great goods to them on the whole." Doubtless many acted out of a desperate ambivalence, one that instinctively clings to life while writing off its positive prospects as a lost cause; one that sees the narrative of one's life—its hopes and dreams, relationships and projects—as hopeless wreckage and yet seeks whether there is not something worthwhile that one can yet do. The cosmic irony is that the (even partial, temporary, and transient) exercise of detaching from one's own good to pay respects to another (whether to another human being, to Beauty, to the excellence of the cosmic whole, or to God) confers dignity on the one who performs it. When the reach is to God—whether in worship or in blasphemy—it can be the stuff of objective (even subjective and appropriated) symbolic defeat (see Chapter 8).

2. Divorcing Theory from Praxis?

The discussion launched by Mackie was tightly focused on whether the existence of evils (in the amounts and of the kinds and with the distributions found in this world) is logically compossible with the existence of God. Plantinga and Swinburne widen the syllabus to evidential considera-

---

2. See my paper "In Praise of Blasphemy," forthcoming in a volume from the Tel Aviv University conference on *The Silence of God* (1994). In that piece, I analyze the book of Job in some detail, by way of commending candid blasphemy as a practical posture for some participants in horrors. See also John K. Roth, "A Theodicy of Protest," in *Encountering Evil,* ed. Stephen T. Davis (Atlanta: John Knox Press, 1981), 7–37.

3. Elie Wiesel, *Night* (New York: Bantam Books, 1982), 31–37, 41–50, 63–66, 71–73, 78, 82, 84–85, 87, 89–91, 94–96, 99–107.

tions. Yet, major participants agree in drawing a sharp distinction between theoretical concerns, on the one hand, and practical and existential concerns, on the other. Thus, in *The Nature of Necessity,* Plantinga is concerned to separate the logical and evidential from the religious problem of evil, chiefly, the difficulty of maintaining "a right attitude towards God" in the face of horrendous suffering and in the absence of knowledge of God's specific reasons for permitting it. On Plantinga's characterization, the spiritual problem resolves into the deontic fact that there are certain attitudes it is not right to have toward God and into the psychological difficulty of avoiding these attitudes (such as mistrust and rebellion) in the face of horrendous evils. Confronted with horrors, he agrees, his own arguments—that evils do not tell logically or probabilistically against the existence of an omnipotent, omniscient, and perfectly good God—offer "cold and abstract comfort." He takes this to show, not that his analyses of the logical and epistemic problems are somehow deficient, but that psychological problems with evil "call for pastoral rather than philosophical counsel."[4] John Hick sounds a similar warning: "A Christian theodicy . . . offers an understanding of our human situation; but this is not the same as offering practical help and comfort to those in the midst of acute pain or deep suffering."[5] Likewise, Swinburne insists, it is important to divide rational reflection upon from emotional reaction to his free will–defending conclusions that some people will be everlastingly excluded from heaven and that God accepts horrendous suffering for millions as the price of Hitler's getting the chance to determine his own destiny.[6]

All three authors acknowledge that their philosophical reflections don't automatically work pastoral cures; all concur that the criterion of pastoral effectiveness is irrelevant to their enterprise. Theological critics of a more continental and/or Wittgensteinian orientation seize on such self-assessments as proof that what analytic philosophers of religion have to say about evil is both conceptually confused and morally pernicious. Many overlapping objections are mounted. For convenience I divide these into three families, leaving until last those distinctive of political and liberation theologies.

4. Alvin Plantinga, *The Nature of Necessity* (Oxford: Clarendon Press, 1974), 35, 195.

5. John Hick, "An Irenaean Theodicy," in Davis, ed., *Encountering Evil,* 39–68, esp. 68.

6. Richard Swinburne, "Knowledge from Experience, and the Problem of Evil," in *The Rationality of Religious Belief: Essays in Honour of Basil Mitchell,* ed. William J. Abraham and Steven W. Holtzer (Oxford: Clarendon Press, 1987), 167.

3. The Immorality of Theodicy?

I have framed the problem of horrendous evils in terms of personal meaning (see Chapter 2). But meaning-making and its disruptions, objectors insist, occur within the sphere of personal engagement. In this connection, some charge "theoretical theodicy" with immorality because it treats persons as things and human problems as topics for analysis instead of meeting persons as persons to be loved and healed. Regard for the suffering person calls for empathy that enters into that person's predicament to "taste and see" just how bad it is, whereas theoretical theodicy remains aloof and discusses evil at an abstract and general level.[7] As an antidote to this, some critics contend that—where horrors are concerned—it would be morally wrong to say anything that would not be credible in the presence of the children burning at Auschwitz, anything that would be morally inappropriate to address to people at the most intense moments of their torture.[8] Particularly noxious are putative justifications of God, which—like the "consolations" of Job's friends—fail to respect the depth of suffering by domesticating it under some overarching scheme.[9]

Stepping back from the brink of required silence, these same critics charge that "theoretical theodicy" is irrelevant because it is the wrong genre, trading as it does in metaphysics and logical relations among propositions, whereas meaning-making operates at the level of *narrative*. When horrendous evils leave participants floundering, what is needed is not ontological reflection but plot invention! Moreover, individual sufferers are historically situated and so require a response tailored to their particular circumstances, whereas theoretical theodicies (such as best-of-all-possible-worlds and free will approaches) sacrifice specificity on the altar of generality. Returning to their moral accusation, critics lay down the rule that nothing should be said about horrendous evils unless it is praxis engendering. Talk that does not aim at action implicitly sanctions what goes on. Thus, *theoretical* theodicy is immoral by definition, insofar as it aims at under-

---

7. Kenneth Surin's book *Theology and the Problem of Evil* (Oxford: Basil Blackwell, 1986) typifies this genre of objection, which has become widespread in English theological circles. It seems to inform Rowan William's "Reply: Redeeming Sorrows," in *Religion and Morality,* ed. D. Z. Phillips (New York: St. Martin's Press, 1996), 132–48.

8. Kenneth Surin quotes Irving Greenberg to this effect with evident approval; see *Theology and the Problem of Evil,* 146–47, 149. The event is recorded by François Mauriac's "Forward" (p. ix) to Elie Wiesel, *Night* (New York: Bantam Books, 1982); see also 30–32.

9. Kenneth Surin, *Theology and the Problem of Evil,* 53–54, 66, 162.

standing for its own sake, rather than analyzing the causes of suffering with a view to stopping it.[10]

4. False Dichotomies, Haul of Red Herring!

It is one thing to find Plantinga, Hick, and Swinburne overzealous in their metalevel comments, driving as they do a firm wedge between theoretical and practical considerations of evil. It is quite another to dismiss philosophical reflection on such matters as irrelevant and therefore immoral. In writing this book, I have meant to chart a *via media* that rejects any dichotomizing of philosophical reflection on horrors, on the one hand, and *praxis* that copes with them, on the other. If they are not the same, I nevertheless envision a marriage between them.

To appreciate their partnership—my unoriginal idea that there can be "consolation" in "philosophy"—it should be enough to consider that personal meaning-making is an *engaged* praxis. The individual trying to shape the materials of his/her life into a meaningful whole, can scarcely be aloof, since s/he is the person being molded; s/he is working to become her/himself. Nor can s/he confine her/himself to a posture of analytical observation (like psychologists observing interactions through one-way mirrors), nor one of aesthetic contemplation (as a museum-goer of a Monet painting). S/he is both painter and canvas, her/his actions—to adopt and pursue goals, to relate her/himself to others, to change directions in such a way as to redeem failures—add content and determine form. Like the expert artist, however, s/he may bring theoretical knowledge to bear, step back and analyze where s/he has got up to now, appreciate what s/he has so far become, the better to know how to continue, to discern what s/he wants to do, how s/he wants to develop next.[11] Such "self-invention" is usually a collaborative project involving a wide variety of intimate and distant human relations. Some may influence us from afar, through what they write (for example, Aristotle or Seneca through their ethical works, John of the Cross through his mystical discourses, Locke through his treatises on civil government, Shakespeare through his plays, Marx through *Das Kapital*) and through what others say about them (George Washington and Abraham Lincoln as represented in grammar school legends), through public example (Gandhi, Mother Teresa, Martin Luther King), and so forth. Typically, in-

10. Ibid., 21, 24–27, 47, 48, 50–51, 60, 67, 70, 130, 155.
11. Rowan Williams, in "Reply: Redeeming Sorrows," 133–38, mistakenly interprets my appeals to aesthetic analogies as evidence that I think it is appropriate to solve the problem from a posture of detached aesthetic contemplation.

timate friends and family, psychotherapists and spiritual directors—are the closest collaborators—Christians would add the Holy Spirit (cf. Chapter 5)—precisely because they are empathetically engaged, make such an effort to get inside to experience how the other sees and values things that they can sometimes feel the other's thoughts ahead of her/him. Yet, once again, engaged praxis is not opposed to theory. Rather, like the well-trained and attentive physician, the individual and his/her intimates have a privileged feel for which parts of theory apply.

Ironically, these theological critics, who fault analytical philosophers' approaches to evil for "abstracting" from "the concrete historical situatedness" of suffering, make the same mistake when they caricature professional philosophers and theologians as "ivory-tower," "armchair" thinkers, or as disembodied minds absorbed in the analysis of abstract objects! This leaves out the fact that professors are also persons who suffer, who even number among participants in horrors; that they love other persons who are likewise vulnerable to horror; that as family members, friends, and teachers, they are involved in the pastoral care of those around them. Critics ignore what is very often the fact: that they are drawn to write on the topic precisely because they know from experience whereof they—we—speak!

Oddly, these critics also abstract from the concrete complexities of crisis and the dynamics of pastoral care. There *is* a time to drop philosophical reflection, to forget about questions of meaning, in order to act to get the suffering to stop. Able-bodied swimmers who fail to interrupt their writing to rescue the child crying for help from the pool are morally censurable. Physicians don't stand around discussing why God allows allergies when they should be administering the life-saving injection. Of course, there are also times when we are unable to get the suffering to stop—such as when cancer or AIDS is taking *this* person's life *today,* despite the best medical efforts; or when we are slaves or children in abusive households. And there are times when removing the original cause does not cancel the seemingly ruinous effect. Aharon Appelfeld's post-Holocaust novels document how, in many cases, liberating the concentration-camp prisoners and resettling them in Jerusalem or New York City were certainly necessary but scarcely sufficient to restore psychic wastelands to fertile gardens.[12]

My point is that many (though, to be sure not all) participants in horrors, sooner or later, not at every stage but eventually, over and over, raise questions of meaning: of why God allowed it, of whether and how God

12. See Aharon Appelfeld, *The Immortal Bartfuss* (New York: Harper and Row, 1989); and Appelfeld, *For Every Sin* (New York: Weidenfeld and Nicholson, 1989).

could redeem it, of whether or how their lives could now be worth living, of what reason there is to go on? They demand of us, their friends and counselors, not only that we sit *shiva* with them, but also that we help them try to make sense of their experience. They look to us for hints, beg for coaching as they embrace, struggle to sustain the spiritually difficult assignment of integrating their experiences of the Goodness of God and horrendous evil into the whole of a meaningful life. Delicate and perilous as this assignment is, participants in horrors themselves often thrust it upon us. Philosophical reflection on horrors takes up the challenge. Put otherwise and more bluntly, it remains appropriate for philosophers to say things it would be inappropriate to voice in the presence of burning children because participants in horrors are themselves not always in the presence of burning children. Survivors have to deal with their experiences afterward. And here philosophy can be a help.

Plantinga, Hick, and Swinburne are right to admit that a comprehensive lecture on their solutions to the problem of evil would be unfeeling, cold and abstract comfort at best. They are also right to believe this does not, by itself and thus abstractly considered, expose faults in their analyses (although I have found other faults with the distinctive contents of their approaches; see Chapters 2 and 3). To suggest that philosophical "solutions" to the problem of horrors are arrogant and insensitive because they would not be the right thing to say on every occasion is like throwing out medical recommendations on courses of chemotherapy, because the patient would die if s/he swallowed all those drugs at once. To charge that they are irrelevant is like dismissing the apparatus of theoretical mathematics because it isn't the place to begin in teaching arithmetic to first graders. It is rarely appropriate for philosophically reflective friends and counselors to lecture *more geometrico* because the pedagogy of recovery is Socratic. The effort is to midwife the individual's own insight and personal integration. Hints are piecemeal by their very nature. Timing is everything when it comes to assisting the individual in tumbling to a resolution for him/herself.

While I disagree with such theological critics about the general irrelevance and immorality of philosophical reflection on evil, the peculiarities of my own treatment of horrors reveal some shared concerns. I, too, have eschewed justification of horrors for the double reason that (as Ivan Karamazov contends) horrors are "too big" to be rectified by justice (see Chapter 3) and God is "too big" to be networked into our systems of rights and obligations (see Chapters 5 and 6). I, too, have charged that attention to evil that abstracts from its worst cases produces irrelevant solutions (Chapter 2), and I have identified the category of horrors in such a way as to force at-

tention to their effect on the individual participant's life. I have made empathetic engagement of evil a criterion for adequately conceiving of it, for
understanding how bad it is (see Chapter 3). I have tried to respect the
depth of horrors, measuring them *epistemically* by Plantinga's observation
that we can't even think of plausible candidate reasons why God permits
them, and *metaphysically* with the claim that no package of merely created
goods would suffice to balance off, much less defeat them. Insofar as I think
the logical problem of horrendous evils can have a solution, I have not paid
horrors the compliment of indefeasibility. To say of the category "evils only
incommensurate Goodness could defeat" that it "trivializes" the worst this
world has to offer seems to me to reflect an insufficient appreciation of
what "incommensurate" means.

The direction of my attempted solutions lies in pointing to the incommensurate Good that God is and to ways that God could be and act to ensure that participants in horrors have lives full of positive meaning. Here, I
have agreed that horrors interrupt life narratives and leave participants at a
loss as to how to continue, and I have appealed to God's talent for plot resolution (see Chapters 6 and 7). But theological critics posit another false di-
chotomy when they celebrate the concreteness of narratives in contrast to
abstract and general metaphysics. On the contrary, structuralists hypothesize
that human beings are naturally capable of generating plots as variations on
only a dozen or so themes. Even if their thesis cannot be proved, the point
that we can abstract plot lines and see them as capable of multiple instantiation and minor variation seems secure. At the very least, Biblical religion
and its worship take for granted strong analogies between Bible stories
about past Divine-human interactions and the lives of present believers,
who are invited to read themselves into its narratives and see its plots as suggestive for the meaning and continuation of their lives (for example to see
themselves as wandering Aramaeans in the desert who are wrestling for
blessing like Jacob; or to understand, with Joseph, how God meant past be-
trayals for good and will resurrect their failures into surprising new life).[13]
Scholars help us to identify this practice within the Bible itself by demon-
strating how prophetic oracles uttered at one time and place and taken to
be relevant there and then can be reused and heard as God's Word for later
contexts. *Reasons* why God permits suffering and *explanations* how God can

---

13. Oddly, Surin recognizes this function of religious narrative but fails to draw the
conclusion that plots are likewise abstract and capable of multiple instantiation (see *Theology and the Problem of Evil,* 27). Paul Fiddes makes a similar point about the religious function of Biblical narrative in *The Creative Suffering of God* (Oxford: Clarendon Press, 1988),
147–49.

make good on it are as much the stuff of narrative as of premiss–conclusion arguments.[14] The story of the fall in Genesis 2–3 is meant to explain the origin of pain in childbirth, the difficulty of earning a living, and legless snakes in terms of human disobedience. The honor code and apocalyptic theology forward the plot suggestion that God won't step in before His enemies do their very worst, so that God can put them definitively to shame.

I want to register one more complaint: that in the hands of these theological critics, the requirement that discourse about suffering be praxis engendering is a slippery one. Sometimes it is construed as the unreasonably strong claim that philosophical theodicy would be legitimate only if it entailed, all by itself, that particular courses of action should be taken in a given concrete situation.[15] As Aristotle observed about practical syllogisms, the universal premiss (for example, 'Dry food is good for health') cannot dictate a particular action without the addition of a particular premiss (such as 'This oatmeal is dry food'). But that scarcely makes the universal irrelevant to action.

Other times, the praxis-engendering requirement is understood much more loosely as satisfied whenever discourse so much as *"motivates"* or *"mediates"* action.[16] Not only is this claim very weak; it is readily satisfied by all putative solutions to the problem of evil discussed so far. Unsurprisingly, each general perspective combines with "particular premisses" to evoke contrary responses in different believers. Swinburne's free will approach may inspire the confident to roll up their sleeves and embrace the challenge ("I am the master of my fate; the captain of my soul"), while driving those gripped by the unenlightened habits of a bad upbringing to indifference or despair. The threat of hell may keep the tempted on their obedient toes, but may also provoke rebellion against Divine harshness. Best-of-all-possible-worlds approaches with their corollary, Divine determinism, may comfort the afflicted and the perpetrators of horrors with the thought that God will make everything turn out for the cosmic best, while leaving others feeling robbed of their agency. Lest theological critics grasp this straw as one more proof of pernicious philosophical abstraction, note that Jesus' parables and aphorisms also opened room for opposing responses, because—in effect—different particular premisses were supplied by the hearer's own heart!

Certainly, it is possible to represent my efforts in this book as "practical" in a Kantian sense. Where Kant argues, in his *Critique of Practical Reason,* that God and immortality are conditions of the possibility of the highest good

14. See Surin, *Theology and the Problem of Evil,* 52–53.
15. Ibid., 13.
16. Ibid., 50, 162.

(morally upright persons being rewarded in proportion to their goodness); I have contended that—given human vulnerability to and participation in horrors—God, immortality, and some organic relation between participation in horrors and the participant's personal relation with God, are conditions of the possibility of each created person's having a life that is a great good to him/her on the whole and one in which any participation in horrors is not merely balanced off but defeated! I will return to this issue in section 6, when I consider the objections of political and liberation theologians, who give the praxis-engendering requirement yet another and more precise meaning.

5. Undermining Morality?

Even if consolation from philosophy were deemed possible, it might be charged that distinctive features of my approach—so far from being praxis engendering—actually obstruct praxis and undermine morality. For in my effort to make vivid how bad horrors are, I have stressed their disproportion to human agency—how our power to produce them exceeds our capacity to shoulder responsibility for them; how they prima facie stump our imaginations and stalemate our attempts to defeat or even to balance them off. In my attempt to block classical free will approaches and to stimulate appreciation for the size gap between God and creatures, I have repeatedly likened human agency to that of infants and small children. Like Mackie, I have emphasized Divine responsibility for horrors and pondered whether there is anything God can do to make good on them. Surely such claims underwrite a quietist posture: it fosters among those plagued by horrors a sense of powerlessness, a sense that everything depends on a heavenly rescuer for whom they should passively wait. The notion that horrors are easy to produce and hard to avoid, the contention that our agency is not fully competent, erodes our sense of responsibility, invites apathy or carelessness, instead of urging us to create family services for the abused, to work for social and political change, to struggle for world peace.

My response comes in two layers. First, the size gap implies, not only that there is a vast difference between Divine capacities and human agency, but also that there are major disanalogies between the relations of humans to God and our relations to one another. Here I have taken a page from Julian of Norwich in supposing that our personal capacities are too limited in relation to Divine powers of thought and will for it to make sense for God to hold us responsible to *God* for what we do, any more than it makes sense for a mother to hold her infant responsible to her for dirty diapers. Responsibility requires that agents be approximate peers, the way statistically normal adults are, the way parents and their adolescent children almost are. To estimate the competence of human agency in the region of the Divine and in relation to other humans, thus requires a "developmental double take."

Second, I have no quarrel with what is in any event an obvious fact: namely, that human society involves role expectations and some system(s) of mutual evaluation and accountability. Relative to my opponents, I have celebrated this fact by dwelling on how humans have invented and deployed a variety of such schemes—the purity and defilement calculus (Chapter 5), the honor code (Chapter 6), and, most recently, morality. Each of these schemes has proved its usefulness in contributing to social order and stability. Each is illuminating, but none is congruent with the others. Because they identify different evaluative loci and lay down contrasting criteria, they focus complementary evaluative pictures of human interactions. I have not denied morality a place at the table or contested its usefulness in regulating contemporary societies. Nor have I doubted that we have moral obligations to refrain from genocide, from domestic violence, from starving or maiming other human beings. Nothing I have said calls into question our duty not to support demagogues or our moral obligation to promote more equitable distributions of this world's goods. Hence, I plead innocent to undermining morality in any of these ways.

Where horrors are concerned, however, I have not only refused to give morality pride of place, I have contended that moral categories are not always relevant (both because sometimes neither perpetrator or victim does anything morally wrong and because we are not related to God as one moral agent to another); that where moral categories apply, their grasp of what is bad about horrors is superficial; and that moral categories and principles are impotent to conceive how truly to remedy horrors. Put polemically, conceptualizing horrors in terms of moral categories is not likely to engender praxis of the most relevant sort, because it will not grasp horrors at their root.

While I am at it, I may as well confess to the suspicion that moral categories never get to the evaluative heart of the matter. Mother Teresa, her life and activities, *can* be subsumed under moral categories. Surely, she fulfilled the human duty to respect other persons, performed what some would regard as supererogatory actions in cleaning the houses of the poor and washing maggots off dying street strangers. Surely, her work gave evidence of virtues—kindness, courage, perseverance, and faithfulness. But just as surely, she did not conceive of herself in any of these ways. She saw herself as a recipient of Boundless Love, which paid her the incredible honor of intimate presence, of the opportunity to touch Christ every morning in the Eucharist under forms of bread and wine. Believing as she did (on the basis of Matthew 25:34–46) that Christ was mystically identified with the poorest and the least, she experienced it as a further honor to continue to touch and handle Christ all day long in the outcaste persons for whom she cared. She responded to (what she believed to be) her very particular call from God, not as a soldier to commanding duty, not with any virtue-theory concern about whether she was thereby becoming a fine human being, but as a beloved daughter returning love's initiative. Nor was she less motivated to act for eschewing moral categories. On the contrary, her zeal was unstinting. Neither the conviction that without God she could do nothing (see John 15:5), nor the recognition that she could not defeat horrors by herself held her back. God was (as she thought) doing something beautiful for her. Her eager longing was to do something beautiful for God![17]

I do not say that human collectives should replace moral evaluation with Mother Teresa's outlook. Impressed as I am with Niebuhr's low estimate of human social competence, I suspect that large-scale collective attempts to aim at something better than justice would reduce in practice to "loving those who love us" (see Matt. 5:46–48) and promote something even worse than what we have now. But the fact that morality is a more useful framework for evaluatively challenged human collectives scarcely commends it as penetrating to any normative core!

6. Antisocial Narcissism?

My main claim to practical relevance lies in my focus on the positive meaning of *individual* lives. But many would find this merit entirely canceled by my failure to give the social dimensions of evil their due. To take the friendlier objections first, Philip L. Quinn points to social wholes, intermediate between the cosmos and individual persons' lives, as another target of Divine attention. Denying any reductive relation between features of societies and those of their individual citizens, Quinn insists that the former have goods of their own (such as just institutions), aptly referred to as the common good, and ills of their own (such as slavery; "slavery would be a terrible evil even if all slave owners were benevolent and all slaves were happy"). Moreover, according to biblical religions, social goods and evils figure importantly among the objects of Divine concern.[18] Quinn might

17. While Mother Teresa was not a writer of books, some of her sayings have been collected in *A Mother Teresa Treasury,* comp. Malcolm Muggeridge (New York: Harper and Row, 1975).
18. Philip L. Quinn, "Social Evil: A Response to Adams," *Philosophical Studies* 69 (1993): 190, 192, 195–208.

have gone on to add that Divine *goodness to* the nation of Israel is a primary issue in the Hebrew Bible!

If Quinn intends to identify a lacuna in my treatment, Rebecca S. Chopp, along with some of the political and liberation theologians she discusses, would find my neglect of the social arena culpably naive, so insideous as to skew my account of individual suffering itself.[19] Have I not joined continental existentialists in ripping individuals out of their social context and thus offered my readers and contented myself with a highly abstract appreciation of horrendous suffering?[20] Sounding the theme of praxis, Chopp insists, it is a theologian's duty to recognize and advertise the social roots of massive collective suffering. Some writers—like Miguez Bonino and Gustavo Gutiérrez—urge theologians to look for their major tools, not to philosophy, but to the social sciences, the better to analyze systemic causes and propose remedies for particular situations, whether revolution or reforms.[21] Insofar as baptized Marxian accounts prove useful, its hermeneutics of suspicion finds me easy prey. By "dehistoricizing" the subject of suffering, have I not blinded myself to the consequences of my own social location among the world's economically privileged? Has not Johann-Baptist Metz already unmasked the existentialist subject of suffering, in the throes of its battles for authenticity, beset with anxiety, loneliness, and despair, as really the bourgeois individual with an enormous vested interest in social arrangements that foster horrendous suffering on a grand scale?[22] Don't such reflections expose my claim to broader coverage as one more self-interested attempt to call down Divine authority to secure the well-being of my own class?[23]

---

19. Rebecca S. Chopp registers such criticisms in her pungent survey of a variety of positions (those of Gustavo Gutiérrez, Johann-Baptist Metz, José Miguez Bonino, and Jürgen Moltmann) including her own, in *The Praxis of Suffering: An Interpretation of Liberation and Political Theologies* (Maryknoll, N.Y.: Orbis Books, 1986), esp. 3–4, 38–39, 48–49, 58, 64.

20. Johann-Baptist Metz, "Facing the Jews," in *Faith and the Future: Essays on Theology, Solidarity, and Modernity,* ed. Francis Schlüssler Fiorenza (Maryknoll, N.Y.: Orbis Books, 1995), 39.

21. Miguez Bonino, "Historical Praxis and Christian Identity," in *Frontiers of Theology in Latin America,* ed. Rosino Gibellini, trans. John Drury (Maryknoll, N.Y.: Orbis Books, 1974), 262; *Doing Theology in a Revolutionary Situation* (Philadelphia: Fortress Press, 1975), 95. See also Chopp, *The Praxis of Suffering,* 84–87. Gustavo Gutiérrez, "Theology and the Social Sciences," in *Essential Writings,* ed. James B. Nickoloff (Maryknoll, N.Y.: Orbis Books, 1996), 43–49.

22. Chopp, *The Praxis of Suffering,* 38–39, 58–59, 71–74, 149, 151. Johann-Baptist Metz, *Faith in History and Society,* trans. David Smith (New York: Seabury Press, 1980), 35, 37, 101, 169–72; and Metz, *The Emergent Church,* trans. Peter Mann (New York: Crossroad Publishing, 1981), 29, 32.

23. Gustavo Gutiérrez, "The Limitations of Modern Theology," in *Essential Writings,* 36–42. See also Chopp, *The Praxis of Suffering,* 3–34, 130.

If bourgeois individual identity is in part a construct of capitalist societies, experience shows that there is a plurality of social systems. Chopp infers that because we have constructed these, it should be within our power to dismantle existing ones and invent others, or at least to work towards that end. Like Carnap, she believes that theoretical justifications cannot decide among the competing schemes; rather choice must be made on pragmatic grounds.[24] For Gustavo Gutiérrez and other liberation thinkers, the norms are clear and summed up in "the preferential option for the poor." Once we recognize that our present social arrangements produce massive collective suffering by marginalizing and excluding persons from social participation that benefits them, morality requires us to choose against the status quo. The right thing to do is to mobilize the marginalized "nobodies" to become active agents by incorporating them into "base communities" whose social arrangements confer on them the dignity of self-determination. So, too, the bourgeois haves must become self-subversive, by working in solidarity with the poor for systemic social changes that will "deconstruct" their privileged social roles![25] How could the discussion started by Mackie—my own writings included—contribute anything to these aims?

7. Liberating Limitations

I share with political and liberation theologians the political aim of social reform to end massive collective suffering and to bring marginalized persons into full participation in the benefits of society. I would not want to deny human beings have a moral obligation to work to do so. Moreover, I believe these authors are right to point out how much horrendous suffering has systemic causes. Socio-politico-economic structures serve as a megaphone that distorts and magnifies the consequences of individuals' actions beyond their power to conceive (see Chapter 3). Indeed, I agree with Reinhold Niebuhr that human collectives perpetrate things far worse in kind and not simply in scope than human individuals would deliberately and consciously do.[26] Few bourgeois citizens would take it upon themselves to starve children until malnutrition-induced chemical changes in their

24. Rudolf Carnap, "Empiricism, Semantics, and Ontology," in *Philosophy of Mathematics: Selected Readings,* ed. Paul Benacerraf and Hilary Putnam (Englewood Cliffs, N.J.: Prentice-Hall, 1964), 233–48.

25. Chopp, *The Praxis of Suffering,* 21, 27, 47, 49, 58. See also Johann-Baptist Metz, "Messianic or 'Bourgeois' Religion?" in *Faith and the Future,* 28–29.

26. This is Niebuhr's main point in his *Moral Man and Immoral Society* (New York: Charles Scribner's Sons, 1960).

brains produced mental retardation. Few would drop flaming napalm to burn the skin off another human being, or plant land mines to blow off arms and legs. Not many would take the initiative to pull the switch on the electric chairs in our prisons. Yet all United States citizens are collectively responsible for such things, and to that extent we are all stained by collective perpetration of horrors. I concur with Quinn that slavery would remain a terrible evil even if all of the owners were benevolent and all of the slaves happy—that is, even if owners saw to it that the slaves were satisfied with their level of concrete well-being. But apparently unlike Quinn's, my reason does not have fundamentally to do with what makes for good or bad institutions but rests on considerations about what is good or bad for individuals at the symbolic level. Slavery dishonors and degrades, sends the lying message that one adult human being has so much less value than another as to be appropriately controlled by another. It is an insult to personal dignity, whether or not the insult is recognized or taken to heart.

Throughout this book, I have in effect insisted upon approaching the logical problem of evil from the view point of participants in horrendous evils. I count it a merit that my characterization of horrors is just abstract enough to capture what is so bad about horrors while yet subsuming the worst evils for the economically prosperous and poor, the socially central and the marginalized alike. At the level of concrete participation, I have preserved a certain incommensurability among horrors, insofar as I hold that participants in one sort of horror (such as being an unintentional but salient cause in the ruin of those one most loves) may not be able fully to conceive horrendous evils of a another (such as being raped and partially dismembered). But I make no apology for the assumption that the Latin American poor and the European bourgeois are alike meaning-makers, even if as members of different cultures they might have dissimilar values and symbolize them in highly varied ways.[27] Nor do I renege on the notion that— at a sufficient level of abstraction—there are strong analogies between the problems horrors cause for the Latin American poor and marginalized middle-class African Americans and gays, not to mention women in sexist societies. Insofar as I take some pages from social anthropology (in Chapters 5 and 6), I cannot be justly accused of dismissing the social altogether. Nor have I been a conceptual imperialist about bourgeois categories; on the contrary, I have commended conceptual frameworks more at home in Latin American village life (that is, purity and defilement and the honor code) as being better able to grasp both horrors and their remedy.

27. In her last chapter, Chopp says that liberation theology also regards human beings as meaning-makers, but gives the existentialist version a political twist by identifying meaning-making with group action to change society (*The Praxis of Suffering,* 149–51).

If my theoretical disagreements with political and liberation theologies are much too broad and deep for systematic development here, my principal plea is the modest one that philosophical reflection and strategic political action, that focus on the individual and attention to the social, that consideration of what we ought and what God is able to do are not really in competition but complementary. What I have tried to contribute is an analysis of what makes the worst evils so bad for the individuals who participate in them, on the one hand, and a general assessment of what it would take to make good on such prima facie personally ruinous participation, on the other. I believe that the former is presupposed by judgments that social reform or revolution is needed, while the latter furnishes a regulator that stands in judgment of political programs and their aims.

7.1. Social Vision, Inverted Priorities

Thus, Chopp's opening gambit is that *because* massive collective suffering is intolerable, social systems that produce it must be changed.[28] To an unreflective Lockean, this makes perfect sense: massive collective suffering of the sort instanced is bad because it multiplies individual horrendous suffering literally beyond our powers to conceive (see Chapter 3); since government is "of, by, and for the people," such malfunctioning social arrangements can and should be replaced. Here the assessment of what is good or bad *for individuals* is prior in the order of explanation to that of the excellence or defectiveness of political systems. Unfortunately, it is not clear whether Chopp or other liberation thinkers should be entirely comfortable with or entitled to this account, given their substantial (but not wholesale) appropriation of Marxian ideas.[29] Marx and Hegel shared the reverse belief that the body politic is prior in the order of explanation to individuals, evaluations of political arrangements prior to those about individual welfare.[30] Their followers would have to explain why social systems productive of massive collective suffering are bad without appealing to the fact that horrors are prima facie ruinous for individuals—a task for which I do not hold out much hope for success!

28. Chopp is still muddying these waters toward the end of her reflections, acknowledging that Christian action aims at the "formation of individuals and communities," while insisting that it "places the personal always in relation to the communal" (*The Praxis of Suffering*, 127). Perhaps Chopp's desire to promote effective praxis as theology's aim, explains her lack of concern with any precise accounting of borrowings from Marxism, much less with any detailed examination of their theoretical fit with other (faith) commitments.

29. Gustavo Gutiérrez, "Theology and the Social Sciences," in *Essential Writings*, 43–49; "The Historical Power of the Poor," in *Essential Writings*, 106–7; Gutiérrez, "Conflict in History," in *Essential Writings*, 115–16, where Gutiérrez rejects Marx's economic determinism. Also see Chopp, *The Praxis of Suffering*, 122–23.

30. In expressing her own views, Chopp several times refers to the individual as essentially social (*The Praxis of Suffering*, 39, 43, 124–25).

Evidently, Chopp applauds Bonino's recommendation that theology turn to the social sciences—to social, political, and economic theory—for insight into the systemic causes and cures of inequality.[31] Metaphysics aside, many such theories understandably consider individuals in highly abstract ways—as holders of social roles, as producers or consumers, as possessed of more or less political power—under the descriptions relevant to their overarching and general theoretical concerns. Their categories are no more equipped than those of biochemistry to conceptualize the impact poverty or cancer, health or freedom has on the meaning of individuals' lives. This is what one would expect of specialized disciplines, whose subject matter targets the dynamics of social, political, and economic systems. Like relativity theory narrowing its universe of discourse to space-time points, so also the social sciences may permit themselves the simplification of a reductive thrust where individuals are concerned. Yet, for this very reason, they shed no light on, but presuppose some other account of what is so bad about horrors in the first place.

7.2. Trimmed Hopes or Division of Labor?

If political and liberation thinkers focus on Christian praxis and so on what humans can do to bring horrendous evils to an end, my analysis of what it would take to defeat horrors within the context of individual lives furnishes an estimate of how much there will be left for God to do when we have given the attempt all we've got. Surely the record of this century (with its recurrent bouts of brutality and genocide) belie any claims of human competence to produce utopia. To whatever extent unjust social structures caricature the prosperous and powerful as well as the down and out, it would be wrong to suppose that all ills are social: mortality and susceptibility to biological and psychological disease arguably go with the turf of personal animality. Better social systems in the future would do nothing to make good on the horrors suffered by inmates at Auschwitz, by tortured and massacred Latin American villagers, and by dismembered Hutus and Tutsis in East Africa. If Chopp follows Metz in recommending that we use the memory of their suffering as a tool for disrupting the offending social order, and thereby—like Hartshorne's God—add positive symbolic value to their lives, this would not be enough to make their lives great goods to them on the whole.[32] No amount of human political action can make the

---

31. Chopp, *The Praxis of Suffering*, 124–25, 136–38, 144–48.

32. Johann-Baptist Metz, "Future in the Memory of Suffering," in *Faith and the Future*, 6–16; Chopp, *The Praxis of Suffering*, 44–45, 74–79. Cf. Gustavo Gutiérrez, "The Historical Power of the Poor," 96–99.

past not to have been or raise the dead.[33] In addition, history seems more supportive of Niebuhr's verdict that human skill at political organization is even worse than that at managing small-scale interactions in the private sphere. And as I have contended in Chapter 5, horrors invade, contaminate those sanctuaries, not through some mere fluke, but through a vulnerability rooted in human nature itself. *Divine* competence is needed to organize the Kingdom of Heaven, and it will take more than new social frameworks for God to make good on horrors within the context of each and every individual life: God will have to grant postmortem survival, and other Divine presence into organic relation with the creatures' participation in horrors. For me, given my low estimate of human nature, the urgency to work for social justice arises not from any positive hope that we can bring in utopia, but from the negative consideration that inaction will make things even worse. This pessimism explains why I have not envisioned any Divine commitment to be *good to* humanly organized social wholes: all of them fall short of utopia by oversimplifying to rule some in and others out!

7.3. *Playing What Sort of Favorites?*

My universalist requirement on Divine *goodness to* individual created persons also sounds a cautionary note about liberation theology's "preferential option for the poor." For Gutiérrez the phrase is shorthand for a political agenda that aims to convert marginal nobodies into mainstream somebodies. Further, it signals a pedagogical and rhetorical strategy. Where the perspective of the haves has been the de facto norm against which social policies are measured, it is a startling corrective to put the poor in that normative place.[34] This helps the poor unlearn the lie forced down their throats by ruling-class ideology—namely that it is appropriate for them to be excluded. It also crashes through bourgeois complacency, forcing middle-class persons to confront how very, very different social arrangements look from the bottom up. Conversely, it would be counterproductive to dwell on bourgeois suffering of the salvation of the oppressors because the reigning ideology has already trained the poor to have solidarity with the upper crust, to sacrifice their own needs for the luxuries of others. And it is just these patterns that liberation movements seek to undo.

So far, these considerations are compatible with the utopian aim (which Gutiérrez endorses) of integrating the good of each and every person with

33. John Roth puts this poignantly in terms of surd losses on the slaughter bench of history, in his article "A Theodicy of Protest," in *Encountering Evil*, ed. Stephen T. Davis (Atlanta: John Knox Press, 1981), 7–37.
34. Chopp, *The Praxis of Suffering*, 46–47, 49–50.

the welfare of the whole.[35] Taken at face value, however, rhetorical appeals to the Magnificat (Luke 1:46–55) compromise universal salvation, since this hymn envisions an apocalyptic reversal in which haves and have-nots simply switch roles. We have already noted (in Chapter 7) how this logic fails to provide any salvation for the oppressor, who will eventually get what s/he deserves—find him/herself socially marginalized, consigned to outer darkness where there is weeping and gnashing of teeth (cf. Matt. 13:42, 50; 22:13; 25:30, 41, 46). Equally disturbing is the way Magnificat logic romanticizes the poor, with its implication that mere inversion of the economic hierarchy would set everything right. Yet, as human beings living in a climate of scarcity, the poor also have a built-in vulnerability, not only to suffer but also to perpetrate horrors. They will carry the motivational complications of this into whichever social role they go. Reflecting on his concentration camp experiences, Elie Wiesel could remark, "Deep down . . . man is not only executioner, not only victim, not only spectator; he is all three at once."[36] The very text of the Magnificat, their song *in extremis,* proves this point. Living among the poor as he does, Gutiérrez is sensitive to these worries and explicitly maintains that what entitles the oppressed to top priority on everyone's political agenda is not that they are good but the fact that they are miserably deprived.[37]

By the same token, the epistemological privilege accorded to the view from below should not be confused with infallibility. What the poor are expert on is how bad social marginalization has been for them. Lurid apocalyptic rhetoric can be respected as a colorful measure—it is *so* terrible, that only eternal torment for the oppressor could make up for it. It does not follow further that such declarations are normative for what ought to happen to the oppressor. *A fortiori* poverty and marginalization do not automatically confer the socio-politico-economic expertise needed to design "a new world order."

35. Gutiérrez distinguishes exclusion from preference in "Conflict in History," 120–22; cf. Gutiérrez, "Preferential Option for the Poor," in *Essential Writings,* 145; Gutiérrez, "Eschatology and Politics," in *Essential Writings,* 201–6; and Gutiérrez, "The Liberating Mission of the Church," in *Essential Writings,* 266. Cf. Metz, who also distinguishes preference from exclusion in "Messianic or 'Bourgeois' Religion," 20.

36. Elie Wiesel, *The Town Beyond the Wall,* trans. Stephen Barker (New York: Avon, 1970), 174. Quoted by Surin with approval in the course of arguing that solidarity with the poor will not suffice to rid the world of evils because victims have flawed motivational structures, too (*Theology and the Problem of Evil,* 120–22).

37. Gutiérrez, "The Historical Power of the Poor," 104–5; and "Preferential Option for the Poor," 146.

7.4. *The View from Where?*

Standing as I do within the analytic philosophical tradition, I take philosophical reflection, social science analysis of the causes of oppression, and
political rhetoric to have different functions and to require different postures. As a skeptical *realist,* I believe there is a way things are independent
of our individual and collective constructions. Philosophical reflection—
including Christian philosophy and philosophical theology—seeks to understand and to value it aright. If political rhetoric and pastoral care are
alike *occasional,* philosophical reflection seeks a wider and more balanced
view. As a *skeptical* realist with a low estimate of human agency, I take to
heart the Marxist lesson and add social location to my list of the many
things that distort our vision and put certainty beyond our reach. I agree
that aloofness is humanly impossible. In my judgment, God is not aloof either, is not only essentially omniscient—the One "to Whom all hearts are
open, all desires known, and from Whom no secrets are hid"[38]—but com-
passionate and Incarnate, the One Who—so far as metaphysically possible—experiences what it is like to be created persons from the inside (see
Chapter 8). If preferential option for the poor serves the liberation political agenda, its very partiality renders it inadequate for the rhetoric of universal salvation and insufficient for the philosopher's task. I suggest that the
way forward is not feigned detachment ("the view from nowhere") but
the praxis of multisite solidarity, which cultivates the intellectual and
personal flexibility to enter deeply into each of many different positions. For Gandhi, this spiritual exercise was integral to his nonviolent
political strategy (*ahimsa*). Hindu that he was, Gandhi assumed that each
person had within him/herself the capacity to develop and live out a
distinctive angle on Absolute Truth. Political oppression insists on the lie
that the oppressors can't speak their truth without distorting or silenc-
ing that of the oppressed. Not only did resisters organize into groups
that acknowledged their worth and the importance of their angle on
Absolute Truth, they had to prepare themselves by taking the further
step of entering into their oppressor's points of view with such empathy that they would neither attribute unworthy motives to their opponents nor take advantage of their weakness. They were then ready to
"speak the truth in love," confident that their message was the good
news for everyone, because the oppressor had done violence to him/her-

38. From the Collect for Purity of Heart at the beginning of the Eucharist; *Book of Common Prayer* (New York: Church Hymnal Corporation, 1979), 323.

self as well as them.[39] My point is not that this strategy ought to be thrust upon the worst off as a replacement for liberation approaches. Rather I am commending it as an ideal for philosophers who write about evil, who wish to understand and rightly value what horrors do to persons and envision how all of it might be made good on by God.

39. Ready access to these ideas is found in Mohandas K. Gandhi, *Autobiography: The Story of My Experiments with Truth* (New York: Dover, 1983). See also Glyn Richards, *The Philosophy of Gandhi* (Totawa, N.J.: Barnes and Noble, 1982).

Conclusion: Horrors,
Disruptive and Disrupting

The main lines of argument in this book have already been drawn together in Chapter 8. I want to close, however, with a few remarks about
horrors and their disruptive power.

Horrendous evils are disruptive by definition, first and foremost of personal life. For they are evils, participation in which—whether as victim or
perpetrator—constitutes prima facie reason to doubt whether the participant's life could be (given their inclusion in it) a great good to him/her on
the whole. Corollary to this, horrendous evils are also disruptive of the con-
ceptualities within which we frame our experience of the world, locate our
place in it, and identify its possibilities for positive meaning. At the practical or existential level, the disruption of horrors is definitely to be dreaded;
actual participation means prima facie ruin and can reasonably bring participants to the point of despair. To the chagrin of some (see Chapter 9), I
have held out the hope that even horrors could be given a dimension of
positive meaning and sketched scenarios in which participants would be
brought to the point of accepting them and so no longer retrospectively
wishing to erase them from their life stories. But I have not envisioned
postmortem cries of *"felix culpa!"* or imagined participants in horrors would
ever think it reasonable to have consented to them in advance as constituent and/or instrumental means to the goods God brings from them. We
are too small and horrors are too great for that!

At the theoretical level, however, it's a different story. For given the facts
of horrors and entrenched human vulnerability to them, disruption of con-

ceptual frameworks that marginalize them is a good thing because it jolts us out of our complacency and propels us to search for deeper, more complicated truths. I began (in Chapters 1 and 2) by diagnosing how a set of tacit conventions in effect conspired to cover up entrenched horrors and the problems they cause. I tried to show how turning the tables by riveting attention on horrendous evils explodes the cover-up assumptions, first by forcing a distinction between two dimensions of Divine Goodness to expose how global and generic approaches attend to one at the expense of the other (cf. Chapter 2); and second, by smashing conceptions of personal agency and the dignity of human nature that underlie classical free will approaches (see Chapter 3). My conclusion (in Part 1) is that neither of these principal approaches solves the logical problem of (entrenched) horrors, when Divine Goodness is understood to include *goodness to* each and every created person.

Horrors belie the pretense of morality conceptually to manage all issues of adult human agency as well as its claim to subsume all interpersonal relationships in a system of rights and obligations. Human agency has to be resized in relation to horrors because our capacity to be salient causes in their production unavoidably exceeds our ability to conceive of and so to be fully morally responsible for them and because their disproportion to human agency renders the calculus of just deserts powerless to set things right (see Chapter 3). Just so, and all the more so, human agency requires remeasuring in relation to the Divine, where the metaphysical gap shows how human persons stand to God more as infants to their agency-enabling mother than as late adolescent or adult children to their parents whom they are roughly as competent as and with whom they are in competition (see Chapter 5). Yet, the suggestion that God has no moral obligations to creatures does not dissolve but rather relocates the problem of entrenched horrors. Divine *goodness to* created persons is not a matter of moral obligations flaunted or fulfilled, but of how God treats, benefits, helps, nurtures, and restores client children (see Chapter 6).

Many outside the tradition of analytic philosophy insist that the worst evils find their true measure in being utterly surd, permanently incomprehensible, and absolutely nondefeasible—not just prima facie but also all things considered, whether by human or Divine power. They warn that any attempt to domesticate them insults participant victims and so constitutes not merely a cognitive but also a moral mistake (see Chapter 9). My contrary intuitions are that the very worst evils are the ones that demand the most to be defeated and that Divine *goodness to* created persons cannot be sustained if God permits horrors beyond the reach of Divine defeat. I pay my respects to *the depth of horrors* by abandoning the search for morally sufficient reasons why God permits them. I pay my respects to the persons who participate in horrors (as well as to Divine resourcefulness) by insisting that a perfectly good God would guarantee each a life that is a great good to him/her on the whole, a life in which horrendous evil is not only balanced off but endowed with positive meanings, meanings at least some of which will be recognized and appropriated by the participant him/herself (see Chapters 4, 7, and 8). At the same time, I make horrors a negative measure of Divine agency, of God's Goodness, power, and imagination (see Chapters 4 and 7). Thus, my position is that horrors smash Humpty Dumpty so badly that only God can put him back together again. Because God can, however, the occurrence of horrors and their entrenchment in human nature neither permanently frustrates participants' attempts to make sense of their lives nor philosophers' attempts to solve the logical problem of (horrendous) evil.

My angle of approach to the problem of horrendous evils consciously upsets other methodological apple carts as well. First, it tips over the hopes of neo-Humean and ordinary language philosophers to conduct the argument about the logical compossibility of (1) God and (2) evil on a philosophically minimalist budget. On the one hand, I have argued that confining the discussion to "religion-neutral" ground shared by atheologians and religious believers, risks irrelevance and equivocation. If it is the internal coherence of the religious belief system that is at stake, other aspects of that framework must be allowed to interpret (1) and (2) and to explain how they have seemed compatible within the wider network of beliefs (see Chapters 1 and 2). On the other hand, as Pike points out, even religion-neutral approaches appeal to fundamentally controversial assumptions in metaphysics and value theory, to theses that are necessary if true but unintelligible or impossible otherwise, to claims that cannot be proved or disproved by arguments every rational person would accept. My contention has been that this "trespass" de facto redefines a methodological common ground, a philosophical stock exchange that trades in packages of assumptions and theories that compete with respect to clarity, coherence, simplicity, fruitfulness, and explanatory power. If even religion-neutral approaches such as Pike's and Plantinga's are thus "fallen," why should not Christians press their more distinctive claims into service—for example, the doctrines of the Incarnation and the Trinity, which lie at the heart of Christian attempts to explain how God redeems human beings from the evil in which we are enmired. Doing so has the pedagogical advantage of displaying the nuance and texture of Christianity's theological resources, as well as exhibiting its explanatory power (see Chapters 5–8).

Second, my strategy for dealing with horrendous evils carries the corollary consequence of blurring the boundary between philosophy and theology and consequently between the roles of philosophers of religion, Christian philosophers, and philosophical theologians as well. In this I "sin boldly." For the dividing line enforced by foundationalists and neo-Thomists is epistemological: philosophy confines itself to what can be grasped or proved by natural reason alone, whereas theology takes from revelation premises that would not be available *sola ratione,* where the doctrines of the Incarnation and the Trinity are items of "revealed" theology *par excellence! Skeptical* realist that I am (see Chapter 8), I find this distinction inept. Instead, I propose a content criterion which counts philosophy theological if God is numbered among its ontological commitments and is presented as doing one or more theoretical jobs—such as in value theory, where God is the ground of created goodness or Divine commands of obligation; in philosophy of mathematics, if the Divine essence is the reality that makes necessary truths true; in metaphysics, if God explains why there is something rather than nothing. So, too, theology is philosophical if philosophical conceptuality and assumptions are deployed to formulate, explain, and/or defend theological claims. Just as Goldbach's conjecture—that every even number is the sum of two primes—belongs to mathematics because it is *about* mathematics, whether or not it can be proved in mathematics; so I count claims philosophical because they are *about* philosophy (for example, about the relation between substance and accident, about the possibility of certain knowledge, or whether right reason grounds its judgments in natural goodness) and/or theological because they are *about* theology (about God's being and goodness, about Divine acts in relation to creation and redemption, and so forth). Understood this way, both restricted standard and expanded theisms qualify as philosophical theology, and Christian philosophers who mobilize distinctive items of their belief systems in formulating philosophical theories could be characterized as philosophical theologians as much as philosophers of religion.

Third, I further muddy value-theory waters with my arguments that moral categories are inadequate for conceptualizing horrors and their likely remedies. Secular ethics already wrestles with the difficulty of giving ordinary moral intuitions any elegant systematization. If strict deontological or consequentialist approaches are at best in tension and at worst incommensurate or mutually contradictory, what are we to make of the fact that eval-

uative schemes no longer dominant in Western industrial societies—the purity and defilement calculus and the honor code—do a better job of han-
dling the horrendous than morality does (see Chapters 5 and 6)? How can
value theory accomodate these facts even when we would not wish to underwrite such schemes as a whole (because of, for instance, the honor code's
"double-standard" gender evaluations) or reestablish them as the principal
evaluative schemes of our societies? For philosophical adherents of Biblical
religion, these data and difficulties are the more difficult to dismiss because
both the honor code and purity and defilement conceptuality shape the
Biblical message of sin and salvation; indeed, the honor code is decidedly
more entrenched in both Hebrew Bible and New Testament texts than is
anything resembling modern moral theory (see Chapters 5 and 6). Also, the
aesthetics of the horrendous and its defeat underscores the importance of
acknowledging the intimate connections of aesthetics with other members
of the value-theory family (see Chapter 7).

Finally, struggling with the problem of entrenched horrors has driven me
to straddle, indeed intentionally begin to kick down the dividing wall of
hostility that some have erected between philosophical and Biblical theology. Philosophers have tended to exclude appeals to the Bible on the above-
mentioned epistemological grounds—that it is a piece of revelation whose
contents are not generally conceded to be true. Against this, I have maintained that lack of self-evidence or widespread consensus about truth does
not automatically undermine its relevance for exhibiting internal coherence and explanatory power. Some neo-Reformation theologians would
ban philosophy as an alien and incommensurate conceptuality and insist
that theology work within the confines of *the* Biblical world view. The literature is full of commendations of this stance based on the putative di-
chotomy between "Hebrew" and "Hellenistic" mind-sets and such. Here, I
respond with a series of otherwise widely conceded points. First, the Biblical texts as we find them have been distinctively shaped by the culture and
outlook of their human authors (see Chapters 5 and 6 for evidence of how
the Bible's soteriological plot lines are cast in terms of purity and defilement and/or are deeply imbedded in the honor code). Second, since the
human tellers and retellers of Bible stories (oral or written) span several
millennia and many widely different cultures, there is no such thing as *the*
Biblical worldview which all the texts reflect. Third, we can see the conceptuality adapting itself cross-culturally in the New Testament, especially
in the Epistles but also in the Gospels. Among the Gentile influences turned
to positive use are philosophical ideas (such as Stoicism within Pauline and
deutero-Pauline materials, and Platonism in the letter to the Hebrews). Nor

was this a Christian innovation. Philo of Alexandria pioneered an impressive integration of Judaism with Platonism, and some scholars maintain that at the turn of the era, there was no such thing as unhellenized Jewish thought.[1] Fourth, the earliest (apostolic and patristic) Christian theology was at once biblical and philosophical. Finally, Biblical theologians can't keep from dirtying their hands with philosophy because textual renderings are always a function of hermeneutical assumptions, and hermeneutics is itself a branch of philosophy! In this book, I make no attempt to develop a theory of how to integrate philosophical with Biblical insights. But I believe the preceding chapters do illustrate some ways in which this might fruitfully be done.

Naturally, I hope to have convinced many readers of my central theses—that horrendous evils can be defeated by the Goodness of God within the framework of the individual participant's life and that Christian belief contains many resources with which to explain how this can be so. But I have also intended—like horrors themselves—to disrupt: in this case, a family of discussions. There is so much to be learned about the meaning of suffering and the Goodness of God, why should we ever stop where we are? If along the way I have said something to offend almost everybody, I can take satisfaction that my effort has succeeded in its aporetic aims!

---

1. Cf. Victor Paul Furnish, *Theology and Ethics in Paul* (Nashville, Tenn.: Abingdon Press, 1968), 44–51; Wayne Meeks, *The First Urban Christians: The Social World of the Apostle Paul* (New Haven: Yale University Press, 1983), 33; Daniel Boyarin, *A Radical Jew: Paul and the Politics of Identity* (Berkeley: University of California Press, 1994), 6–7, 13–14, 59–69.

Works Cited

Adams, Marilyn McCord. "Horrendous Evils and the Goodness of God." In *The Problem of Evil,* edited by Marilyn McCord Adams and Robert Merrihew Adams, 209–21. Oxford: Oxford University Press, 1990.

———. "Julian of Norwich on the Tender Loving Care of Mother Jesus." In *Our Knowledge of God,* edited by K. J. Clark, 203–19. Kluwer Academic Publishers: The Netherlands, 1992.

———. "The Metaphysics of the Incarnation in Some Fourteenth-Century Franciscans." In *Essays Honoring Allan B. Wolter,* edited by Girard Etzkorn, 21–57. St. Bonaventure, N.Y.: Franciscan Institute Publications, 1985.

———. "Ockham on Truth." *Medioevo* 16 (1990): 143–72.

———. "Relations, Subsistence, and Inherence, or Was Ockham a Nestorian in Christology?" *Nous* 16 (1982): 62–75.

———. "The Resurrection of the Body according to Three Medieval Aristotelians: Thomas Aquinas, John Duns Scotus, William Ockham." *Philosophical Topics* 20 (1993): 1–33.

———. "St. Anselm on Truth." *Documenti e Studi sulla Tradizione Filosofica Medievale* 1, no. 2 (1990): 353–72.

———. "Separation and Reversal in Luke-Acts." In *Philosophy and the Christian Faith,* edited by Thomas Morris, 92–117. Notre Dame, Ind.: Notre Dame University Press, 1988.

———. "Theodicy without Blame." *Philosophical Topics* 16 (1988): 215–45.

———. *William Ockham.* Notre Dame, Ind.: University of Notre Dame Press, 1987.

Adams, Marilyn McCord, and Robert Merrihew Adams, eds. *The Problem of Evil.* Oxford: Oxford University Press, 1990.

Adams, Robert Merrihew. "Middle Knowledge and the Problem of Evil," reprinted in *The Problem of Evil,* edited by Marilyn McCord Adams and Robert Merrihew Adams, 110–25. Oxford: Oxford University Press, 1990.

Adkins, Arthur W. H. *Merit and Responsibility: A Study in Greek Values*. Chicago: University of Chicago Press, 1960.

Allen, Diogenes. "Natural Evil and the Love of God." In *The Problem of Evil*, edited by Marilyn McCord Adams and Robert Merrihew Adams, 189–208. Oxford: Oxford University Press, 1990.

Alston, William P. "The Inductive Argument from Evil and the Human Cognitive Condition." Philosophical Perspectives 5, *Philosophy of Religion* (1991): 26–67.

Anselm. *Opera Omnia ad fidem codicum recensuit*. Edited by F. S. Schmitt. Edinburgh: Thomas Nelson & Sons, 1938–1961.

Appelfeld, Aharon. *For Every Sin*. New York: Weidenfeld and Nicholson, 1989.

———. *The Immortal Bartfuss*. New York: Harper and Row, 1989.

Aquinas, Thomas. *Opera Omnia*. Rome: Typographia Polyglotta S. C. de Propaganda Fide: Commissio Leonina, 1982–1996.

Augustine. *Augustine of Hippo: Selected Writings*. Translated by Clark, Mary T. New York: Paulist Press, 1984.

———. *De libero arbitrio: Libri Tres*. Edited by William M. Green. Vol. 74, *Corpus Scriptorum Ecclesiasticorum Latinorum*. Vienna: Hoelder-Pichler-Tempsky, 1956.

Bonaventure. *The Breviloquium*. Translated by José de Vinck. Vol. 2, *The Works of Bonaventure*. Paterson, N.J.: St. Anthony Guild Press, 1963.

———. *Collations on the Six Days*. Translated by José de Vinck. Vol. 5, *The Works of Bonaventure*. Paterson, N.J.: St. Anthony Guild Press, 1970.

———. *The Soul's Journey into God; The Tree of Life; The Life of St. Francis*. Translated by Ewert Cousins with an introduction by Ignatius Brady, O. F. M. New York: Paulist Press, 1978.

Bonino, Miguez. *Doing Theology in a Revolutionary Situation*. Philadelphia: Fortress Press, 1975.

———. "Historical Praxis and Christian Identity." In *Frontiers of Theology in Latin America*, edited by Rosino Gibellini and translated by John Drury. Maryknoll, N.Y.: Orbis Books, 1974.

Bourdieu, Pierre. "The Sentiment of Honour in Kabyle Society." In Honor and Shame: The Values of Mediterranean Society, Edited by J. G. Peristiany, 193–241. London: Weidenfeld and Nicolson, 1965.

Boyarin, Daniel. *A Radical Jew: Paul and the Politics of Identity*. Berkeley: University of California Press, 1994.

Brown, Frank Burch. *Religious Aesthetics: A Theological Study of Making and Meaning*. Princeton: Princeton University Press, 1989.

Burrell, David. "Human Freedom in the Context of Creation." In *The God Who Acts: Philosophical and Theological Explorations*, edited by Thomas F. Tracy, 103–9. University Park: Pennsylvania State University Press, 1994.

Carnap, Rudolf. "Empiricism, Semantics, and Ontology." In *Philosophy of Mathematics: Selected Readings*, edited by Paul Benacerraf and Hilary Putnam, 233–48. Englewood Cliffs, N.J.: Prentice-Hall, 1964.

Chisholm, Roderick. "The Defeat of Good and Evil." In *The Problem of Evil*, edited by Marilyn McCord Adams and Robert Merrihew Adams, 53–68. Oxford: Oxford University Press, 1990.

Chopp, Rebecca S. *The Praxis of Suffering: An Interpretation of Liberation and Political Theologies*. Maryknoll, N.Y.: Orbis Books, 1986.

Cooper, David, ed. *A Companion to Aesthetics.* Oxford: Basil Blackwell, 1992.

Cousins, Ewert H. *Bonaventure and the Coincidence of Opposites: The Theology of Bonaventure.* Chicago: Franciscan Herald Press, 1978.

Craig, William. " 'No Other Name': A Middle Knowledge Perspective on the Exclusivity of Salvation through Christ." *Faith and Philosophy* 6 (1989): 172–88.

Creel, Richard. *Divine Impassibility: An Essay in Philosophical Theology.* Cambridge: Cambridge University Press, 1986.

Delattre, Roland Andre. *Beauty and Sensibility in the Thought of Jonathan Edwards: An Essay in Aesthetics and Theological Ethics.* New Haven: Yale University Press, 1968.

Denzinger, H. H. *Enchiridion Symbolorum et Definitionum.* Freiburg-in-Brisgaw: B. Herder, 1911.

Douglas, Mary. *Purity and Danger: An Analysis of Concepts of Pollution and Taboo.* London: Routledge and Kegan Paul, 1966.

Elliott, John H. "Patronage and Clientism in Early Christian Society." *Forum* 3, no. 4 (1987): 29–48.

Fiddes, Paul. *The Creative Suffering of God.* Oxford: Clarendon Press, 1988.

Furnish, Victor Paul. *Theology and Ethics in Paul.* Nashville, Tenn.: Abingdon Press, 1968.

Griffin, David. *God, Power, and Evil.* Philadelphia: Westminster Press, 1976.

Gutiérrez, Gustavo. *Essential Writings.* Edited with an introduction by James B. Nickoloff. Maryknoll, N.Y.: Orbis Books, 1996.

Harries, Richard. *Art and the Beauty of God: A Christian Understanding.* London: Mowbray, 1993.

Hartshorne, Charles. *Omnipotence and Other Theological Mistakes.* Albany: University of New York Press, 1984.

Hayes, Zachary. *The Hidden Center: Spirituality and Speculative Christology in St. Bonaventure.* New York: Paulist Press, 1981.

Hick, John. *Evil and the God of Love.* New York: Harper and Row, 1978.

———. "An Irenaean Theodicy." In *Encountering Evil,* edited by Stephen T. Davis, 39–68. Atlanta: John Knox Press, 1980.

Hospers, John. "Aesthetics, Problems of." In *The Encyclopedia of Philosophy,* 1: 35–56. New York: Macmillan, 1967.

Howard-Snyder, Daniel, ed. *The Evidential Argument from Evil.* Bloomington: Indiana University Press, 1996.

Julian of Norwich. *A Book of Showings to the Anchoress Julian of Norwich.* Edited by Edmund Colledge. O.S.A., and James Walsh, S. J. Toronto: Pontifical Institute of Medieval Studies, 1978.

———. *Revelations of Divine Love.* Translated by Clifton Wolters. London: Penguin Books, 1966.

Leibniz. *Discourse on Metaphysics.* Indianapolis, Ind.: Hackett, 1991.

Levenson, Jon D. *Creation and the Persistence of Evil.* San Francisco: Harper and Row, 1988.

Lewis, C. S. *The Problem of Pain.* New York: Macmillan, 1979.

Lewis, David. "Evil for Freedom's Sake." *Philosophical Papers* 22, no. 3 (1993): 149–72.

Mackie, J. L. "Evil and Omnipotence." In *The Problem of Evil,* edited by Marilyn McCord Adams and Robert Merrihew Adams, 25–37. Oxford: Oxford University Press, 1990.

Maimonides, Moses. *The Guide for the Perplexed.* Translated by M. Friedlander. New York: Dover, 1956.

Malina, Bruce J. *The New Testament World: Insights from Cultural Anthropology.* Atlanta: John Knox Press, 1981.

———. "Patron and Client: The Analogy behind Synoptic Theology." Forum 4, no. 1 (1988): 2–32.

Martin James Alfred, Jr. *Beauty and Holiness: The Dialogue between Aesthetics and Religion.* Princeton: Princeton University Press, 1990.

Meeks, Wayne. *The First Urban Christians: The Social World of the Apostle Paul.* New Haven: Yale University Press, 1983.

Metz, Johann-Baptist. *The Emergent Church.* Translated by Peter Mann. New York: Crossroad Publishing, 1981.

———. "Facing the Jews." In *Faith and the Future: Essays on Theology, Solidarity, and Modernity,* edited with an introduction by Francis Schlüssler Fiorenza, 38–48. Maryknoll, N.Y.: Orbis Books, 1995.

———. *Faith in History and Society.* Translated by David Smith. New York: Seabury Press, 1980.

———. "Future in the Memory of Suffering." In *Faith and the Future: Essays on Theology, Solidarity, and Modernity.* Edited with an introduction by Francis Schlüssler Fiorenza, 3–16. Maryknoll, N.Y.: Orbis Books, 1995.

———. "Messianic or 'Bourgeois' Religion?" In *Faith and the Future: Essays on Theology, Solidarity, and Modernity.* Edited with introduction by Francis Schlüssler Fiorenza, 17–29. Maryknoll, N.Y.: Orbis Books, 1995.

Mill, J. S. "Mr. Mansel on the Limits of Religious Thought." In *God and Evil,* edited by Nelson Pike, 37–45. Englewood Cliffs, N.J.: Prentice-Hall, 1964.

Moltmann, Jürgen. *The Crucified God: The Cross of Christ as the Foundation and Criticism of Christian Theology.* Minneapolis, Minn.: Fortress Press, 1993.

Moore, G. E. *Principia Ethica.* Cambridge at the University Press, 1960.

Mothershill, Mary. *Beauty Restored.* Oxford: Oxford University Press, 1984.

Muggeridge, Malcolm. Introduction in *A Mother Teresa Treasury.* San Francisco: Harper and Row, 1975.

Niebuhr, Reinhold. *Moral Man and Immoral Society.* New York: Charles Scribner's Sons, 1960.

Ockham, William. *Opera Theologica.* Vol. 3. Edited by Girard J. Etzkorn. St. Bonaventure, NY: St. Bonaventure University, 1977.

Otto, Rudolf. *Idea of the Holy.* New York: Oxford University Press, 1958.

Penelhum, Terence. "Divine Goodness and the Problem of Evil." In *The Problem of Evil,* edited by Marilyn McCord Adams and Robert Merrihew Adams, 69–82. Oxford: Oxford University Press, 1990.

Pereboom, Derk. "Stoic Psychotherapy in Descartes and Spinoza." *Faith and Philosophy* 11 (1994): 592–625.

Peristiany, J. G., ed. *Honour and Shame: The Values of Mediterranean Society.* London: Weidenfeld and Nicolson, 1965.

Pike, Nelson. "Hume on Evil." *Philosophical Review* 72 (1963): 180–97. Reprinted in *The Problem of Evil,* edited by Marilyn McCord Adams and Robert Merrihew Adams, 38–52. Oxford: Oxford University Press, 1990.

———. *Mystic Union: An Essay in the Phenomenology of Mysticism.* Ithaca, N.Y.: Cornell University Press, 1992.

———, ed. *God and Evil.* Englewood Cliffs, N.J.: Prentice-Hall, 1964.

Pitt-Rivers, Julian. "Honour and Social Status." In *Honour and Shame: The Values of Mediterranean Society,* Edited by J. G. Peristiany, 19–77. London: Weidenfeld and Nicolson, 1965.

Plantinga, Alvin. *God and Other Minds.* Ithaca, N.Y.: Cornell University Press, 1967.

———. *The Nature of Necessity.* Oxford: Clarendon Press, 1974.

———. "The Probabilistic Argument from Evil." *Philosophical Studies* 35 (1979): 1–53.

———. "Self-Profile." In *Alvin Plantinga,* edited by James E. Tomberlin and Peter Van Inwagen. Dordrecht: D. Reidel, 1985.

Quinn, Philip L. "God, Moral Perfection, and Possible Worlds." In *God: The Contemporary Discussion,* edited by Frederick Sontag and M. Darrol Bryant, 197–215. New York: Rose of Sharon Press, 1982.

———. "Social Evil: A Response to Adams." *Philosophical Studies* 69 (1993), 195–208.

Rad, Gerhard von. *Genesis: A Commentary.* Philadelphia: Westminster Press, 1972.

Rolt, C. E. *The World's Redemption.* London: Longmans, Green, 1913.

Roth, John K. "A Theodicy of Protest." In *Encountering Evil,* edited by Stephen T. Davis, 7–37. Atlanta: John Knox Press, 1981.

Rowe, William L. "The Empirical Argument from Evil." In *Rationality, Religious Belief, and Moral Commitment,* edited by Robert Audi and William Wainwright, 227–47. Ithaca, N.Y.: Cornell University Press, 1986.

———. "Evil and the Theistic Hypothesis: A Response to Wykstra." *International Journal for Philosophy of Religion* 16 (1984): 95–100.

———. "The Problem of Evil and Some Varieties of Atheism." *American Philosophical Quarterly* 16 (1979): 335–41.

———. "Ruminations about Evil." *Philosophical Perspectives* 5, Philosophy of Religion (1991): 69–88.

Sherry, Patrick. *Spirit and Beauty: An Introduction to Theological Aesthetics.* Oxford: Clarendon Press, 1992.

Stump, Eleonore. "The Problem of Evil." *Faith and Philosophy* 2 (1985): 392–435. With comment by Michael Smith and reply by Stump.

Surin, Kenneth. *Theology and the Problem of Evil.* Oxford: Basil Blackwell, 1986.

Swinburne, Richard. *The Coherence of Theism.* Oxford: Clarendon Press, 1979.

———. "Knowledge from Experience and the Problem of Evil." In *The Rationality of Religious Belief: Essays in Honour of Basil Mitchell,* edited by William J. Abraham and Steven W. Holtzer, 141–67. Oxford: Clarendon Press, 1987.

———. "A Theodicy of Heaven and Hell." In *The Existence and Nature of God,* edited by Alfred Freddoso, 37–54. Notre Dame, Ind.: University of Notre Dame Press, 1983.

Tanner, Katherine. "Human Freedom, Human Sin, and God the Creator." In *The God Who Acts: Philosophical and Theological Explorations,* edited by Thomas F. Tracy, 111–35. University Park, Penn.: Pennsylvania State University Press, 1994.

Tillich, Paul. *Biblical Religion and the Search for Ultimate Reality.* Chicago: University of Chicago Press, 1955.

Tooley, Michael. "The Argument from Evil." *Philosophical Perspectives* 5, Philosophy of Religion (1991): 89–134.

Van Inwagen, Peter. "The Problems of Evil, Air, and Silence," *Philosophical Perspectives* 5, Philosophy of Religion (1991): 135–65.

Walls, Jerry L. *Hell: The Logic of Damnation.* Notre Dame, Ind.: University of Notre Dame Press, 1992.

Wiesel, Elie. *Night*. Toronto: Bantam Books, 1982.

———. *The Town Beyond the Wall*. Translated by Stephen Barker. New York: Avon, 1970.

Williams, Rowan. "Reply: Redeeming Sorrows." In *Religion and Morality*. Edited by D. Z. Phillips, 132–48. New York: St. Martin's Press, 1996.

Wippel, John. "Quidditative Knowledge of God." Chapter 9 in *Metaphysical Themes in Thomas Aquinas*, 215–41. Washington, D.C.: Catholic University of America Press, 1984.

Wolterstorff, Nicholas. *Art in Action: Toward a Christian Aesthetic*. Grand Rapids, Mich.: Eerdmans, 1980.

Wykstra, Stephen J. "The Humean Obstacle to Evidential Arguments from Suffering: On Avoiding the Evils of 'Appearance'." *International Journal for Philosophy of Religion* 16 (1984): 73–93.

Index